Investigating Classroom Talk

Social Research and Educational Studies Series

Series Editor
Robert G. Burgess,
Professor of Sociology,
University of Warwick

Investigating Classroom Talk

A.D. Edwards
and
D.P.G. Westgate

Revised and Extended
Second Edition

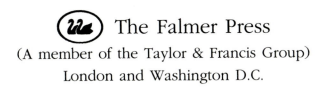 The Falmer Press
(A member of the Taylor & Francis Group)
London and Washington D.C.

UK   The Falmer Press, 4 John Street, London WC1N 2ET
USA   The Falmer Press, Taylor & Francis Inc., 1900 Frost Road, Suite 101, Bristol, PA 19007

First published in 1987
Second edition 1994

A catalogue record for this book is available from the British Library

Library of Congress Cataloging-in-Publication Data are available on request

ISBN 0 7507 0324 5 (cased)
ISBN 0 7507 0325 3 (paper)

Jacket design by Caroline Archer

Typeset in 10.5/12pt Garamond by
Graphicraft Typesetters Ltd., Hong Kong.

Printed in Great Britain by Burgess Science Press, Basingstoke on paper which has a specified pH value on final paper manufacture of not less than 7.5 and is therefore 'acid free'.

Contents

Contents

Series Editor's Preface to the Second Edition

The purpose of the *Social Research and Educational Studies* series is to provide authoritative guides to key issues in educational research. The series includes overviews of fields, guidance on good practice and discussions of the practical implications of social and educational research. In particular, the series deals with a variety of approaches to conducting social and educational research. Contributors to this series review recent work, raise critical concerns that are particular to the field of education, and reflect on the implications of research for educational policy and practice.

Each volume in the series draws on material that will be relevant for an international audience. The contributors to this series all have wide experience of teaching, conducting and using educational research. The volumes are written so that they will appeal to a wide audience of students, teachers and researchers. Altogether, the volumes in the *Social Research and Educational Studies* series provide a comprehensive guide for anyone concerned with contemporary educational research.

The series will include individually authored books and edited volumes on a range of themes in education including: qualitative research, survey research, the interpretation of data, self-evaluation, research and social policy, analyzing data, action research, the politics and ethics of research.

The first edition of this book was very well received and achieved wide recognition as a major text on classroom studies and classroom language. In this new edition, Tony Edwards and David Westgate continue to examine methods of investigation for use in classrooms and ways in which researchers and teachers may advance their knowledge of classroom talk. They have taken the opportunity to add material on oracy and the importance of spoken language in the curriculum. All research evidence and bibliographic material has been revised and updated. *Investigating Classroom Talk* will continue to be an important book for a new generation of students and researchers in language and linguistics, social science and educational studies.

Robert Burgess
University of Warwick
March 1994

Glossary of Essential Terms

In the following list we offer outline definitions of some technical terms, together with an indication of the main points in the book at which a fuller discussion of them can be found. (Page numbers are given in brackets).

ACT. Smallest unit of analysis in Discourse Analysis (*q.v.*), and basic component of higher levels of that system: viz. 'move', 'exchange' and 'transaction'. Related to the theory of 'speech acts' originating with Austin (for example 1962). (pp. 27; 139; 141)

CODE-SWITCHING. Changing from one language, or variety (*q.v.*), to another, according to the speaker's perception of context: for example, when talk in a bilingual community shifts from official business to social matters; or, elsewhere, when a speaker turns from strangers to friends. (pp. 20; 33)

COMPETENCE: COMMUNICATIVE. The socio-cultural as well as linguistic knowledge drawn on by language users in real situations. (pp. 21; 34; 149–62)

COMPETENCE: FORMAL/LINGUISTIC. An essentially abstract conception (Chomsky, 1965) of a 'speaker-hearer's' linguistic knowledge as implied by the ability to engage in language use (or 'performance'). (p. 19)

CONTEXT. Variously defined: as the location of a word, or other linguistic item, amid other words, etc. ('verbal context'); as the total setting in which language use occurs on a given occasion ('context of situation'); more recently, as inclusive of the events themselves, 'created' by the talk rather than 'given' beforehand. (pp. 22–4; 75–6)

CONVERSATIONAL ANALYSIS. A form of talk-analysis which seeks to understand how participants organize turns and topics in less formal types of talk; see also 'ethnomethodology'. (pp. 27–8; 64–7; 116–20)

DISCOURSE. Variously defined: as 'language in use', as a 'stretch of language larger than a sentence', etc.; sometimes distinguished from 'text' as the activity giving rise to it. (pp. 21; 24–7)

DISCOURSE ANALYSIS. The term has both general and particular applications: as any study of 'discourse' (*q.v.*); and as a system of analysis pioneered by Sinclair and Coulthard (1975) and others. *See* ACT above. (pp. 21; 25–7; 138–49; 159–61)

ETHNOGRAPHY. A mode of (originally) anthropological enquiry based on extended observation so as to gain access to the views of reality of those observed. (pp. 14; 75–6; 79; 133)

ETHNOMETHODOLOGY. A mode of sociological enquiry which seeks to identify the perceptions, everyday knowledge and working rules on which people act; basis for work in 'conversational analysis' (*q.v.*). (pp. 27–8; 115)

GRAMMAR: LINGUISTIC. Description or codification of a language at two main 'levels of analysis': phonology and syntax (*q.v.*). (p. 18)

GRAMMAR: SOCIAL. Knowledge of situations and relationships upon which people draw for participating appropriately in social activity. (p. 28)

ILLOCUTIONARY FORCE. The functional meaning of an utterance, sometimes at variance with literal, or 'locutionary', meaning: i.e., what the words 'do' in the interaction. (p. 21)

INTONATION. The organization of sound-sequences, involving for example, pitch, pitch-change and accentuation. (pp. 65; 67–73)

LINGUISTICS. The scientific study of language and languages; its major pre-occupation this century has been on structural descriptions of various kinds. (pp. 3; 18–22; 141)

MONITORING. (as, for example, 'monitoring black') Language variety being self-consciously used to demonstrate group-solidarity or exclusion of 'outsiders'. (p. 32)

MORPHEME. Smallest unit of language having independent meaning; identical with, or smaller than 'word': for example, 'going' contains two morphemes (go + ing). (p. 141)

PHONOLOGY. The range and patterning of sounds ('phonemes') in a language or languages. (p. 18)

PRAGMATICS. Study of language and meaning in relation to contextual, including non-linguistic, factors. (pp. 21–2)

PSYCHOLINGUISTICS. The study of language in relation to mental processes (for example, language and thought) or development (for example, language acquisition). (p. 13)

REGISTER. Set of linguistic features, lexical and grammatical, associated with use in particular settings: for example courtrooms, chemistry lessons. (p. 20)

SEMANTICS. The study of meaning; the systematic organization of word ('lexical') meanings. (pp. 18–19; 22)

SOCIOLINGUISTICS. The study of language in relation to society, and in particular of linguistic variation associated with social factors or settings. (pp. 19–21; 27–33)

SPEECH EVENT. Sociolinguistic term for an identifiable communicative unit, usually recognized as such in common parlance: for example, insult, joke. (pp. 23; 27)

STANDARD USAGE. (or 'variety') Language use associated with high-status users and the transaction of public business. (pp. 5–6; 19; 30–3)

SYNTAX. The organization of words and morphemes (*q.v.*) into larger units (for example, sentences). (p. 18)

SYSTEMATIC OBSERVATION. The observation of behaviour which operates through the marking of categories on a schedule by a trained observer. (pp. 60–1; 83–91; 96–100; 138–9)

TRANSACTIONAL LANGUAGE. That used for getting things done; sometimes contrasted with 'interactional' use which concentrates more on (for example) relationships. (p. 10)

TRIANGULATION. Process whereby certain researchers (for example, in ethnography: *q.v.*) consult participants, for example, about transcripts of their interactions, with a view to establishing a shared perspective on what 'really' occurred. (pp. 76–7)

TURN. One person's turn at speaking; anything from, for example, a single exclamation to a long series of utterances (*q.v.*). (pp. 46–7; 115–6; 145–7)

UTTERANCE. For many, the basic unit of discourse; typically shorter and less complete than a sentence, which is its (idealized) grammatical counterpart. (p. 19)

VARIABILITY. The flexibility in choice of words, etc., available to speakers as they respond to context or realize particular communicative intentions; related to individuals' 'linguistic repertoire' of speech styles. (pp. 20–1; 30–2)

VARIETY. Regularly occurring ways of speaking which are associated with particular categories of user (dialects) or of use (registers: *q.v.*) (pp. 19–20; 29–33)

Introduction

The 'language of the classroom' has become so prominent a topic of academic interest that it is difficult to remember how recent that interest is. For a surprisingly long time, the questions which classroom researchers were most inclined to ask were about the outcomes of teaching. They rarely enquired into the complex interactions through which knowledge is transmitted, displayed, impeded or avoided. When they did so, they even more rarely recorded 'live' the verbal encounters which constitute such a large part of classroom interaction. To find verbatim transcripts of classroom talk produced before about 1970 is difficult (Bellack *et al*, 1966, and Massialas and Zevin 1967, are among the exceptions). While their absence is partly attributable to the relative difficulty and higher visibility of making recordings compared with the discreet cassettes and radiomicrophones available now, it also reflects a confidence that what was happening in the exchanges of teachers and pupils was sufficiently obvious to be noted by a trained observer.

Professional interest in classroom language has grown with the recognition of its centrality in the processes of learning, and its value as evidence of how relationships and meanings are organized. That interest received a powerful stimulus in the UK from the publication of *Language, the Learner and the School* (Barnes *et al*, 1969). In particular, Barnes' account of the predominance of 'closed' questions in whole-class teaching, and the consequently heavy constraints on what pupils could say and mean, led many teachers to reflect for the first time on their routine practices and even make them a matter for investigation. The experience of seeing their methods reflected in Barnes' descriptions and their transcript illustrations might be 'crucifying', but it could lead to extensive recording of interaction in their own classrooms to see first if things were really so bad, and then if they could be made better — 'The more I listened to the tapes, the less I talked in class, and the more my teaching energies went into devising contexts in which learners' talk could take place naturally and fluidly, without my having to interfere with it' (Torbe and Medway, 1981, p. 6). Supported by studies like those of Barnes and his colleagues, more attention was paid to the communicative demands made on children in classrooms, and to the rather limited range of skills they were typically called upon to display. There was interest in how much those demands varied across age groups and across subjects of the curriculum, and in whether forms of learning which were more collaborative and less teacher-dominated could be recognized clearly in the patterns of communication which they generated.

There were obvious attractions in recording classroom talk. Listening to it and transcribing it could reveal characteristics of teacher-pupil encounters unnoticed in the hectic pace of classroom life. Transcript evidence seemed to bring a breath of life into the previously rather arid confines of classroom research. It was also evidence on hand, of a kind which teachers could collect for themselves and so contribute to research rather than waiting for the 'findings' of others (Martin, 1984).

The attractions of recording and transcribing, however, were offset by some formidable difficulties. In the Systematic approach to observation which dominated classroom research until well into the 1970s, and which was itself largely directed towards 'professional self-improvement' (Flanders, 1976), it could be claimed reassuringly that — 'an hour of observation yields an hour of data' (Rosenshine and Furst, 1973, p. 149). Even the analysis of that data could be quickly carried out, and the results fed back to the waiting practitioner as a basis for recognizing both a need for change in teaching strategy and the direction that change might take. In sharp contrast, the taping of lessons and the transcribing of the tapes is 'enormously laborious', and their careful scrutiny is 'arduous' (Torbe and Medway, 1981, pp. 6–7). An hour's audio-recording will take 15–20 hours to transcribe with any thoroughness, and the researcher may then feel overwhelmed by the detail and complexity of the data. Describing how eight teachers in a London comprehensive school set up their own 'talk workshop' to investigate the quality of language used in their classrooms, John Richmond (1984) describes their early feeling of panic about whether there was 'anything there at all' in the tapes and videos they had so laboriously made and, if there was, what they had to do to find it.

Questions immediately arise about how much teachers need to know to overcome that bewilderment, and to make all the hard labour productive. For example, what 'technical' skills are necessary, and how theoretically informed is it necessary to be, to say much that is useful about the complex organization of classroom talk? Is it possible to apply methods of analyzing classroom talk without extensive knowledge of the specialized academic areas of enquiry from which they derive, especially where a thoroughgoing commitment to a particular approach would seem to demand a level of theoretical specialization which the busy practitioner is unlikely to possess in sufficient measure (Atkins, 1984).

Throughout this book, we have tried to keep in mind the busy practitioner, the teacher in training, and researchers (of the 'action' variety and others) whose interest in classroom language may be less direct than our own. We have also been more concerned with methods than with findings, and with setting out a wide range of approaches from which those enquiring into classroom processes can take appropriate examples and modify them to fit their particular purposes.

The range is wide, because so much of the impetus behind investigations of classroom talk came from outside the ranks of educational researchers. It came from linguists, especially those wishing to claim the then recently invented label of socio-linguists, who sought to extend the domain of linguistic study beyond a rigorous concentration on structure abstracted from use to a more 'socially-realistic' concern with 'persons in a social world who must know when to speak, when not, what to talk about, with whom, when, where, and in what manner' (Hymes, 1972, p. 277). They were joined by ethnographers, and specifically 'ethnographers of communication', whose primary theoretical purpose was to discover how talk is systematically patterned in ways which reveal, or define, how the speakers perceive their relationships and situation. Such talk may then become broadly predictable 'on the basis of certain features of the local social system' (Blom and Gumperz, 1972, pp. 421–2).

Given all the subtleties and complexities of human communication, that purpose seemed to be more readily achievable where the 'local social system' was strongly marked, and the talk 'institutionalized' in ways that could be identified in its structure. Thus many researchers have agreed with Sinclair and Coulthard (1975, p. 2) that classrooms represent an attractive research setting precisely because — 'teacher-pupil relationships are sufficiently well-defined for us to expect clear evidence of this in the text'. As part of this general interest in situationally-appropriate forms of talk came numerous investigations of the distinctiveness of classrooms as communicative settings, the nature of the demands commonly made on pupils as they received and displayed school knowledge, and the continuities and discontinuities between those demands and their experience of language being used in the other main settings of their social world (for example, Cazden *et al*, 1972). Since it seemed probable that the dominant role normally taken by teachers imposed severe situational constraints on the communicative options available to pupils, much sociolinguistic work followed the directive addressed by Cazden to those engaged in testing children's language development — 'When a child makes or fails to make a particular kind of utterance, consider characteristics of the situation as well as of the child' (Cazden, 1971, p, 84; also Cazden, 1977).

The practical implications of such research were so clear to those doing it as to make nonsense of any contrast between the 'pure' and the 'applied'. For example, Hymes' (1972) influential discussion of communicative competence was largely directed towards the problems encountered by children from one cultural background who enter classrooms where communicative demands may be defined largely in terms of another. Analysis of such problems necessarily carried researchers far beyond the classroom. They had to examine 'how questions are customarily answered, turns taken, silence is maintained and broken, to understand that part of a verbal repertoire that appears in educational settings' (Hymes, 1979, p. 4). It was the challenge of narrowing the gap between what is known and what needs to be known about the communicative skills necessary (or strategic) for educational success which led Hymes to see the study of 'language in education' as the cutting edge of a fully social-linguistics, and as an 'integrating focus' for many other areas of academic work.

How an informed insight into the 'language of the classroom' might help teachers is a question which we consider in detail. We are both aware from personal experience of the benefits to be gained from working closely with teachers on the analysis of language arising in the circumstances in which they work (Edwards and Furlong, 1978, 1985; Westgate *et al*, 1985; Hughes and Westgate, 1988, 1990). We are also aware of the studies carried out by individuals and by groups of teachers seeking to transform their everyday intuitive experience into deeper, more systematic and more shareable insights. While disclaiming any easy belief that 'knowing more' about classroom language will bring simple recipes for 'better' teaching, we have tried to indicate some of the main sources of such knowledge and some ways in which it can be further enhanced.

During the seven years separating the first and second editions of this book, quite dramatic changes have been taking place not only in the scope of our knowledge about classroom talk, but also (and not uncontroversially) in the educational status of talk — particularly in the UK, although parallel developments are observable, for instance, in North America, Australia and New Zealand. The growth in knowledge and the increased importance accorded to talk have been inter-related. In the UK, it is possible to discern three connected strands of influence, in at least two of which teachers have played an important part. The first is the National Oracy Project; the second, the inclusion of a separate Attainment Target for 'speaking and listening' in the National Curriculum orders for English; the third, the growing recognition within a large section of the educational (including research) community that spoken language plays a central and mediating role in a much wider curriculum. Thus MacLure *et al*, (1988) introduce their valuable collection of essays by making a 'distinction between oracy as a medium of learning in all subjects, and oracy as a subject in its own right — as a further aspect of language competence which teachers now have an obligation to promote, alongside the traditionally recognized skills of reading and writing' (p. 2). Other publications illustrate the prominence being given to that obligation: for instance, Jones (1988), Self (1987), Tarleton (1988) and Wray (1990).

The increasingly wide currency of the term 'oracy' is also in itself indicative, its meaning remaining very much that given to it by its acknowledged originator, Andrew Wilkinson, when he wrote: 'Oracy is not a "subject" — it is a condition of learning in all subjects; it is not a "frill" but a state of being in which the whole school must operate' (1965, p. 58). That is, oracy is a concern within the English lesson but also and essentially beyond that, in all teaching and learning, at every age and phase. The inter-dependency between what MacLure *et al*, call 'oracy as competence' and 'oracy for learning' was also anticipated by Wilkinson. He wrote: 'Where children are . . . placed in situations where it becomes important for them to communicate — to discuss, to negotiate, to converse — with their fellows, with the staff, with other adults . . . This is basically how oracy grows: it is to be taught by the creation of many and varied circumstances to which speech and listening are the natural responses' (1965, p. 59). What has changed since that time, and even since the publication of our first edition in 1987, is the professional acceptance of these propositions, the practical understanding of oracy in a range of settings, and the development of a theoretical rationale to underpin it.

The National Oracy Project can be seen as an embodiment of that acceptance and as an important source of improvements in that understanding. The main part of its work was carried out between 1987 and 1991. It drew its strength from regionally-based groups of teachers and co-ordinators, following a pattern already set by pioneers who had been active as early as the mid-seventies in Inner London (see, for example, Talk Workshop Group, 1982) and the late-eighties in Wiltshire (see, for example, Howe, 1988). Eventually, more than half of the LEAs in England were to be involved at differing levels. Co-ordinated by a national steering committee, like the Writing Project which preceded it, the National Oracy Project was essentially a devolved operation. Many of the insights of those associated with the Project can be found in its numerous publications, notably the collection edited by Norman (1992), but its officially-designated dissemination phase (1991–3) had also been preceded by widely-shared explorations of classroom talk the benefits of which were already being seen in practice. Numerous teachers had been noting, recording and transcribing talk, as well as sharing their interpretations; they had been looking for ways of extending and making more effective their pupils' talk-contexts, of putting pupils into more diverse roles, of relinquishing their own monopoly of expertise, and of gaining a better understanding of such matters as the use of small-group talk, together with its implications for classroom management and equal opportunities issues.

In some ways therefore the Project followed the cyclical model of classroom action research — of reflection, experimentation, evaluation and re-application — but with the added bonus for the teachers involved of working in groups and learning from one another. At the same time, some of the materials produced for discussion were gathered together more formally. Intended to provide talk-related in-service support for Language in the National Curriculum (LINC) on a truly national basis, these materials were nevertheless to remain un-disseminated, the victims of a political agenda and, in particular, of arguments surrounding perceived threats to standard English to which we return.

The story of the emergence, and of the prompt revision, of English in the National Curriculum is well-documented (for example, Stubbs, 1989; Cox, 1992). Among many ironies surrounding these developments is the juxtaposition between the original Working Group's insistence on the importance of oracy to the well-being of a democracy and the reception given to the proposals in a context of right-wing preoccupations with authority. The Group had asserted, for example, the value of future citizens being able to 'discuss, evaluate and make sense of what they are told' and to act on that understanding; without such abilities, the Group continued, there could be 'no genuine participation, but only the imposition of the ideas of those who are linguistically capable' (DES, 1989, 2:17). That message remains severely at odds with the agenda of those politicians preoccupied with the inculcation of standard forms.

A valuable and more general exploration of the 'politics of oracy' is given by Barnes (1988). Of immediate significance in the present context is the welcome given to the English proposals as a whole by those long concerned with the centrality of oracy. Wilkinson *et al*, (1990), for instance, praised its authors for incorporating 'much of the best in theory and practice over the last thirty years' (p. 3). Nevertheless, they (and others) point to problems arising from the adoption for English of a general assessment-led model involving a series of ten ascending levels of attainment. These problems concern, at bottom, the attempt to assess children's essentially non-linear development in speaking and listening by a linear sequence of levels, the very definition of which also creates difficulty. Progress in 'discussion' can be cited to illustrate the point: 'participate as speakers and listeners in a group engaged in a given talk' exemplifies Level 2, while 'Take an active part in group discussion' refers to Level 7, and 'Take part in group discussions actively and critically' indicates Level 8. *How* active is 'active', one might ask? Where does 'critically' stop and 'obstructively' begin?

Between them, however, the National Oracy Project and National Curriculum English, with its equal treatment of spoken and written modes, constitute a measure of official recognition for classroom talk. The notion of oracy as 'talking to learn' has, however, drawn further justification from a cluster of recent studies (see for example, Edwards and Mercer, 1987; Wells, 1987; Newman *et al*, 1989; Maybin, 1991; Mercer, 1992; Norman, 1992) with a common theoretical approach frequently termed 'constructivist'. Key features of this perspective on learning, knowing and (therefore) teaching include: the idea that knowledge is constructed by the individual knower, through an interaction between what is already known and new experience; that knowing is thus not so much a state as a process, and as such is helped by social interaction; hence learning and teaching can helpfully be seen as collaborative and involving the social and cultural perceptions of all parties. Talk is central to this view of learning and knowing, being the primary medium of interaction, and because it helps learners to make explicit to themselves and others what they know, understand and can do. An accessible account of this view and its implications for oracy is given by Wells (1992) and a thorough overview is provided by Wood (1988).

As we make clear in chapter 1, these developments have had the effect of accentuating views of teaching and learning already being articulated in the early work of Barnes (for example, 1976) and in the Bullock Report of 1975. They have a clear pedigree. Wells writes of 'a coherent theory of learning and teaching . . . originating in the works of Piaget and Vygotsky and extended by scholars in a wide range of disciplines' (1992, p. 285), while Britton (1987) also attributes great influence to the work of Vygotsky. In terms of practical pedagogy, processes involving argument, explication, hypothesis testing, justifying, etc., are emphasised, but these influential studies also have important implications for classroom enquiries where talk is the focus and the source of data. If the development of understanding is 'a communicative accomplishment embodied in classroom discourse' (Edwards D, 1990), talk itself has also to be recognized as jointly constructed. Pupil-talk thus provides not so much a window on to the individual pupil's thinking as to a collaborative discourse through which meanings are shared and constructed. It is a perspective therefore to which we give further attention in chapter 5 and, particularly, in chapter 6.

We also have to recognize, however, more clearly than when first writing this book, that the commitment to enabling pupils to talk their way into understanding has been contested from the political Right as part of a campaign against 'progressive' practice. From that perspective, 'real' education is inherently undemocratic because its transactions are properly between a teacher who knows and pupils who do not, and progressive practice defers to ignorance by giving too much respect to uninformed pupil opinion and so too much time to 'aimless chatter'. It thereby replaces authoritative transmission of knowledge with 'easygoing discussion and opinionated vagueness' (Hillgate Group, 1987, p. 3). And it is supposedly aided in doing so by progressive-minded HMI, who are inclined to 'tear into any school where pupils are not in continual conversation with their teacher and . . . not continually questioning everything they are taught' (O'Hear, 1991, p. 24). There could hardly a sharper pedagogic and communicative contrast than between, for example, Barnes' (1992) defence of pupils' talk as critical to their 'trying out' new ways of knowing and understanding, and O'Hear's (1991) argument that, since education is a prolonged induction into established bodies of knowledge, then pupils will have no opinions worth eliciting until their grounding in the subject is already firm.

Most of the research cited in the chapters which follow provides evidence of the potential richness of pupil talk, and much of it originated in teachers' interest in exploring that potential. The first chapter exemplifies some of the more essential technical terms (which appear in the Glossary) in the course of reviewing various rationales for recording and analyzing classroom talk. It also discusses some of the possibilities and difficulties inherent in the task of 'reading off' the managing of relationships and the transaction of meanings from the form and structure of spoken language. Chapter 2 describes some main dimensions of classroom language as these have been studied from different perspectives. It is more directly concerned with substantive than with methodological issues. In contrast, chapter 3 deals with the methods adopted by researchers in relation to their theoretical affiliations and their practical purposes. It reports a diversity of methods for displaying verbal records so as to capture as much as possible of the knowledge and relationships 'behind' them. In the three chapters which follow, the strengths and limitations of different approaches are considered, with an emphasis on their appropriateness to particular topics and problems, and with special reference to particular studies which either illustrate their range and power or which have had considerable influence on classroom research.

The book reflects our own fascination with language in its social contexts, and in particular with its typical forms and functions in classrooms. If there is a single theme which unifies and focuses our interests, it is a concern with the communicative consequences of transmitting knowledge, and a concern for the often limited and limiting quality of language experience which schools offer children.

1 A Rationale for Researching Classroom Talk

All normal human beings are expert in the practical interpretation of talk. Most of our everyday life depends on skills in talking and making sense of the talk of others, as we work or trade or simply pass the time of day.

These skills go far beyond the uttering of sounds related by the conventions of our language to objects, actions or ideas. In our speech we select and organize our utterances according to our sense of what is correct and appropriate in a particular setting. This is partly a matter of grammar, partly of social etiquette, partly of culture, and essentially of assuming that others will be perceiving the same situation as we do. Our largely tacit knowledge of ourselves, of others, and of the conventions which shape interpersonal behaviour, enables us to take part in all kinds of social interaction. In interpreting the talk of others, we routinely make allowance for apparent disparities between what we take them to mean and the actual words they use. We also create coherent conversation out of the seemingly unconnectable —

> Speaker A 'Do you know what time it is?'
> Speaker B 'The train was late.'
> Speaker A 'That's a tall one'.

Readers will have little difficulty in imagining possible contexts for this exchange, a fact which both illustrates the point already made and then extends it by demonstrating our capacity to make hypothetical analyses even of second-hand data. As participants in interaction, we can be generally confident in our interpretations because we can use our ability to attend to fine details of intonation, stress, pitch and tone of voice, pausing and hesitation, gesture, movement, facial expression and other features of body language. We can integrate clues from each source of evidence, and act or react instantly on the basis of our judgment. In our turn, we deploy such signals in ways which are normally consistent with our personalities but are also adapted to our shifting perceptions of those with whom we interact in the circumstances in which we do so. In the act of making statements about the world, or asking or answering questions, we also and simultaneously locate ourselves socially, indicate how we perceive others, and announce, confirm or challenge how the situation is to be defined. As observers of the talk of others, we draw on this everyday knowledge in treating the words as evidence of the meanings, purposes and consequences for those involved.

At a deeper level, this knowledge reflects processes which underlie all social interaction. Cicourel (1973), for example, lists among the basic 'interpretive procedures' which make orderly communication possible an assumed 'reciprocity of perspectives', mutual willingness to 'fill in' meanings which are meant but not stated, and a recognition that what is said now may not become clear until later in the interaction or may have to be reinterpreted in the light of past words and action. From a very different disciplinary perspective, Grice (1975) suggests a similar basis for orderly talk which he calls a 'co-operative principle'. This consists of a readiness to assume that our interlocutors' utterances mean something, and that it is our job to discern what that something may be. We therefore scan both talk and context for relevant evidence. As soon as it is appropriate, we may test our judgment, not (usually) by asking directly 'Do you mean X?', but rather by backing our hunch and basing subsequent contributions on it. The hunch can then be revised if things go wrong. Continuous interpretation, and frequent re-interpretation, are among the intricacies which confer upon talk both its fascination and its intricacy as an object of study.

Although we have begun with conversation, it has been the more evidently purposeful, 'transactional' uses of talk which have received most analytical attention, especially from linguistics, psycholinguistics, and philosophy of language. Sociolinguistics and sociology, however, have been more concerned with the 'interactional' functions of language — its uses to establish and maintain social relationships. From this perspective, talk can often be seen as an end in itself, from its more trivial to its most 'artful' forms. It includes so-called 'phatic' talk through which the participants tell each other little or nothing they did not know already ('Raining again, I see'), but where the mere exchange of words conveys at least a token friendliness and sense of solidarity. It also includes all kinds of deliberate word-play, such as the playground rhyming recording by the Opies (1959, p. 18) — 'I'm a knock-kneed chicken, I'm a bow-legged sparrow, Missed my bus so I went by barrow' — or the ritualized exchanges of insults reported by Labov (1972a, p. 342) — 'At least my mother ain't no railroad track laid all over the country'. Here propositional content is, mercifully, not the point. What counts is style, quickness in repartee, finding old words to fit the context or skilfully creating new content within quite rigidly prescribed forms.

We have begun as though talk was either transactional or interactional. In fact, utterances characteristically convey social and cultural as well as propositional meanings. Some conversations are almost entirely interactional, ways of passing the time of day, while business-talk in public places is almost entirely transactional. In general, however, talk is social action, and represents the fundamentally human way of getting things done. We persuade others to provide us with goods or services, or ask them to tell us what we do not know. We sharpen our own understanding by telling or attempting to explain to others. As we hear ourselves say what we think, or what we think that we think, we can monitor this objectification of our thoughts, judging its accuracy or adequacy and modifying it where necessary. Without plentiful experience of 'talking things through', we would be denied access to that 'inner speech' (Vygotsky, 1962) through which we organize our thinking.

All of us have the temerity at times to instruct others. Some of us are paid to do so, to transmit systematically some selected parts of what we believe we know. The institutionalizing of this process in schools has invested with special status certain kinds of knowing and certain ways of displaying knowledge. The complex relationships between knowing and displaying provide an underlying theme of this book, because pupils and students have to develop the language skills necessary to meet the transactional and interactional demands characteristic of classrooms. Some of these skills have already been learned in the home and are easily transferred to a new setting, some have to be newly acquired, and much of what has been learned already about communication has to be set aside as unnecessary or inappropriate to learning as it is formally organized. Certainly learning to 'become pupils' (Willes, 1983) is very much a matter of mastering an interactional code, the rules of which are regularly acted on by teachers and pupils but rarely explained.

1 The Educational Status of Classroom Talk

We need to begin by examining the nature of the language experience in the dialogue between teacher and class . . . By its very nature a lesson is a verbal encounter through which the teacher draws information from the class, elaborates and generalizes it, and produces a synthesis. His skill is in selecting, prompting, improving, and generally orchestrating the exchange (Bullock Report 'A Language for Life', 1975, p. 141).

Learning from words is, of course, only one form of instruction. There are many societies in which children learn mainly by observing and imitating their elders. Such learning from experience is then practised without adult criticism or evaluation, and its results are displayed publicly only when the learner feels a sufficient sense of mastery to do so (Phillips, 1983; Cook-Gumperz and Gumperz 1982). Formal schooling, however, normally means lessons, and most lessons are 'verbal encounters' orchestrated by the teacher.

It is only relatively recently, however, that the quality of those encounters has received close attention. Although talk has long been the principal medium of instruction in the schools, the aim of fostering pupils' powers of verbal expression and the valuing of their talk for its contribution to learning have emerged much more slowly. Traditional education put its stress on written language; it is the skills of literacy, not oracy, which figure among the '3 Rs'. The transmission of information was achieved mainly through the teacher's 'talk and chalk', and the pupils' note-taking and written exercises. Their talk was largely confined to chanting in chorus, or reciting what had been learned by rote, and answering questions that tested memory and attentiveness. And it was talk from which the 'language of the playground', and in many circumstances the language of the home too, was expected to have been properly filtered out.

Over the last twenty-five years or so, however, the status of classroom talk has changed markedly. It has been accorded a central place in the processes of learning. What linguists term 'the primacy of speech' has been translated by educators into a new respect for talk that has received strong academic support in psychology, child development, sociolinguistics and sociology. An extensive literature on 'language in education' has emerged, much of it focused on problems associated with linguistic 'disadvantage' but much of it looking critically too at how language is organized and used in classrooms. Official reports have urged teachers to scrutinize language 'across the curriculum', and to plan deliberately to extend the range of opportunities available to pupils when listening and speaking no less than when reading and writing. George Sampson's statement of 1934 that 'every teacher is a teacher of English' has acquired, in the UK and the USA, resonances he could scarcely have predicted.

While changes in pedagogic practice have not kept pace with the prescriptions, the ideas themselves have achieved a large measure of penetration into both the initial and in-service training of teachers (for example, Farrer and Richmond, 1981), and have found official sanction at a high level — most notably in the Bullock Report of 1975 and then in the National Oracy Project and the National Curriculum. Although no studies of classroom language were commissioned by the Bullock Committee itself, its Report has particular interest because its terms of reference were set at a time of increasingly fierce debate about 'standards' and the supposed threat to them from over-'progressive' methods of teaching. On the one hand, the Report can be seen as a significant early contribution to a shift towards more central control over the curriculum (Ball, 1985). For the teaching of English especially, it is in this light a 'publicly-conducted procedure of boundary definition', in which some innovations were commended while others were censured as 'excessive'. On the other hand, those innovations which the Report did sponsor can be seen as remarkably radical in their underlying insistence on extending the range of uses to which language is put in classrooms so as to provide richer opportunities for children to 'learn by talking and writing' (*ibid.* 1975, 4.10). What is more, the injunction to take seriously the learner's language (particularly talk) was intended to apply to all areas of the curriculum, and therefore to require 'whole-school policies' in the development of which teachers' consciousness of classroom language would be raised with far-reaching pedagogic consequences. Thus what had been one of several competing models of English teaching — dubbed by Ball (1985) the 'English as language paradigm' — not only received strong backing in itself, but was identified as a relevant model for other subjects.

The first main sources of this view of language as being central to the processes of school learning were psychological and psycho-linguistic. Of particular influence were Kelly, Bruner and Vygotsky, all of whose ideas found eloquent interpretation in the UK through James Britton (1970), himself an important contributor to the Bullock Report. Similar views underlay the early seminal studies of classroom talk by Douglas Barnes (Barnes, Britton and Rosen, 1969; Barnes, 1976). Indeed, something very like Barnes' model of 'exploratory' pupil talk appears in several subsequent Reports. For example, pupils need more opportunities than were observable in most primary classrooms to 'find their own solutions to the problems posed', to follow a sustained argument and discuss it afterwards, and to ask questions as well as answer them (HMI, 1978, pp. 27, 46–7). The 'best work' seen in English lessons, as elsewhere in the secondary curriculum, was marked by 'a teaching style which allowed for the free expression of ideas, refined by frequent and sustained discussion and a good deal of individual contact between teacher and pupils' (HMI, 1979, pp. 74–5). Even very young pupils should engage more often than they seemed to do in most classrooms in 'the kind of talking and listening which is engendered by shared experiences' (DES, 1982, 2.34). Much older pupils often suffered from a sharp decline in orally-based lessons at the very time when they needed to achieve 'a near-adult level of articulation'; teachers should therefore take care to act more often as consultants and less often as mere transmitters of information, should recognize discussion as a proper form of 'real work', and should encourage pupils to generate their own questions and to explore alternative answers (ILEA, 1984, p. 70).

While outlining in the Introduction how 'constructivist' theory has provided a coherent justification for these views, we disclaimed any intention of being prescriptive ourselves. Our concern is with methods of investigating the quality of classroom talk so as to understand more clearly how language is used and organized in various modes of teaching and learning. From this perspective, it has to be admitted that prescriptions, and even diagnoses of what is wrong, have tended to run far ahead of the evidence. We review in later chapters the rapid growth of classroom-based educational research since the late 1960s, and we want here to make only two preliminary comments.

Those early studies which reported scenes from classroom life certainly had a more attractive flavour of 'reality' about them than could be found in the numbers, tables and matrices produced by researchers working in the Systematic tradition (compare, for example Flanders, 1970 and Jackson, 1968). But language received attention only as a more-or-less transparent medium through which to observe and record social interaction. Where language was explicitly the focus of investigation was in the difficult and politically-explosive debate about 'linguistic disadvantage' and its educational consequences. But here the disadvantages from which lower-class or ethnic-minority children were said to suffer in coping with classroom demands were identified with almost no empirical reference to what those demands typically were. Deficiencies or differences identified in their language, or in their experience of using language, were then 'matched' against the very demanding forms and uses of language which it was assumed must face them in school. But almost all the direct evidence relevant to revealing contrasts and continuities came from the language of the home (A. Edwards, 1976, pp. 145–7). While careful investigation of school demands certainly began in the early 1970s (for example, Cazden, 1972; Cazden *et al*, 1972), Stubbs still ended a cogent review of the 'deficit' debate by listing eight broad areas of classroom language in which evidence was almost entirely lacking. He prefaced that list by claiming, justifiably, that — 'We still know very little about what *actually happens in classrooms* between teachers and pupils, and have little basic information about teacher-pupil dialogue in different teaching situations' (Stubbs, 1976, p. 114; original emphasis).

That sentence remains unmodified in the second edition of his book (1983), which seems unfair in the light of the very considerable advances in knowledge and understanding made in the intervening years — advances for which Stubbs himself can take some credit, partly for having pointed the way and partly for his own contributions to developing one of the relevant methods, that of discourse analysis. While there is truth in his observation that research has concentrated too much on formal instruction in conventional contexts, there has been other work too which has advanced both our knowledge of school processes and the power of available research instruments. Most methods of investigating classroom talk which we review have been developed or applied since the early 1970s, so that direct evidence of its forms and functions is no longer as impoverished. Significantly, in their own revised version of persistent problems and gaps in classroom research, Delamont and Hamilton (1984) base their updated cautionary advice on the knowledge that research in real settings has burgeoned so that many of their earlier suggestions of what was needed have now become a kind of orthodoxy (Hamilton and Delamont, 1974). Similarly, Wolcott (1982) worries that the fashion for ethnographic investigation of classrooms in the United States may lead to the approach being 'usurped for the purposes of quick and dirty program evaluation', instead of the careful and detailed 'contextual description' which ethnographers should feel obliged to undertake.

2   The Status of Talk As Evidence

At this point in our account, it may still be unclear why talk, rather than some other indexical features of classroom life, is held to be so rich a source of data. It is because 'the process of learning how to negotiate communicatively is the very process by which one enters the culture' (Bruner, 1984). It is largely through talk that we develop our concepts of self, as members of various social 'worlds' which can be brought into focus and in which we can locate ourselves and recognize the values, rights and obligations which permeate them. As we listen and as we talk, we learn what it is necessary to know, do and say in that area of social life or that setting, and can display the competence necessary to be accepted as a member.

It is for these reasons that talk is so important as a source of data. Since so much is constituted in and through it, its close inspection should reveal the very constituting processes themselves. In classrooms, that means making 'visible' the curriculum in both its 'manifest' and its 'hidden' forms. It should bring into view the declared agenda of lessons, together with those other meanings to be drawn from them about what it is like to enter given areas of human thought, how the apparent experts behave and use their knowledge, how it feels to be inducted into parts of 'their' knowledge, how pupils define and display their sense of their own capacities and personal worth in their struggle to assimilate school knowledge, or to reject it. While all that may be open to scrutiny through analysis of talk, there is much more to see; for participation in classroom events also depends on habits and expectations derived from wider, non-school contexts which are still actively relevant within the classroom.

Reviewing this book, Tony Burgess (1988) commented that our rationale 'tends to slide between "talk" and "language" as the mediating force in people's lives', and that our emphasis on oracy had led us to neglect literacy. Certainly 'presuppositions about literacy and about the forms of written language' shape classroom communication through the relative priority given to speech and writing, and the extent to which talk is treated as preparation for more 'serious' work. A strongly hierarchical view of that relationship was certainly apparent in ministerial reactions to the initial recommendations about English in the National Curriculum, and the English Working Group had to struggle hard to defend the equal weighting it gave to 'speaking and listening' (Cox, 1991, pp. 125–132). The strength of ministerial resistance is only explicable in the context of wider debates about standard language, and about the importance of upholding 'correct usage'. We therefore agree with Burgess that the analysis of classroom language should relate forms of talk to forms of writing, and relate both to 'wider processes of cultural transmission' (Burgess 1988, p. 135). In revising this book, we refer to recent research which has explored the interactions between teacher and pupils from which written texts are eventually produced, and the problems which can arise in moving between spoken and written discourse (Christie, 1987; Jackson, 1988; Pirie, 1991). We have also kept in mind Wells (1987) use of 'literate thinking' to cover all uses of language in which meanings are explored, connected or re-arranged, some of the most interesting research we cite having required investigation of cultural differences in how stories are narrated, jokes told, questions asked and arguments proceed in children's home world, and their conse-quent ease or unfamiliarity with how language is used in their classrooms.

How far is it possible then to 'read' the talk of teachers and pupils as evidence of how they perceive and organize their immediate tasks and how, more broadly, pupils perceive and respond to the demands of school in the light of their other social and cultural knowledge and experience? In asking these questions and emphasizing the possibilities, we are not our-selves treating classroom talk as a transparent, neutral medium through which the relationships and ideas of the participants are easily discerned. As Mehan has argued (1984, p. 181) —

> By treating language as a mediating force in people's lives, socio-linguists have pointed out the importance of looking at the win-dow of language and not just through it. Here, language as a mediator is not meant in the statistical sense of a variable that intervenes between independent and dependent variables in a correlational equation; it is used in the communicative sense that the acts of speaking and listening enable people to make sense of the world. That is, language transforms the world, changing nature into culture.

The exciting potential of talk-analysis is accompanied, however, by for-midable difficulties. There is, first, the sheer quantity of words exchanged. Talk remains the main means of transmitting information, and books and other prepared resources are essentially only adjuncts to it. Then there is all the 'social talk' which surrounds and often submerges the 'language of instruction'. With so much to record, researchers may well feel as though they are drowning in data. Being therefore necessarily selective about what to record, transcribe, analyze and report brings immediate worries about how representative or typical the selections are. Some of the technicalities of transcription, together with some of the dilemmas involved in using transcript as evidence, are discussed more fully in chapter 3.

For all the richness of talk as data, transcripts alone are unlikely to be sufficient. All kinds of experiences, in and out of school, shape classroom interaction and the participants' interpretations of it. How is the observer to know what parts of those experiences are relevant and 'in play' at that time? Since so much more is understood than is ever said, how is that observer to know what the participants are taking for granted about, or reading into, the interaction — whether from their recollections of past encounters of that kind, or from the history of their particular relationships? Can the misunderstandings and occasional bewilderment which may arise when the observer treats too much of what is said at 'face value' be reduced or even overcome by such complementary strategies as 'going native' (in the sense of living with the participants long enough to enter their culture), or consulting them directly about uncertain interpretations? How confident can observers be that what they believe they see in the moments they select is either representative of other comparable events or free from gross distortion due precisely to the participants' awareness that they are being observed?

At least two opposing responses to these questions can be envisaged. One might be to reject an over-reliance on talk as evidence on the grounds that its meanings are so difficult to interpret, and so dependent on local detail and background knowledge which the observer is unlikely to have, that the laborious tasks of recording and transcribing and analyzing are not worth the effort, and that easier sources of data must be found instead. Another might begin with the recognition that while talk is certainly complex, subtle, allusive and often ambiguous, it is about time educational research adopted appropriately complex and sensitive forms of enquiry and explanation. This response might go on to acknowledge that general theories have, as they develop, to be tested against particular reality, that modest claims are usually the most convincing, and that even the most formidable research problems are not to be overcome by pretending that they do not exist. This, roughly, is our own view. We have therefore tried to find a reasonable balance between confronting the difficulties and limitations of various approaches to investigating classroom talk while also identifying their possibilities.

3 Concepts and Terminology

The accounts of various approaches to investigating classroom talk which are given in later chapters involve concepts developed in several disciplines. Some of these concepts and their associated terminology are now introduced so that readers may have a sense of the intellectual contexts for the practices and procedures they will meet, and so that they may gauge the levels of technicality necessary in different kinds of analysis.

Every discipline has its technical vocabulary, and is open in consequence to charges of using jargon. The force of those charges is difficult to establish. Some of the distinctive terms used by specialists are essential tools of their academic trade, discriminating between phenomena and classifying them with a detail and precision not available (because they are not needed) outside it. Other terms can be seen more as linguistic markers of academic territory which, while not strictly needed to organize inquiry in particular ways, serve to reinforce their users' sense of being 'insiders' and non-users' sense of exclusion. Examples can therefore be found in every discipline of technical language which seems unnecessarily mysterious, or which seems to cover conceptual or empirical nakedness with 'verbal substitutions masquerading as knowledge' (Andreski, 1974, p. 58).

Unfortunately, however, the 'smokescreen of jargon' which Andreski so deplores as a display of academic 'sorcery' is more easily denounced than penetrated, one person's mere 'verbal substitutions' being another's necessary clarifications. We take the view that certain concepts are so essential in organizing various fields of language study that they have to be introduced at this stage, although others may well be required (and acquired) in the course of examining particular styles of enquiry. For example, work in discourse analysis demands some general linguistic knowledge and an elaborately technical coding scheme; on the other hand, some classroom observation schedules are designed to need only a few hours' training and no acquaintance with any theory underlying them. In writing about a wide range of methods, we have borne in mind Barnes' (1969) distinction between 'intellectual' usage which usefully and economically encapsulates necessary ideas, and merely 'conventional' usage which may confer a spurious respectability on academic writing at the cost of disengaging the reader. We have therefore tried to avoid unnecessary verbal 'smokescreens'. But the 'special languages' of academic study provide more than new, and perhaps mystifying, labels for familiar things. They also provide ways of 'seeing' what is of particular interest to the observer, and of describing and categorizing it with a consistency and precision not available in everyday language because there is no need for the specialized terms in which that work is done. 'If what distinguishes a subject is its distinctive conventions of thought and particular conceptions of phenomena, the task for teachers is to communicate those conventions as useful . . . ways of understanding the world' (Barnes and Sheeran, 1992, p. 91). That is the task for the rest of this chapter, which attempts to define some key concepts through which to observe and make sense of the complexities of classroom talk.

It has been a primary achievement of twentieth-century linguistics to establish the systematic nature of the structure of language. Whether at the level of units of sound and their organization (*phonology*), of grammar or (more exactly) of *syntax*, or of the meanings which are encoded (*semantics*), rules are seen to operate, and in such a way that meaning itself depends in the first instance not on words alone but on the simultaneous interplay of units and rules at all these three levels. But meaning also depends on other factors of a 'non-linguistic' kind — for example, whether communication is face-to-face or at a distance, and what the relationship or respective social status of the speakers may be. Such 'extraneous' factors have posed a formidable problem for the more strictly linguistic study of language. How could they be ignored if they were so important? But how could they be included when they seemed to have more to do with social science or psychology than with the structure of language, and when their imprecision and ambiguity seemed to contradict that precise description to which structuralist linguistics aspired?

Until the mid- to late 1960s, the line had been drawn round the subject so as to largely exclude the 'non-linguistic'. Even when Chomsky (1965) developed his distinction between *competence* and *performance*, his notion of language users was still at a high level of abstraction. By competence, he meant the set of linguistic rules of which the 'idealized speaker-hearer' must logically be in possession in order to produce or understand sentences of the language; significantly, sentences, not utterances, for there is an essential difference. Utterance implies reality, actual use in an actual context, a contribution to discourse; sentence is usually an abstract grammatical concept, even when it can be sensed as a kind of ideal form behind the actual utterance. For example —

'Who was that at the door?'
'The milkman (was the person who was at the door).'

Chomsky had insisted that he intended no psychological reality for his 'competence', even though it appeared to others to be compatible with far more complex theories of language use than those behaviourist theories which it sought to supplant. Indeed, within what might be called a linguistic-linguistics, Chomsky's innovations were, and remain, revolutionary.

It was partly the study of language varieties which extended the subject's boundaries beyond accounts of linguistic structure, particularly syntactic structure, to include the differential functions of the varieties identified and the 'social meanings' they carried. From the overlapping interests of sociolinguists and sociologists came insights into the social correlates of standard and non-standard usage, of linguistic variation associated with specific purposes or settings, and of how and why the same speakers moved from one variety of language, or even one language, to another. What it had seemed possible to explain away as 'free variation' from a standpoint in structural linguistics now became visible as being itself a highly systematic structure of social and stylistic stratification.

Many of the emergent concepts were to have important implications for education, as we indicate in the chapter which follows. For example, the identification of the *standard* variety of a language as being distinguished by the high status of its users rather than by any inherent linguistic superiority implied that non-standard varieties were no less systematic and no less logical, whatever social disadvantages they might carry. In Dell Hymes' words (Cazden *et al*, 1972, p. xxxi), often cited since, — 'What is at stake is not logic or rationality, but what we think of others and of ourselves.' Attempts were also made to define, alongside the dialects of a language, another range of discrete varieties distinguished by their use rather than by their users — as being defined by setting rather than by speakers (Hasan, 1973). Impossible though it proved to be to describe these registers linguistically as separate entities, their study helped to show how certain forms of speech may become so associated with particular situations or activities as to seem the only forms really appropriate to them, and to emphasize how often (and rapidly) speakers alternated between varieties, such code-switching being a powerful expression of group loyalty or of changing perceptions of the situation and relationships involved (Blom and Gumperz, 1972). It is from this perspective that the registers associated with particular school subjects can be seen as containing both the terms embodying concepts essential to their practice, and markers of academic boundaries between one subject and another, and between school knowledge and everyday knowledge.

Variability is now the term commonly used to conceptualize a continuum, or a complex of intersecting continua, of linguistic choices. Individual speakers are then deemed to operate, not with 'a' language (or even several distinct languages), but with a wide linguistic repertoire, developed through need and experience and appropriately deployed as they move within and between the social networks to which they belong (Milroy, 1982). It is therefore recognized that speakers may exert more or less deliberate control over the social meanings conveyed in their speech — the information it carries about their social origins or affiliations, how they place themselves socially in relation to their fellow participants, and so on. 'Unmarked' usage describes those forms of speech which are produced, recognized and accepted as being normal in those circumstances — indeed, may be so confidently expected as to be not noticeably 'heard'. 'Marked' usage describes departures from conventional expectations, which may be interpreted by others as a display of incompetence (for example, a failure to recognize the situation for what it 'really' is, or inadequate knowledge of the appropriate forms), or as a deliberate bid to redefine the situation into something else (for example, to make it less formal and impersonal). Blom and Gumperz (1972), for example, distinguish between 'metaphorical' and 'situational' code-switching in order to separate such social signalling from alternation between languages in, say, a bilingual context. Hudson (1980, p. 48) has suggested that while individuals' syntax varies relatively little, and thus acts as a 'marker of social cohesion', their much greater variations in vocabulary serve to signal sub-group loyalty while idiosyncrasies in pronunciation may sometimes be preserved to signal individuality. Of course, regionally or ethnically accented speech may arouse strong evaluative responses, the individual speaker being assumed to have those characteristics stereotypically associated with the group in which he or she is placed. Such responses persist when those making them lack any coherent 'theory' of correctness and when they confuse personal taste with public standards (Trudgill, 1979; Milroy and Milroy, 1985).

Such complex variability in use implies a corresponding complexity in the everyday abilities of the user, and requires a very subtle notion of 'competence' to account for them. When Hymes (1972) originally proposed an analysis of *communicative competence*, he had just this perspective in mind. In contrast to Chomsky's account of the 'idealized' user, Hymes' primary interest lay with 'persons in a social world' who need to know 'when to speak, when not, what to talk about, with whom, when, where, and in what manner'. Their knowledge included 'knowledge of sentences, not only as grammatical but also as appropriate', responsive to sociolinguistic conventions. 'There are rules of use', he wrote, 'without which the rules of grammar are useless'.

This attempt to account for sensitivity to context has proved very powerful, not least in the study of language development where it links infants' pre-linguistic behaviour to their gradually evolving use of words. And it has grown to include further dimensions of interpretive and adaptive skills which characterize interactive, as against one-way communication. Regularities at the level of social structure, expressing speakers' knowledge of appropriate usage, are then seen as being as much a part of language ability as is knowledge of grammatical rules; indeed, syntactic ability becomes part of, or even secondary to, more general social abilities (Cook-Gumperz and Gumperz, 1982; Kress, 1985). Thus Saville-Troike (1982) defines communicative competence as embracing three sets of components: interactional skills, linguistic skills, and cultural knowledge. In this form, the concept has evident application to accounts of the communicative skills demanded of pupils, and to the identification of contrasts and continuities between the contexts of home and school.

Other developments within linguistics itself have similarly contributed theories and techniques to the analysis of real talk. They were at first philosophical in nature, and can be traced back to the seminal suggestions made by J.L. Austin (1962) for clarifying 'what can be done with words'. His threefold distinction between the *locutionary* and *illocutionary* force of an utterance, and its *perlocutionary* effect, brought a new clarity to analysis of the kinds of work which language can perform. The locutionary function can be taken as being broadly synonymous with 'semantic', as the literal meaning of an utterance. The second distinction contains the vital recognition that the form of an utterance is often at variance with its illocutionary force — for example, when a question is intended to have the force of a command, as is commonplace in classrooms ('Can you open the window for me?', or 'Are you listening in the back?'). Both the locutionary and illocutionary meanings are to be distinguished from the perlocutionary effect which is produced — the window being opened, or a properly attentive silence achieved. The concept of illocutionary force in particular opened the way for two highly relevant further lines of thought. The first led, by way of Grice and his theory of 'implicature', to *pragmatics*; the second, to the allied field of *discourse analysis*. Both have their origins in speech act theory, and both have much to contribute to the analysis of classroom talk. They will be considered briefly at this stage.

Grice (for example, 1975) confronted a central and problematical feature of so much talk, that the meanings conveyed may be far more extensive and complex than might appear from the words that are used. Indeed, a brief utterance may be especially eloquent in what it leaves out. Imagine the answer 'It makes an excellent doorstop' to the question, 'What do you think of "David Copperfield"?' Whether you think the reply reveals a philistine or a wit, either intended meaning would gain in force from being unstated. Grice used the term 'conversational implicature' to contrast with logical implication, and to refer precisely to those inferences which the speaker intends to be recognized, and to be recognized as intentional. He proposed a set of 'maxims' which can be seen being observed in conventional conversations based on the 'co-operative principle', maxims which the speakers will normally follow and expect to be followed. Deviations from them are then seen as deliberate floutings, designed to reveal what the speaker intends to be inferred. In our hypothetical example, Grice's maxims of Quantity and Relevance are both broken: the answer is shorter than would be expected, and is much less directly linked with the meaning of the question. Its probable meaning is clear enough, though in practice this would be reinforced by intonation, tone of voice, and facial expression.

The importance of conversational implicature is stressed by Levinson (1983, p. 87) because it offers 'functional explanations of linguistic facts' and thereby makes possible the study of pragmatics — '... it allows one to claim that natural language expressions do tend to have simple, stable and unitary senses ..., but that this stable semantic core often has an unstable, context-specific pragmatic overlay — namely, a set of implicatures' (*op. cit.* p. 99). Indeed, the purpose of pragmatics is to 'predict the meaning', in the broad Gricean sense, of an utterance in a specified context; it is 'a theory of language that takes context into account to complement semantics' (*op. cit.* p. 27). It can therefore be seen as logically prior to semantics in that the semantic elements of meaning can only be tackled when the pragmatic ones are known. Since no utterances are entirely context-free, the scope of pragmatics is both fundamental and far-reaching. Ochs and Schieffelin (1983), for example, use the term 'developmental pragmatics' to refer to what others would call the acquisition of communicative competence. Either way, the reference is to learning to communicate appropriately in a variety of settings, 'situational competence' being the 'full set of linguistic, interpersonal and social knowledge skills required by the demands of communication in a specific context' (Borman, 1979a, p. 82). As we have argued already, that 'full set' includes knowing the rules of social order as well as the rules of grammar.

It is therefore to pragmatics and to sociolinguistics that those investigating classroom talk can turn for a fuller understanding of *context*. That concept has been enriched, and complicated, by the developments we have outlined. The traditional notion of 'context of situation' usually had assigned to it such background information as the observer was aware of, without any firm criteria for assessing either its adequacy or its precise bearing on how the talk was organized and interpreted by the participants. It could easily become then an ill-defined dumping ground for assorted bits of social information of unspecified relevance to the analysis. From a perspective informed by pragmatics and sociolinguistics, attention was focused on evidence in the talk itself of what the speakers 'must have been' assuming about their situation and relationships. Context is also seen much more dynamically — not as a set of factors or constraints already 'there' at the outset of the talk, but as being brought into being, maintained, modified or challenged through the talk itself. From this perspective, contexts are seen as 'mutually shared and ratified definitions, and the actions taken on the basis of those definitions' (Erickson and Schultz, 1981, p. 147). It is a perspective which has strong links with reaction of ethnomethodologists against treating people (in Garfinkel's memorable phrase) as 'cultural dupes' who simply follow the rules, and their insistence on studying the everyday knowledge and reasoning procedures through which they construct the orderly, comprehensible interactions of everyday life (Atkinson and Heritage, 1984). For example, there is a strong tendency in medical discourse to classify patients so that the condition becomes more and more salient, and the person recedes; such progressively impersonal discourse is not seen simply as reflecting the 'underlying' doctor-patient relationship, but as an active and powerful constituent of it (Kress, 1985, pp. 141–2).

This view is highly relevant to the very contexts in which language is often elicited for research purposes. Labov's (1972b) 'methodological paradox' is now widely recognized, if not resolved; a researcher interested in habitual, everyday speech is probably recording it in a context which excludes real informality, not least because of the researcher's own presence. If it is so difficult, even impossible, to record entirely 'natural' speech through anything resembling an interview, it may be more sensible to treat the research interview as being itself a 'speech event', defined by one participant's right to ask questions and the other's obligation to answer them, and to make allowance for those situational constraints when assessing the quality of the talk which has been elicited. Those allowances may well include recognizing that speakers from different social backgrounds are unlikely to perceive the 'same' situation, however carefully the researcher has tried to standardize the questions, prompts and cues, and may feel very differently challenged or threatened by it (Edwards, 1976, pp. 116–22; Romaine, 1984, pp. 15–35).

Testing the linguistic or cognitive development of young children is especially sensitive to contextual influences where the tasks are presented verbally 'abstracted from any supportive system of meaningful events' (Donaldson, 1978, pp. 69–76). But neutral, standardized and 'scientific' assessment of language skills is impossible wherever the child's relationship with the tester, and insight into the test-situation, are in fact part of the task. What is then being tested is 'the ability to match speech and social strategies inventively' to the tasks, and in the situation, as these are perceived (Barnes, 1980, p. 128).

The complex and dynamic view of context which we have outlined makes the assessment of talk inherently difficult, given that talk is naturally not a solitary activity, and that its 'products' are normally a joint achievement rather than a solo performance. If an individual's contribution is as sensitive to each and any of the variables (such as topic, relationship with other participants, test-related stress, etc.) as we begin to realize it will inevitably be, there appears at the very least to be a need to take a variety of contexts into account in arriving at a judgment. In the context of National Curriculum English assessment, as with judging individual contributions to group-talk in GCSE examinations, the dangers lie in a possibly mechanistic approach, or in replicating the worst practice in traditional assessment of written language: namely, a concentration on form at the expense of function. Wilkinson *et al*, (1990) see a way forward in tentative, cross-curricular moves away from assessment *of* talk towards 'the assessment of overall language competence *through* talk' (p. 167). An approach to evaluating group-talk (rather than that of individuals in a group-setting) has also been offered by Wilkinson (1991), using criteria derived from Halliday: i.e. interpersonal (How effectively do participants listen to and build upon each other's contributions?), ideational (How effectively is content dealt with?) and textual (How clear and effective is the language itself?). The whole field is ripe for development.

These points have obvious general implications for investigating children's competence in coping with the communicative demands typical of classrooms. In so far as 'normal' classroom discourse has generalizable features which, in their nature or frequency, constitute distinctive sets of interlocking rights and obligations, then how and how quickly do children acquire the necessary knowledge and skills to display themselves as competent participants? How directly are these skills taught and learned? Since they are likely to be more easily acquired and displayed by children from homes within the cultural 'mainstream' of the society, what allowances do teachers make for the additional learning required of children from other cultural groups? These are questions to which we return at length in later chapters. Provisional answers to them have been strongly shaped by the perspectives on context which we have briefly described.

It will be helpful here to clear up some confusions about the term 'discourse'. We broadly agree with Stubbs (1983b, pp. 9–10), who finds no great need to distinguish 'discourse' from 'text', except in so far as that the latter is regarded as describing equally both oral and written products. Nevertheless, it is sometimes necessary to be explicit as to whether what is being considered is the verbal record of a communicative event, or the event itself. On such occasions, it is useful to follow Brown and Yule

(1983) in defining text as the verbal record, and keeping discourse to mean 'language in use'. That basic distinction is commonly made. Halliday (1978), for example, writes of language being 'actualized' or 'realized' in text. Leech (1984, p. 4) considers discourse to be the whole 'interpersonal transaction' composed of 'messages' largely carried in the text.

It would be wrong, however, to imply a general definitional consensus. An interesting variation is found in Kress (1985), who criticizes the tendency to equate discourse with 'any extended piece of language', and prefers to align the term with styles or registers (as in, for example, 'medical discourse'). 'Texts . . . are constructs produced in the relatively constrained inter-relation of discourse — the way of talking on a given matter — and of genre, the formal structure which gives the text its material form' (Kress, 1985, p. 144). This view can perhaps be seen as a refinement of the basic distinction between speech events, the discourse which largely constitutes them, and the text in which the discourse is objectified. Such distinctions can be important for analyses of classroom talk, particularly when discourse structure is examined for the meanings and purposes 'beneath' the product. Not that all linguistic study of discourse is oriented towards process. The cohesion of linguistic elements within texts-as-products (Halliday and Hasan, 1976), and the whole field of text-linguistics, can be contrasted with the discourse-as-process view exemplified by Widdowson (1979) and by Brown and Yule (1983). It is the latter which holds particular attractions for investigating classroom talk, for — 'Unless we believe that language users present each other with prefabricated chunks of linguistic strings (sentences) . . . we must assume that the data we investigate is the result of active processes', and that text serves illocutionary and interpersonal functions in revealing 'dynamic means of expressing intended meaning' (Brown and Yule, 1983, pp. 23–4).

In spite of a pedigree going back in part to speech act theory, discourse analysis has not always avoided the simpler, static view of context we have criticized. Those analysts whose roots are most firmly in linguistics have certainly argued strenuously among themselves about how predominantly 'linguistic' their procedures can be, and how sociologically sensitive to context. Common ground might be found in Stubbs' comment that 'a coherent view of language must take account of its everyday use in connected discourse'. Thus where earlier linguists sought to identify structural regularities at the level of the sentence, discourse analysts seek to identify (if they can) the rules governing 'the actual mechanisms by which communication, understanding and interaction are maintained over longer stretches of talk', and to justify those intuitions or impressions we often have about a passage of recorded text by finding the 'specific linguistic mechanisms' through which its particular character is produced (Stubbs, 1983b, p. 30; Burton, 1980, pp. 9–12). In other words, they ask whether there are definable criteria for 'well-formed' and coherent sequences of discourse and, if so, whether such criteria have predictive power.

Clearly, there are stylistic devices for producing cohesion between utterances which may be placed some way apart in the spoken text. For example,

'On the one hand . . . on the other hand . . .', or
'As I said earlier . . .', or
'I'll give you three reasons why you shouldn't do it. First . . . Second . . . Finally . . .'

Then, too, cohesion derives from the links which speakers establish with specific words, or intonation, used by their conversational partners. They often echo, or directly cite, previous utterances or details from them. They also repeat themselves, or find themselves completing an utterance in words which were not foreseen when they began it but which are selected by the grammatical structure on which they embarked. However, the kinds of reference which confer cohesion on discourse usually involve the integration of textual and contextual clues — they include both the references back to previous lexical or grammatical or other items, and references 'out' to features of the context which are assumed by one participant to be apparent to the other(s). Shuy refers to the 'wonderful redundance that context brings' (1984, p. 170) — the many ways in which contextual clues build up and reinforce the meanings of what is actually said. But there is also a 'wonderful' economy that context also makes possible. The integration of textual and contextual clues is illustrated in the following brief exchange, recorded by one of the authors.

Tom (aged 5½): (looking at a 'Star Wars' book),
'I didn't know Darth Vader had a sword'.
Father: (not looking up from his newspaper), 'He does in that picture, though, doesn't he? (rising tone at the end)
Tom: Mmm. (affirmative tone)

The father's utterance blends knowledge of both his son and 'Star Wars' books with the verbal message heard; at the same time it offers to Tom, through the intonation used, the choice of confirming or rejecting his interpretation. The existence of such cohesiveness in everyday discourse is by no means remarkable or contentious. What is at issue is the possibility of writing rules upon which to predict or evaluate given elements in a sequence. It is just such problems which discourse analysts explore. As our simple example (above) shows, the cohesiveness of discourse often depends largely on what speakers take for granted, or what they read in to what others say. Consequently, it may be necessary to adopt the 'working assumption' of Coulthard and Brazil (1981, p. 82) — that 'in the co-operatively produced object we call discourse, there is no direct equivalent to the concept of grammaticality'. It may also be helpful for analytical purposes to distinguish between two kinds of connectedness — 'cohesion' with respect to lexis, syntax and so on; and 'coherence' with respect to functions. Writing a 'grammar' for either poses problems enough.

Nevertheless, we have referred several times to 'social abilities' and 'rules of social order' when commenting on communicative competence, and much early work in sociolinguistics relied implicitly and even explicitly on some notion of 'social grammar' to summarize that knowledge of 'the world' on which speakers rely to participate appropriately in a wide range of situations and relationships. Indeed, discourse analysts have often chosen to begin their search for structure in settings where roles were relatively clearly marked, and where the consequent inequalities in the communicative rights of the participants are relatively 'evident in the text' and serve to remove many possible ambiguities of meaning (Sinclair and Coulthard, 1975). Their work has therefore been both 'pure' and 'applied'; it has brought new insights into the organization of educational discourse, especially into the extent and nature of the teacher's dominance of typical instructional encounters, and in doing so has developed methods for analyzing talk in other 'unequal' settings (Coulthard, 1987). In subjects such as Second and Foreign Languages, where co-called 'communicative' methods of teaching are in vogue, there have also been benefits in applying concepts of discourse analysis in order to obtain feedback for teachers concerning the communication which their teaching actually creates. Particular attention has been given to the 'authenticity' or otherwise of the tasks which students perform (see, e.g., Allwright, 1988; Brumfit and Mitchell, 1989; McCarthy, 1991).

At least in conventional school settings, a lesson can be treated as a convenient (if non-linguistic) unit — a speech event with clear boundaries. It also lends itself to further sub-division into a hierarchy of transactions, exchanges, moves and acts. That hierarchy can be compared, loosely, with the division of a written text into paragraphs, sentences, clauses, and words, each 'rank' in the hierarchy being realized by elements from the one beneath. While it has been the more traditionally teacher-centred lessons which have seemed most amenable to such analysis, modifications have also been suggested which would extend its scope to less formal settings (Burton, 1980; Brazil, 1981).

Although similarly concerned with the complex organization of discourse and its subtle indirectness, conversational analysis draws much less on linguistics than on anthropology and especially ethnomethodology. As we mention in the following chapter, and then describe more fully in chapter 5, its name reflects a primary concern with everyday talk and with conversation, defined as 'talk between equals' in which no participant has special rights, allocated in advance, on which the management of the talk is based. Its scope has extended to talk in power-marked settings like courtrooms and classrooms, where the power differences can be identified, clearly and in detail, in how that talk is organized (Edwards, 1980;

Dillon, 1990). In relation to the problem of achieving cohesion through long stretches of talk, the focus of attention is not on quasi-syntactic ties between utterances, but on how the speakers display their expectations of how sequences are 'opened' and 'closed', and of what follows what. In classroom talk, for example, there is a pervasive expectation that pupils' answers will be followed by the teacher's evaluation of them. The frequency with which this occurs is a salient characteristic of a 'speech exchange system with particular local characteristics' (Atkinson, 1981, p. 112).

The extent and distinctiveness of those 'local characteristics' is the theme of the next chapter. We lead into it by returning to the notion of situational competence, and to a difficult theoretical issue arising from the distinction we have made between talk in equal and unequal settings and from the question of 'what constitutes a context'. We have argued that context is often used as a shorthand term for whatever social knowledge the participants perceive as relevant to organizing words and meanings in that setting. It includes knowledge of the respective social identities of the speakers (for example, their respective age, gender, race, occupation or other status) where this is seen as being generally relevant to what can be said and how it can be said. It includes knowing what forms of talk are appropriate within particular role-relationships, such as that between doctor and patient. And it may also include knowing the rules which normally govern specific speech events, such as an interview for a job, or a cross-examination in a courtroom, or a practical lesson in chemistry. Communicative competence includes all these things. The 'communicative map' which children build up has both its precisely delineated routes and its more general signposts. Or, to revert to the notion of a 'social grammar', there are both specific rules for specific occasions and basic (or 'ground') rules from which to generate performances appropriate to types of relationship and situation. At their most general, such rules can be seen as enabling speakers to cope with a great diversity of encounters along fundamental dimensions in social life — those of 'power and solidarity', hierarchy and equality, intimacy and social distance (Edwards, 1976, pp. 73–6 and 1980; Hudson, 1980, pp. 122–8). Teacher-pupil relationships appear normally to be high in power and low in solidarity, and classroom talk represents from this perspective the working-out of a power relationship. It is to some of the details of that working-out that we now turn.

2 Characteristic Patterns of Classroom Talk

> Any school child playing teacher will produce most of the behaviours used by most teachers . . . standing in front of a group of relatively passive onlookers, doing most of the talking, asking questions to which they already know the answers, and evaluating by passing judgments (Simon and Boyer, 1970, volume 2, p. 2).

That sketch of how teacher behaviour is commonly 'mirrored' by its audience prefaced an extensive collection of classroom observation schedules. In visual form, a similar image of typical classroom encounters appears on the cover of many books about teaching, sometimes in instances where the authors intend to describe or prescribe much less teacher-directed approaches. There is an ironic example of its inappropriate persistence in a Teachers' Guide to the skills needed to chair unobtrusively and neutrally those discussions of controversial issues which figured so prominently in the Nuffield Humanities Project. The pupils portrayed on its cover are certainly not in desks; they are arranged in an informal circle without any apparent 'director's chair'. But it is the teacher who is shown talking, and both his posture and their expressions suggest that he will go on doing so for some time (Schools Council, 1970).

In this chapter, we describe the deep grooves along which most classroom talk seems to run, even in settings designed for the breaking of new ground. We use some of the organizing ideas outlined in the previous chapter to explore the distinctiveness of classrooms as communicative contexts, and the skills and knowledge they demand of communicatively competent participants.

1 Varieties of Classroom Language

Among the main achievements of sociolinguistics have been the detailed description of the structural complexity of non-standard language, and the extension of the notion of linguistic competence to include knowledge of how to speak, and to interpret the speech of others, in ways appropriate to a wide range of settings. Both these closely-related areas of research have been strongly impelled by efforts to explain the high rates of educational failure among children from outside the cultural, economic and political mainstream of their society. The first provided the main source of criticism of those theories of 'verbal deficit' or 'verbal deprivation' which were widely used in the 1960s to account for learning difficulties. The second, by giving such prominence to the notion of situational competence, drew attention to the importance of looking beyond the school at the communicative demands which children regularly faced, and the skills they routinely displayed, in other settings. As one black mother complained to Shirley Heath (1982, p. 107) about the difficulties her son was having with language at school — 'My kid, he too scared to talk, cause nobody play by the rules he know. At home, I can't shut him up'.

It is not our intention here to review, even cursorily, the long, fiercely contested debate over linguistic explanations of educational failure. (For commentaries on the evidence and its interpretation, see A. Edwards, 1987; J. Edwards, 1989). Instead, we extract from that debate several issues relating directly to the kinds of language which predominate in classrooms, and the tolerance or intolerance shown towards other varieties.

Standard language is that variety which is normally used in the transaction of public business. Some command of it is likely to be 'a prerequisite for full social effectiveness', a necessary part of the linguistic repertoire of those in (or aspiring to) positions of power and authority. And where a great deal of public business is transacted in writing, then the language of the more powerful is likely to resemble 'the written mode being used in speech' (Kress, 1985, p. 148). The definition of standard language as 'the speech of educated people' is therefore necessarily circular. Something approaching it, or not departing too widely from it, is often assumed to be necessary for the serious business of formal education, both in the social sense of being more fitting, and in the cognitive sense of being structurally superior. Too much tolerance of non-standard varieties is then seen as a threat simultaneously to linguistic and educational standards, as Peter Trudgill discovered from the many fiercely critical responses to his earlier defence of those varieties as being no less well-ordered and no less logical (Trudgill, 1979). Similarly fierce arguments surrounded the reports of two national enquiries into the teaching of English (DES, 1988; 1989). Both were urged from within the political Right to restore respect for 'correct' usage. Both disappointed their hecklers by making a clear and necessary distinction between the equally rule-governed structures of non-standard varieties, and the social advantages which may be conferred by facility in Standard English. As defined by the Working Group on English in the National Curriculum, Standard English is a social dialect 'of a special kind'. It is not to be confused with 'good' English because its users can speak as 'badly' as anyone else, but it has such a 'wide range of public purposes' that all children should have the opportunity to 'learn to use it competently' (DES, 1989, chapter 4, paras. 9–12).

Reflecting on the travestying of its position which the Group suffered, its chairman notes that 'the task of overcoming arrogance about accents is formidable', and that 'correct grammar' had become a Right-wing shibboleth inseparable from broader campaigning for traditional values and respect for authority (Cox, 1991, pp. 25 and 34). Certainly rational debate is difficult when departures from 'correct' usage are not only dismissed as errors rather than as forms governed by different rules, but are commonly treated as evidence of individuals' intellectual incapacity and (more generally) of cultural and even moral decline (Milroy and Milroy, 1985; Stubbs, 1989; Corson, 1991). The essential fact, to which we return, is that languages and varieties of a language may be 'different but equal' from a linguistic perspective, and yet be very unequal in the social worlds to which they give ready access.

Whatever the expectations may be about standard language as the 'proper' language of instruction, few classrooms will contain more than a handful of pupils fully practised in its use, and many will contain none. In their survey of twenty-eight London secondary schools, Rosen and Burgess (1980) reported that 79 per cent of pupils spoke some form of London-English (London-Jamaican being a particularly prominent variety), and that over sixty varieties of English could be identified. Many pupils spoke habitually a variety which diverged quite sharply from standard forms, while many more could switch into one on appropriate occasions while remaining fluent in something approaching more closely to standard English. Alongside these dialectal and bi-dialectal speakers were the substantial minority fluent in at least one other 'named world language', the most frequent being Bengali, Urdu, Gujerati, Punjabi, Chinese, Arabic, Turkish, Italian, French, Spanish, and Portuguese. The ILEA's own language census (1983) indicated that one pupil in seven was bilingual, while there were particular districts (most notably Haringey) where the proportion was as high as one in three. London schools represent, in heightened form, a common reality in urban areas (Linguistic Minorities Project, 1985; but see Nicholas, 1988).

The association of non-standard languages and varieties of language with low-status occupations and political powerlessness is commonly treated as a causal relationship, linguistic differences being treated as deficiencies and then used to 'explain' high rates of educational and occupational failure on apparently impartial grounds (Hymes, 1979, p. 14). Before turning to some of the problems and tensions which linguistic diversity can create, especially through the capacity of formal schooling to make pupils lose confidence in their vernacular speech, we recognize a growing tendency to regard that diversity as being, at least potentially, 'a source of strength, an access of new resources' (Rosen and Burgess, 1980, p. 10; see also Bullock, 1975, para. 20.17; Miller, 1983; ILEA, 1984, pp. 45–9; Craft and Atkins, 1985). It can make available to a school class both knowledge of other languages and new insights into how richly and subtly language works, while pupils struggling with so much new learning become temporary experts when given opportunities to display proficiency in their home-tongue. Those bilingual speakers may also be encouraged to develop that reflective, analytical stance towards language which (as we argue later) is often seen as being highly 'strategic' for educational success.

But where success, or even classroom survival, seem to depend on learning a new 'language' — and we include here some more prestigious variety of the 'same' language — then its adoption often marks and re-inforces a growing cultural distance between children and parents. A facility in its use which is taken (and often intended) as evidence of successful assimilation into another culture or sub-culture, may well be suspected or resented by those 'left behind'. Where it brings more prizes within reach, it may be welcomed regretfully by parents, even to the extent of discouraging their children from using the language to which they remain loyal themselves because of the material disadvantages of sounding like an outsider, or (metaphorically and sometimes literally) like a 'peasant' (V. Edwards, 1986; Walker, 1984; Corson, 1991). Conversely, their children's awareness of the pain caused to parents by their cultural uprooting may lead them, in the settings of their home world, to depress their otherwise skilled performance in the second language and display a deliberately cultivated incompetence in the hope that it will be temporarily reassuring (Miller, 1983, p. 131).

More fully documented, however, is the deliberate accentuating of non-standard forms as a marker of resistance to assimilation. 'Monitoring black' refers to such shifts towards Black-English vernacular, whether to demonstrate solidarity with fellow insiders, or to maintain or increase social distance in interaction with outsiders. It implies an explanation of why pupils of West Indian origin in British schools often use more non-standard features, and use them more consistently, when they are aged eight than when they are fifteen, and why London-Jamaican is such a 'magnetic political, social and peer group dialect' (V. Edwards, 1979; Rosen and Burgess, 1980, p. 57). 'Monitoring working-class', or 'Liverpool', or 'Brooklyn', are clearly variants on the same theme, and illustrate what a powerful (and economical) resource linguistic features provide for displaying similarity or difference, solidarity or opposition, assimilation or resistance. They also illustrate the notions of repertoire and variability which were introduced in the previous chapter by reminding us how swiftly and deftly speakers may move along whatever linguistic continuum constitutes their repertoire, doing so according to their perceptions of the setting, their fellow participants, their own sense of identity in that setting, and their purposes in the interaction.

In the example which follows, the interviewer is white (a fact evident in some of the speech addressed to him), and the pupils are black. They are talking to John Furlong in school, but about decidedly non-school matters. There is a considerable linguistic distance between some utterances by the same speaker, but it is the fluency of the code-switching — or code-sliding, as Rosen and Burgess call it to emphasize its fluidity — which is particularly interesting because it is switching between standard and non-standard.

P1 'Why don't you play him Dubb?'
P4 'Yeah, bounce a record for him.'
P3 'Cool, cool, cool'. (They turn on a cassette)
P1 'This is a classic example of what we play in our Reggae clubs.'
P2 'Strictly rockers.'
P1 'The reason why I like Reggae — Dubb I call it, Reggae is what the old people call it — it's harder . . . You see, Soul to me it's too fast, it's stupid, you know what I mean? It's kina womanish.'
P2 'Scene, scene.'
P1 'It's got nothing to it, you know what I mean.'
P2 'Womanish.'
P1 'Soul is American, Dubb is rockers — Jamaican, you know.'
P4 'You think Soulies are weakhearts, don't you? Weakhearts.'
P2 'Yeah, most of them are.'
P4 'You don't know nuttin', you don't know nuttin.'
P1 'You know they more peaceful than us.'
P4 'If you peaceful, that mean you weak. We ain't weak.'
(from Furlong, 1984, p. 220)

Similarly rapid code-switching has been recorded when adolescent girls moved from talking about school to talking about pop music, and so from fairly standard English to a 'code' so elliptical and allusive as to be intentionally 'unanalyzable' by an adult listener (Rutherford, 1976), or when children switched between the heavily dialect-marked speech of the playground and variants more appropriate for classroom purposes (Reid, 1978; Cheshire, 1982). All these examples are of speech on occasions when group membership may seem more important than identity as an individual, and the talk becomes in that sense impersonal, an expression of common knowledge and common loyalties. This was a main theme in the Opies' marvellous record of the 'lore and language of school children' (1959), which they saw both as offering 'a constant welcome to innovation' and as reflecting a very strong oral tradition (see also I. and P. Opie 1975; 1985). Much of the language is intended to protect activities from adult understanding and intervention, and there are appropriate forms for almost every time and purpose in group life — for fun, for licensed obscenity, for challenging and conciliating, for bargaining, and for mocking the adult world. Through using them, children demonstrate their knowledge of that sub-culture and their adherence to its norms.

From this perspective, the notions of communicative competence with which we shall be largely concerned have to be considerably extended. In relation to classrooms, competence is usually defined by the demands of instructional encounters which are dominated by teachers. But pupil competence is also a matter of being judged and gaining acceptance by one's peers. It has to be regularly demonstrated in the kinds of talk through which common definitions of teachers, classroom activities and other pupils are displayed and reaffirmed, rules of 'fair play' confirmed, relief from boredom is sought by 'having a laugh', and the teacher's authority tested by the routine deviance of replacing work with chatter (Woods, 1990; B. Davies, 1983; Beynon and Atkinson, 1984; Pollard, 1984b). Since one of the main functions of such talk is to reinforce group solidarity at the expense of outsiders, it is particularly inaccessible to researchers. Andrew Pollard's use of pupils themselves as 'investigators' was therefore especially ingenious where the focus of his enquiry was playground life (Pollard, 1985a, chapter 4; 1985b, pp. 226–30).

We have left until last some of the educational consequences attributed most often to discontinuities between the 'languages' of home and school. Most of the relevant research has been concerned not with evidently multi-lingual classrooms, but with those in which pupils are seen as being disadvantaged in some way because their variety of the same language does not match their teacher's expectations, or is perceived to be restricted in form or functional range. Take, for example, the flat assertion by John Edwards and Howard Giles (1984, pp. 119–20) that — 'As an institution of the middle class, school is one of the obvious places in which to investigate language and class contact'. Or the 'new theory' of a 'lexical bar' confronting pupils from backgrounds where those words of Graeco-Latin origin which carry most specialist and abstract meanings in English are likely to be seen as 'bizarre, highbrow and difficult'; lack of familiarity with that lexicon, and of facility in its use, impedes their access to school knowledge as normally transmitted and limits their capacity to display what they know in the forms expected by their teachers (Corson, 1985). Or the assertions that what is at issue is conflict, not contact, and that the forms of speech deemed suitable for purposes of instruction act as a social filter controlling access to educational opportunities and the occupational advantages likely to arise from them (Hymes, 1979; Bourdieu and Passeron, 1977, pp. 72–6, 108–12). We now refer briefly to some of the dimensions of classroom language which have been seen as the source of significant educational difficulties.

In initial reaction against theories of verbal deficit or deprivation, it was firmly argued that the evidence for them greatly exaggerated both the extent and structural significance of non-standard features, and failed to recognize that those features which did occur were produced from different but no less systematic rules. The social significance given to such features made them conspicuous even in the speech of those who could both understand the standard variety without difficulty and produce something like it when they felt situationally constrained to do so. This reaction may have underestimated the breakdowns in communication which can occur when (for example) interference between one system of sound-rules and another leads teacher and pupil to mishear what the other says, and when answers to questions or the saying of words in a test of reading proficiency are judged incorrect only for that reason (Milroy, 1984). But while sociolinguists sought to demonstrate the structural equivalence of non-standard varieties and their merely 'social' superiority, they also drew attention to the consequences of 'sounding disadvantaged'. Any realistic perspective on language differences had to reconcile 'the essentially neutral or arbitrary nature' of those differences with 'the social stratification of languages and levels of speech unmistakeable in any complex speech community' (Sankoff, 1976, cit. Hudson, 1980, p. 119). Whatever complexities and subtleties might be revealed in non-standard varieties, their more habitual speakers were often at risk of not being taken seriously, or of arousing expectations of failure. Teachers were therefore warned against basing their judgments of pupils' general abilities on linguistic 'evidence' irrelevant for that purpose, and against confusing differences in speech with differences in logic and rationality. There was the wider danger too that children whose vernacular speech was pointedly excluded from the classroom might further lose confidence in their cultural group, or feel still more strongly that the knowledge they are being offered on others' terms has little to do with them or for them (Rosen, 1982; Walker, 1984).

Yet the question has continued to be asked, in increasingly sophisticated form, whether the kinds of language which normally predominate in classrooms present many pupils with cognitive as well as social difficulties (Winch, 1985). The characteristic identified most often as the main source of difficulty is the high level of abstraction which pervades so much classroom talk (and, of course, classroom writing). It is argued that most of the expositional language of teachers, and of textbooks, is 'language at the apex of a pyramid of experience' — that is, language which offers summaries of, or generalizations about, objects and actions and events (Rosen, 1967). That would not be a problem if more of the pyramid had earlier been in view, because we are all accustomed to first 'telling a story' and then 'giving the gist' of it. Problems arise where there has been no 'story' — where the abstractions are free-floating, unattached to those detailed empirical referents which can alone give them life (Barnes *et al*, 1969; Edwards, A. 1978; Hull, 1985). Such language can too easily become formalistic, a display of words about words which some pupils may manage so fluently as to provide false evidence of an understanding which they do not have, while others resort to what Rosen called a 'desperate mimicry' or simply give up. Where teachers recognize a failure to understand, they may try to bridge the gap by shortening and 'simplifying' their exposition, and thereby make things worse by reducing the empirical referents (or circumstantial details) still further in the hope of highlighting the 'essential points'.

We return now to the more general debate because of its implications for research focusing directly on classroom language. When children become pupils, and increasingly as they move through the school system, they face a multitude of tasks 'abstracted from any supportive context of meaningful events', and unsupported by a back-cloth of shared assumptions or practical activities (Donaldson, 1978, p. 76; Romaine, 1984, pp. 166–70). It has long been argued that middle-class children are, in general, better prepared to cope with this large move towards 'disembedded' language — language which feeds largely on itself. They are more accustomed to making their ideas verbally explicit, and to responding to tasks presented through words alone; they are also more practised in answering, or more disposed to answer, questions to which the questioner already knows what needs to be known — especially when those questions are about names, and what things are called.

Yet similar assumptions about classroom language may lead to very different diagnoses of the consequences for many working-class pupils, and for others who come from backgrounds outside the cultural mainstream. These diagnoses are discussed more fully later in the book, especially in chapter 6. But the essential divergence is between those who see classroom language as being too demanding for children whose other communicative experience is restricted in its range, and those who see 'instructional dialogue' as creating serious difficulties in recognizing what some of those demands are (or accepting them as reasonable) for those children whose other experience is simply very different. Differences were strongly opposed to deficits in the reaction against the culturally insensitive accounts of language problems which predominated in the 1960s, the basis for doing so being something like Dell Hymes' (1972, p. 287) formal statement of a formidable educational problem — 'When a child from one developmental matrix enters a situation in which communicative demands are defined in terms of another, misperception and misanalysis may occur at every level'.

Early empirical applications of this approach were usefully collected together in a book edited by Cazden, Hymes and John (1972), and they illustrate vividly the importance of extending the notion of competence from the linguistic to the communicative. For a speech community consists of those who share both the 'same' language and similar (or at least compatible) ways of using it. In this wider sense, teacher and pupils may sometimes be communicative strangers, and they be so without realizing it. As a black parent told Shirley Heath (1983) — 'Miss Davis, she complain about Ned not answerin' back. He says she ask dumb questions she already know 'bout'. And as Thomas Kochman (1981) has suggested, from his own experience of teaching in multi-ethnic classrooms, different 'etiquettes of communication' can cause problems with much older pupils. A 'black mode' of public discussion which is 'high keyed, animated, interpersonal and confrontational' may contrast so sharply with a 'white mode' which is relatively cool, dispassionate and quiet that black pupils are seen as being less thoughtful and more hostile than they are, especially if a cultural preference for strong argument as a way of testing views leads black pupils to compete more forcefully for the next turn than is usual in classroom settings (Evans, 1988; Biggs and Edwards, 1991).

An especially powerful and influential analysis of discontinuities between the communicative systems of home and school has been developed over the last thirty years by Basil Bernstein (Bernstein, 1990; Atkinson, 1985; Edwards, 1987). The scope of the analysis is huge, and we take from it here only its explanation of why pupils from some cultural backgrounds are placed at a disadvantage because the 'orders of meaning and relevance' with which they are familiar, and towards which they are orientated, are significantly different from those which predominate in schools. The explanation has focused on social class differences. Briefly, middle-class children are described as being more likely to respond to even apparently open questions from the teacher as tests in which their answers will be evaluated, and so to be verbally explicit about objects and events even when the listener knows about them already. More generally, they have less difficulty in recognizing the differences between instructional contexts and therefore in producing the kinds of specialized language appropriate to them.

As a theory about the nature and sharpness of the boundaries between school knowledge and everyday knowledge, and within the curriculum itself, it contained some large assumptions about what classroom communication is normally like. And when this book was being written, it remained a theory rarely tested against classroom practice. Since that time, however, it has shaped several substantial investigations. Harry Daniels (1989) explored the sensitivity of 'slow-learning' children to the rules regulating communication in particular curriculum areas and particular classroom activities. But while his study illustrated how classroom tasks may be detached from children's everyday experience and yet make sense as the kinds of things which go in school, it also raises questions about how explicit teachers should be about the requirements of appropriate classroom communication if they are not to discriminate against children who have difficulty in recognizing the rules. There is a further question, central to Bernstein's theory, about whether teachers differentiate between children from different social class backgrounds in the 'orders of meaning and relevance' which they themselves make available and familiar even within the framework of a supposedly common curriculum. That they do so is the main finding of Portuguese research designed to test that possibility through detailed analysis of classroom language. Thus working-class pupils had greater difficulty in applying the scientific knowledge they had acquired to new problems, so that increasing the level of abstraction in classroom tasks increased social class differences in achievement. But they had also had much less classroom experience of tasks involving 'understanding' rather than 'acquisition'. There was evidence that the level of conceptual demand made by the teachers was strongly related to how they characterized their school's intake, which prompted the conclusion that teachers need such 'sociological knowledge' if they are to correct the depressing effect of sociocultural context on how what is ostensibly the same syllabus is transmitted (Domingos, 1989, 365; Moraes *et al*, 1992).

2 Varieties of Classroom Discourse

In the Introduction, we referred briefly to the possibilities of 'reading off' social relationships from even brief transcripts of interaction in institutional settings which are open to anyone with the cultural knowledge needed to recognize the situationally-appropriate forms of talk. We now trade on that possibility. We assume that the following extracts will be 'read' as examples of normal teacher-pupil talk, without preliminary information about the contexts in which the talk was recorded. The likelihood of recognition is high, and it comes from the ways in which the talk is organized rather than from its style. Yet, as we go on to suggest, the examples are deliberately taken from contexts in which rather differently organized talk might well have been expected.

1 T   Maybe you could hold it out. I want you to notice a lot of things about the hamster. We can notice a couple of things right away. When we look at the hamster, what do we notice right away?

   P   It has pink feet.

   T   It has pink feet. Yes. What does he have on the end of his pink feet?

   P   Claws.

   T   He's a digging animal. Do you notice he's sniff, sniff, sniff, sniffing all over. Why does he do that?

   P   It's a girl.

   T   Why does she do that? What? Maybe she smells Chrissy's lettuce (laughter), Don't be afraid, he won't bite — she won't bite.

   Pp She won't bite.

   T   Must like Troy. Guess she's not hungry right now. They usually eat at night. What's the word we use when an animal is trying to find out everything? It's sniffing around looking at everything. What's the word?

   P   Curious.

   T   Curious. I think that's a perfect words for our hamster . . .

(Dillon and Searle, 1981, pp. 31–2)

2 T   Can you tell us what fossils are, do you think?

   P   Sir, sir, a long time ago animals — there was animals, and when they died, er, the rain and wind came over them and then the bodies disappeared and left the shells and that.

T   Good. Why do you think the bodies disappeared and the shells stayed?

Pp   Sir, sir, they rotted.

T   And what about the shells?

P   Sir, they got harder — er, the clay dried, they made marks in the clay.

T   Right.

P   The clay dried hard.

T   Right, OK, thank you. Can anybody add anything to that at all? It's a very good description . . .

(Edwards and Furlong, 1978, p. 17)

3   T   All right then, now, can you please pay attention. You remember what happened when we burnt a candle under a bell. What happened? Well?

P   The water came up, sir.

T   Yes, but why did the water come up?

P   Because er, there was a vacuum.

T   Yes, but why was there a vacuum?

P   Well, the candle kind of sucked up the water, sir.

T   How did it do that? Yes?

P   Some of the air got burned up.

T   That's not right is it?

Pp   Sir, sir, oxygen, sir.

T   It was the inactive air that was left, the oxygen that was used up. What's the oxygen called? Come on (silence). It's called the reactive part, isn't it. What's it called, Jane?

P   Reactive.

T   Why is it called reactive? (Silence) It's called reactive because it reacts, isn't it.

(Carré, 1981, p. 28–9)

4   T   Why do people have discussions?

P_1 It's just natural, kind of — it's natural.

T   That's right, it's natural to talk to people about things, but why? Why do people discuss?

P_1 Cos it's easier than writing it all down on paper.

Pp   (laughter)

T   Yes (doubtfully), it's natural to talk but I think there's some other reasons too.

P_2 To get each other's opinions.

T   Good, to get each other's opinions . . .

(And, from much later in the same lesson)

T   What should you do in a discussion? Christine?
P   You've got to say what you want to say, not what other people
    want you to say.
T   Good girl!
(Young, 1984, pp. 231 and 234–5)

The first example is of a teacher who had been picked out for the researchers as an exemplar of good 'progressive' practice with very young pupils.
The second is a similarly structured 'object lesson', given in an explicitly
innovative comprehensive school. The third is of a teacher working within
a science syllabus overtly directed to giving pupils more scope to carry out
their own investigations. And the final example is of a discussion about
discussion which, as the researcher notes, manages to avoid being a 'real'
discussion at all. In all four examples, communication is firmly centred on
the teacher. It is he or she who talks and decides who else is to talk, asks
the questions, evaluates the answers, and clearly manages the sequence as
a whole. These are all main ingredients in any commonsense view of what
classroom communication is normally like.

There are certainly dangers in assuming too narrow a range of normality, given the possibility to be discussed later that it may reflect as much
on the insensitivity of research methods as on the uniformity of classrooms.
But there is no doubt that the evidence so far available supports a high
level of generalization, and no doubt either that it provides grounds for
concern about the very limited communicative and semantic options
normally available to pupils. Far from being too demanding, the assumption
made in much of the debate outlined in the previous section, the evidence
suggests that many classrooms most of the time are not demanding enough.
Briefly, appropriate participation requires of pupils that they listen or appear to listen, often and at length. They have to know how to bid properly
for the right to speak themselves, often in competitive circumstances where
a balance has to be found between striving so zealously to attract attention
that the teacher is irritated, and volunteering to answer so modestly that
their bid is ignored. They have to accept that what they do manage to say
in answer to a teacher's question will almost certainly be evaluated (if only
by repetition), may well be interrupted if judged to be irrelevant to the
teacher's purposes, and may be so heavily modified and translated to fit
the teacher's frame of reference as to be no longer recognizable as their
own contribution at all. Since the teacher usually knows the right answer
already, they learn to focus on the many clues and cues which the teacher
provides to narrow the area of search within which that answer is to be
found. Their task is to respond, rarely to initiate, and it is for the teacher
to say what has 'really' been learned from the words which have been
exchanged. These are all aspects of the organization of classroom talk
which we explore in later chapters.

By way of contrast, it is useful to consider whether the presence of a teacher is immediately obvious in the extracts which follow, and (if so) where that teacher's contributions occur.

1 The speakers are discussing the dangers to health in towns in the early stages of the industrial revolution

P   It says here erm . . . that pigs were slaughtered like they could have got a disease from somewhere and all the filth could have gone down the drains

C   Yeah and then from there on people could have caught it off them somehow

D   But in here by the top when it rains filth and dirt and that's the hygiene really . . . and dirt. . . . those sewers. . . . off the filth that just had nowhere to go

P   And then the people . . . all the kids playing about. . . .

C   Kathy, can I just . . . ?

P   . . . . start going round the streets

C   Here it says 44 deaths on Bank Street . . . now must be . . . This is Warrington. . . . Where's Bank Street, Kathy?

D   It seems that . . . it's just like . . . insanitary houses

C   But it says here it's got like a list of deaths . . . how do you spell . . . ?

A   That's right, that's the . . . spelling . . . Kathy, did you find Bank Street yet?

K   No

D   You see round here it seems like where there is water there is not so many fatal incidences . . .

A   Where there is water . . . clean water . . . I see, how do you explain then the. . . . it's overcrowded then possibly . . . that's interesting — so when it's overcrowded . . . so there's more likely to be an incidence of dirty water . . . what about here? Is there anything here that might . . .

C   If like some are groups and some are isolated . . .

P   Well, there's a pig slaughterer

A   Pig slaughter houses yet?

C   See the number of deaths on here in each street

A   You got a pump here and a pump there . . . and slaughter houses . . .

D   Round here there's sewers so whan it rains . . . filth and dirt left and it's got nowhere to go

A   So link that together. Overcrowding. . . . .

(transcript provided by our colleague Frank Hardman from his work in the Cheshire Oracy project)

2 The group is discussing what merchants in a medieval town are to do to defend themselves against lawless lords.

B   Gordon's the leader, right, Gordon should go to the king and ask . . .

A   He's only our chairman — sorry to interrupt.

B   Chairman. He could go to the king and ask the king can he have some of his army . . .
C   But he could . . .
D   Wait Johnny.
B   Could he control his army so we can fight the lords and win?
C   But he's too weak to control his army.
B   Gordon will. He's goona go up to the king and ask him
E   We can ask him that of his own he wants to get off the throne now and somebody else take his place. 'Cos he might be tired himself.
D   All right. You're all saying, right, that you need a new king. Who's the king that's got everything — soldiers, everything?
F   Not a king, a man.
?   I mean a man.
G   You don't need a king that has soldiers, you need a king that's strong enough to control the soldiers.
H   But then again, right, we don't need . . . or don't really need a king do we?
P   We do. (confusion of voices)
A   The reason we need a king is that we need peace, we need order. Now if the king can make the laws of the land, most people are loyal, most people will obey the laws. . . .

(Burgess, 1984, p. 19–21)

In both these examples, the teacher is 'A'. The unusual quality of the transcripts then becomes evident in the infrequency of the teacher's turns, and in the frequency with which pupils take initiatives. Perhaps less obviously, they ask questions as well as answer them, sometimes take the lead in moving from one topic to another, and are able to respond directly to the contributions of other pupils rather than doing so through the teacher's mediation. Turns are not allocated by a single 'director', but seem rather to be negotiated as the talk proceeds. And while the teacher may still be evident, if only by verbal style, some of those moves which teachers normally monopolize are clearly being taken by others. It is certainly less clear than usual that one participant has the sole or main responsibility for repairing breakdowns in communication, clearing up misunderstandings, and defining what is to be learned.

In drawing attention to some of the differences between these extracts and the four cited earlier, we have deliberately mixed features from several of the analytical approaches which we examine later. At this point, we are concerned more descriptively and generally with departures from the familiar grooves of classroom talk, and (in the final section of the chapter) with the difficulty of making them. 'Normal' descriptions are often useful as a basis from which to highlight patterns of communication more characteristic of particular classroom activities, areas of the curriculum, or stages of schooling, or from which to identify 'real' innovations in pedagogy through such comparative analysis.

For example, accounts of traditional whole-class teaching, in which almost all 'official' talk is channelled to or by the teacher, has little obvious relevance to nursery or infants classes or to the more 'progressively' organized classrooms in primary schools, where a high proportion of teacher interaction is with individual children and the rest of the class 'get on with their work'. Either that teacher will 'move rapidly round the tables, checking work, clarifying instructions and giving information, or she will remain seated at her desk while the pupils form a queue' (Galton and Willcocks, 1983, pp. 161–2; see also Bennett *et al*, 1984; Tizard and Hughes, 1984). Laboratory-based subjects are also likely to involve the teacher in more individual, and more physically-close encounters with pupils, and to generate far more talk among pupils themselves (Reid, 1980). Teaching designed to give pupils a taste of, and a taste for, scientific investigation should leave more 'space' than is usual for their questioning and problem-solving, and for practical activity (Hacker *et al*, 1979; Eggleston, 1983; Brook *et al*, 1988). Mixed-ability grouping might be expected to move teachers away from a single communication system centred on themselves and towards more varied encounters with pupils who are at very different stages of activity and understanding (Evans, 1985; Kerry, 1982). And while modern-language teaching directed at correctness of detail will generate highly teacher-centred sequences of question and answer, English teaching of the kind which gives priority to pupils' reflections on their own experience should generate discussions during which the teacher's authoritative role is at least temporarily relaxed (Westgate *et al*, 1985; Burgess, 1984). Computing, whether taught as a subject or in permeated form, is more likely than most curriculum areas to produce challenges to the teacher's 'power to know' because there are pupils who may know more and be more confident in their knowledge. It has therefore prompted investigation of the communicative consequences of pupil expertise and — a matter to which we return — of whether the consequences are different for girls than for boys (Culley, 1988; Underwood *et al*, 1990; Singh, 1993).

As the references indicate, there are research studies relevant to these expectations and predictions. But as we have argued already, there remains a dearth of detailed description of communication in its less orthodox forms, and so of the ways in which alternative conceptions of teaching and learning are manifested in classroom talk. What evidence there is, at a sufficient level of detail, suggests a strong tendency to preserve more traditional patterns of classroom talk under the appearances of organizational or curriculum change. For example, whole-class teaching has proved resilient in primary schools, despite the strictures of its critics and the anxieties expressed by others at its relative demise (Simon, 1981; Barker-Lunn, 1984;

Pollard, 1985a). Even where interaction is organized more individually, whether in line with 'progressive' practice or in response to mixed-ability groups, the scope for pupil initiatives and for more demanding encounters with the teacher is not necessarily increased nor is the teacher's interactional and semantic control consistently loosened (Galton, 1979; Pollard, 1984a; Edwards and Furlong, 1978; Evans, 1985). Settings which are less physically trammelled than the traditional rows of desks within closed rooms are not too predictably associated with more open styles of teaching, and of teacher-pupil interaction (Bennett *et al*, 1980).

In any form of research, there are problems of selection in defining the relevant objects of enquiry and the relevant data. However, as we hinted earlier, it may be that the pervasiveness of closely teacher-directed forms of classroom talk has been unwittingly exaggerated by researchers because these are the forms which are easiest, or least difficult, to record and to interpret. The more the interaction is centred on the teacher, the more obvious will seem the focus of eye or camera, and the direction of the microphone. It will then be tempting to believe that what is happening around the edges of the 'official channels' can be ignored for practical purposes. We have emphasized the importance for pupils of all the unofficial talk which accompanies, competes with, and often subverts those channels, but we have also emphasized its inaccessibility. 'Decentralized' teacher-pupil talk is also difficult to record or overhear. Of course, researchers often choose on principle to avoid the typical, and to select for study unusual forms of teaching, or teaching in unusual settings, so as to 'make the familiar strange' and thereby gain a clearer view of what is too easily taken for granted (for example, Delamont, 1981; Burgess, 1984, chapter 1). But to make sense of the unfamiliar is so evidently expensive in time that it is beyond the reach of most researchers, even if they had the analytical tools to catch the nuances of unfamiliar forms of teacher-pupil talk.

Despite all these cautionary notes, however, there are strong reasons why the familiar forms of talk have remained so persistent. In considering them, we have found it useful to extend the range of comparisons beyond types of classroom to other social settings in which very unequal communicative rights are created and sustained by the unequal knowledge accredited to or claimed by the participants.

3 Status, Knowledge, and Unequal Communicative Rights

We begin with a more general comparison, that between talk in any 'status-marked' setting and what conversational analysts call for practical purposes talk between equals. When McHoul (1978) was seeking to account for the impression of formality which is given by most transcripts of talk in classrooms, he drew from that analytical frame of reference its basic

distinction between talk which has to be organized as it goes along because none of the participants has any special rights or obligations to take
the decisions necessary to achieving orderly interaction, and talk which is
organized largely through unequal rights and obligations arising from status differences between the participants. In conditions of such inequality,
there may be pre-allocated rights (for example) to speak first or most or
last, to decide who else shall speak and when and for how long, and to
interrupt or correct or discard the contributions of others. It is part of the
participants' competence to know their place, or (if they wish) to challenge
it in ways which others will recognize as being a challenge and not a
display of incompetence. We want to examine this broad distinction briefly,
if only because recommendations for more 'real' discussion in classrooms
may be seeking to carry teacher-pupil talk unrealistically far towards the
informal end of the continuum which McHoul describes.

Towards the formal end of that continuum are such settings and occasions as public lectures, committee meetings, court-room interrogations
and job interviews. In each of these examples, expectations about which
turns belong to whom may be made very clear indeed — as in the common
penultimate move in job interviews, 'We've bombarded you with questions, is there any question you'd like to ask us?'. But of course, conversations do not always take place in conditions of perfect equality either.
For example, adults often act as though they 'own' their interactions with
young children. They decline to listen at all when they have 'better things
to do', insist on being heard themselves, exclude or curtail topics which
are 'silly' or arise from an at least temporarily inconvenient curiosity, and
decide unilaterally when the talking has 'gone on long enough'. These
rights would cause offence in adult company, and their young conversational partners may have to struggle hard to initiate the encounter in the
first place, and then to sustain it through the adult's flagging interest (Speier,
1976). Even in the extended, inventive and mutually rewarding conversations between mothers and young children recorded by (for example)
Tizard and Hughes (1984), the child is often dependent on having his or
her meanings interpreted appropriately by an authoritative adult. Another
pervasive source of inequality, now extensively documented, is the un-
even share of communicative space taken by women in mixed groups,
their much greater vulnerability to interruption than men, and their relative
tentativeness in bidding for turns and determining or changing topics
(Cheshire, 1984; French and French, 1984; Graddol and Swann, 1989; Swann,
1992).

Conversational analysts do not ignore such inequalities, but insist that
they have to be 'evident in' the text of what is said, and so 'warranted' by
that evidence, if they are to be included in the analysis of how the talk was
organized and understood. Their main interest, however, has been in talk
where the achievement of orderly transitions from one turn and topic to
the next is treated as being a collective responsibility, not something which

is seen from the outset as 'belonging' to one participant. In classrooms, the fact that such decisions are normally made by and conceded to the teacher, places them immediately towards the formal end of McHoul's continuum.

The notion of 'instructional conversation' may therefore be misleading in so far as it implies a dialogue between equals. It is useful in drawing attention to how turns and topics are managed when the talk is so goaldirected by a single speaker that negotiation is largely replaced by rights claimed and conceded to make the required decisions. In orderly classrooms, the teacher takes turns at will, allocates turns to others, determines topics, interrupts and re-allocates turns judged to be irrelevant to those topics, and provides a running commentary on what is being said and meant which is the main source of cohesion within and between the various sequences of the lesson.

The most obvious contrast in conditions between ordinary conversation and ordinary classroom talk is one of numbers. For conversation is not only 'talk among equals'; it is also talk among a few. Where more than three or four are gathered together, the managing of turns is likely to become so complicated and the frustrations of waiting one's turn so great, that the group breaks up into more 'manageable' units. Teachers are likely to have thirty or more potential speakers to manage, often within a central communication system in which whoever is speaking is supposed to be heard by all. It is not surprising, then, that 'irrelevant talk' and 'excessively noisy talk' figure so prominently in reports of pupils' misbehaviour (Wragg, 1984, pp. 37–9), or that such a high proportion of teachers' disciplinary actions are directed against talking out of turn — 'No talking when I'm talking', 'Come on, stop the chatter', 'Are you listening? What have I just said', and so on. For pupils, of course, the strain of not talking out of turn is considerable, when there is so much in their lives in and out of school of more direct and immediate interest than is on the official agenda. And where the class is being taught 'as one', pupils' unofficial talk has a visible and public quality which requires swift preventative action from the teacher if it is not to be imitated. More 'decentralizing' of classroom communication has therefore been seen by some observers, from this standpoint, as reducing the occasions for confrontation by allowing more scope for tolerated conversation, and as thereby reducing the effectiveness of noise as the main weapon to be used against the teacher (Edwards and Furlong, 1978; Denscombe, 1980). It also makes it possible to avoid 'spotlighting' misbehaviour by making more of the teacher's interaction with pupils a relatively private affair — an advantage which has been especially emphasized in several studies of multi-cultural classrooms (Philips, 1972; Erickson and Mohatt, 1982).

Most teachers, however, have seen close and persistent control over classroom communication as a precondition for reaching their educational objectives, and challenges to it are unlikely to be far from their minds. This is not only because of the immediate problems of managing turns and topics in such crowded conditions, but also because their failure to 'keep the noise down' is likely to be severely judged, both by their pupils and their colleagues. As Martyn Denscombe (1985) has argued, teachers are rarely observed by other teachers while actually engaged in instruction. But they and their classrooms can usually be overheard. Even without the danger that excessively noisy classrooms make the task of other teachers more difficult, it is the absence of more subtle and direct evidence of professional competence that gives the apparent capacity to keep order its significance. A common consequence is a wariness of pupil activities which are likely to generate a great deal of noise, even 'productive noise', and of curriculum innovations which promise (or threaten) an unusual frequency of such activities. A more general consequence is a managerial constraint on teachers to ask the kinds of questions which make it 'natural' to regain the floor at regular intervals, which commonly extends to doing so every other turn, in order to evaluate the answers and redirect the questions. There are clearly constraints against asking 'open' questions, because of the unpredictability of what may follow. Indeed, the more successful the teacher is in initiating 'discussion', the more the ensuing talk may move towards the structure of conversation. While this may be organizationally feasible in conditions where small-group teaching is commonplace — for example, in higher education and in the style of teaching often associated (without much evidence of frequency) with sixth forms — it will pose a formidable challenge to the teacher's skills in the normally crowded conditions in which so much classroom communication occurs.

Making conditions less crowded by breaking up the single communication system centred on the teacher may be a necessary condition for less teacher-dominated interaction. It will be insufficient without some accompanying relaxation of control over the meanings being exchanged so as to allow interplay between alternative frames of reference. For conversation is not only 'talk between equals' in the organization of turns and the determining of topics. It is also talk without a predetermined expert, and without constraints to reach authoritatively defined conclusions. It is not normally 'an enterprise designed to yield an extrinsic profit'; at its best it can be 'an unrehearsed intellectual adventure'; and there is neither an unavoidable arbiter, nor a 'door-keeper to examine the credentials of entrants into the flow of speculation' (Michael Oakshott; cited in Hadley, 1980).

Most classroom talk which has been recorded displays a clear boundary between knowledge and ignorance. Pupils are mainly or merely receivers of knowledge, and there are heavy constraints on what they can say and mean because it has to be confined within the limits of what the teacher treats, for practical purposes, as being relevant and correct. These constraints are most apparent in the kinds of questions which they are normally asked. To be asked a question by someone who wants to know is to be given the initiative in deciding the amount of information to be offered and the manner of its telling. But to be asked by someone who already knows, and wants to know if you know, is to have your answer accepted, rejected or otherwise evaluated according to the questioner's beliefs about what is relevant and true (Young, 1984). If 'the typical preschool does not nurture dialogue' (Sylva *et al*, 1980, p. 82), there is little evidence that other kinds of classroom nurture it either.

From this perspective, classrooms can be aligned with other contexts in which a participant has, or claims to have, prior or superior knowledge of the matters in hand. Where the other participants accept that claim, then the talk will be organized by reference to that hierarchy, and will be 'evident in the text' in ways which we explore in detail in chapters 4–6. Broadly, the 'expert' will 'control knowledge' by asking the questions, evaluating and shaping the answers in the light of what he or she needs to get the other(s) to say, discarding those which are thereby irrelevant or redundant, and terminating the exchange when enough information has been obtained for the practical purposes of that encounter. For example, a doctor questions a patient about symptoms until at least a provisional diagnosis can be made. A barrister questions a witness long enough, and 'leadingly' enough, to obtain a damaging admission or an exonerating alibi (Dillon, 1990). An investigative journalist, or a self-consciously formidable television interviewer, will also ask leading questions which deny the informant the normal conversational control over the length and content of the answer, and does so by acting on at least an implicit claim to superior knowledge or insight. And teachers regularly ask questions to which they already have answers, or have 'established the parameters in which a reply can properly fall'; the pupil then has to match the questioner's knowledge, or fall within those parameters (Mehan, 1979b, p. 286).

The following example illustrates that shaping of what is said towards the predetermined ends of one participant. The second example, also from class 'discussion', shows a teacher relinquishing the normal role of expert in order to receive information about the topic which he seems not to possess already.

1   T   What do you know about it so far?
    P   You can have a skin on top of the water.
    T   A kind of skin on top of the water, but remember it's not a skin like the skin on boiled milk, you can't scrape it up and take it off and leave it on the side of your plate — you can't do that with it. But it is a kind of skin and various insects can make use of it. Think of an insect that makes use of the skin — Michael?
    P   Mosquito.
    T   Good, a mosquito. How does a mosquito use this skin? Janet?
    P   It lays its larva underneath it.
    T   Well, yes, the eggs are laid in water and then what happens to the larva? What does the larva do? Well?

P   Hangs from the surface tension on top of the water.

T   Good, it hangs from the surface of the water. Why? Why can't it lie under the water altogether? Why does it need to hang from the surface?

P   It wouldn't be able to breathe.

T   Yes, it wouldn't be able to breathe. What it does is to put a breathing tube up into the air and breathes that way. . . .

(Taken from a lesson on surface tension recorded in a middle-school by one of the writers).

This second example is from a science lesson on evolution, with pupils aged eleven —

2   T   And how do scientists know, or reckon they know, that fossils are so old?

P   Sir, they're given chemical tests.

T   Good. Would anybody like to add to that?

P   They found the shapes in rocks, and the only way the rocks could have formed over them was over a lot of years.

T   Very good, excellent.

P   Say you've got something in the water, like a dolphin. If it died it would land in water so nobody else — the water would disappear and all the earth would grow above it. And they can tell how old it is by how much the earth covers it.

T   I see. Very interesting. Any other comments on it?

P   Sir, another thing that explains how fossils came about is the mystery of the Tollund Man.

T   Mmm?

P   This man, sir, he done something wrong, and he was left on the ground and put in a pit. And they put earth over him. And his body was preserved. And his fossil is his actual shape.

T   Can you explain that again?

P   They think he died from hanging. There was a rope round his neck.

T   And how old do they think this is?

P   Sir, the scientists even know what his last meal was.

T   Really?

P   Maybe the food was preserved in the stomach and they took some samples.

T   And the stomach was well enough preserved?

P   It was preserved in peat.

(From Chilver and Gould, 1982, pp. 52–3)

Even in the second extract, it is evident who is managing the interaction, though some of the information being transmitted is volunteered rather than directly elicited. It is the possibility of giving pupils more responsibility for managing the talk which underlies much of the advocacy of small-group discussion, when the pressures of trying to contain so many participants within a single communication system are significantly reduced, or of discussion in which the teacher either adopts an unobtrusive chairing role or is only present indirectly in the task which the pupils have been set.

Of course, placing pupils in small groups is more often 'a convenient seating arrangement than a specific site for teaching', an organizational device 'rather than a technique for promoting enquiry-based learning using collaborative methods' (Bennett *et al*, 1984, p. 220; Galton, 1990; Bennett and Dunne, 1990). But where pupils are encouraged to explore meanings collaboratively, the absence of clearly-marked asymmetrical relationships, and the consequent lack of pre-allocated rights and obligations, make it necessary for them to negotiate the terms of their interaction as it goes along. They have to give and receive more information about the functions of utterances and how they are to be heard as 'going together' than in those usual occasions when there is a single source of authoritative decisions to rely on. And that information has often to be subtle and indirect if it is not to be resented as unjustified domination. Acts normally monopolized by the teacher, such as the repairing of breakdowns in understanding and the providing of regular summaries of where the talk has 'got to so far', have now to be shared around. Such conditions of relative equality make possible something like conversation, even conversation in the form of 'unrehearsed intellectual adventure', although the salience of friendship in classroom life may also exert its own pressures. Unwillingness to take the social risks of disagreement with friends may lead discussion groups to close down their talk prematurely by reaching a contrived consensus. In the rare studies where such talk has been recorded, a particular focus of interest has been how pupils manage their relationships with one another in the course of tackling some academic task (Barnes and Todd, 1977; Salmon and Claire, 1984; Halligan, 1988; Phillips, 1985).

The next transcript illustration has been chosen because it displays in a single discussion both hierarchical and relatively equal forms of organizing the talk. As in the original, it is presented with none of the conventions for marking (for example) pausing and intonation which are outlined in the following chapter, and without reference to anything more systematic than the reader's intuitive sense of its organization. The extracts are from different stages in a discussion of 'success and failure' between six second-year girls in a London school, and the recording was one of many made by a group of teachers who worked collectively to monitor and improve the quality of language in their classrooms (Talk Workshop Group, 1982; pp. 14–19). The topic is clearly the teacher's choice, and during the opening stage Marcia S. acts out what is almost a parody of a teacher's directing role. The discussion then develops into something approaching a state of conversational equality, before reverting again (with one digression) to a more 'teacher'-controlled interaction.

Marcia S	Audrey, what does success mean to you?
Audrey	I don't know what it really means to me.
Marcia S	Beverley, what does success mean to you? Does it mean a good job?
Beverley	Yes.
Marcia S	Marcia, what does success mean to you?
Marcia R	Success, it means when you're doing something and you're sort of nervous about doing it. You don't know whether you're going to pass or not. If you pass, that mean you succeeded but if you didn't pass that mean you fail.
Marcia S	Yes. So what does succeeding mean to you. A lot?
Marcia R	Yeah, it mean a lot, it makes you feel better, sometimes people when they succeed in a thing they start to cry. They fool aren't they?
Audrey	Yeah, yeah. I would like to succeed in that test I'm gonna have soon. You know that test . . .

(from a later stage in the discussion)

Audrey	Did you know there's lots of policemen and lots of coloured ones round Brixton, did you know that?
Beverley	No.
Marcia R	They feel embarassed. If you — see a coloured policeman, right, and you look at him, he feels embarassed, you know he does, because when me and my brother were walking along — you know Gladstone my big brother — and we saw a coloured policeman, and the man he was looking at us you know, and when my brother started looking at him he bent down his face like that.
Marcia S	Do you think black people, black policemen round London, just show you how successful people can be if they try?
Marcia R	Er — I wouldn't like to be a policewoman.
Marcia S	Because — we didn't have any before, but do you think it's being successful, just showing how successful you can be?
Marcia R	I think the white police are using the black police for, er, beating, er black youths in the street.
Ann-Marie	You can say that again.
Marcia R	You know what I mean.
Marcia S	So you don't they're being successful, they're just being used?
Marcia R	No — yeah, just being used . . .

An initial attempt by Marcia S to return to interrogating the others about their ideas of a 'really successful job' was briefly diverted back to an issue of much more immediate concern to them. Marcia then regained control as surrogate teacher, and the rest of the 'discussion' became a steady tramp through the official task.

Beverley	You know about black policemen, I think er, why they go to be police in the first place is to show white people how good they can be.
Audrey	Be a success, that's why they go round Brixton in those uniforms.
Marica S	And tell me something. Do you think that the more black people go — get really good jobs, they're showing we're just as equal?
Audrey	Yeah, showing them how successful they can be when they get all those big jobs.
Marcia S	Oh yeah. So success really matters a lot. Okay. So just gonna go on and talk about failure. What does failure mean to you? How do you feel? Do you feel depressed after you failed something like an exam . . . . . .

The placing of commas around 'discussion' is intended to suggest that the label is often attached to activities which are something else. When the teacher is neither telling nor testing, it is often assumed that the interaction will be less teacher-centred and that the pupils will be doing more of the communicative work. Nowhere is the recording and close analysis of classroom talk more useful as a check on such assumptions. For what it commonly reveals is another way of leading pupils towards a predetermined conclusion, the route still shaped by the teacher's questions and by his or her evaluations of what pupils say in response. If the questioning 'genre' is less likely to be the WDPK (What do pupils know) type because the knowledge being transmitted is new to the pupils, it is quite likely to be of the WDTT (What does teacher think?) type in which the search is for what is already in the teacher's mind (Young, 1992, chapter 8). We cite part of Young's transcript illustration of the WDTT genre on page 37, the extract having added force because it is taken from a 'discussion' of 'discussion'. Our own argument is not that teacher-led and teacher-managed explorations of ideas should be avoided, for they have their place and may be managed with great skill, but that they should not be mistaken for something else. If the teacher intends an 'open' discussion and what occurs is 'collusion' in reaching a consensus 'that accords closely with what the teacher already knows' (Edwards, 1990, pp. 61–2), then the difference may only become apparent from close examination of (for example) how and by whom contributions are made, elaborated, contested, and built upon.

We have already cited examples of 'real' discussion in which the teacher contributes to but avoids dominating a collaborative search for meaning (pages 38–40), and there are other examples in chapters 5 and 6 of teachers managing such events even with a whole class of potential contributors (see also, Howe, 1988). But the pressures of habit and custom which make the teacher a normally authoritative source of answers has led many teachers to explore the possibilities of teacher-less discussion, thereby defying that belief which we mentioned earlier that the outcome will be 'aimless chatter' (for example, Berrill, 1988; Howe, 1992; Maybin, 1991; Phillips, 1988, 1990; Wray, 1990). As in the previous extract, pupils' talk may still be constrained by the unseen teacher's directives. The requirement to make contributions relevant to the set task may be tight where there is a 'conclusion' to be reported back to the whole class, though there can be advantages in leaving room for some divergence into 'irrelevance' (Phillips, 1988; Westgate and Corden, 1993). But the talk will be governed by rules closer to those which regulate everyday conversation — for example, don't hog the floor, don't interrupt, listen to others and make some reference to what they have said, and so on — and responsibility for maintaining those rules will be shared. This may usefully extend pupils' awareness of, and willingness to comment explicitly on, how the talk is managed (Hardman and Beverton, 1993).

Our final example is of talk shaped by the teacher's task, but in which pupils are enabled to take on responsibilities normally reserved for the teacher, and to draw on personal experience to challenge generalizations. Berrill (1990, pp. 166–7) is concerned here to justify the place of argument in classroom talk, provided that it avoids 'assertive pummelling' and encourages (for example) 'valuing and eliciting differences', justifying opinions, and 'challenging ideas without criticizing people'. The pupils here have already exchanged experiences about the nature and extent of parental supervision.

Bimal	Right, go on then. Should they be able to control our lives?
Stephen	Er, yes and no. Yes they should and no they shouldn't 'cos it's our life in'it When we get maried, we're not gonna have all the time to do what we want, are we? So let's (?) now while we can.
Sheryl	I think if you tell them what time you're coming in it doesn't matter so much
Leanne	It does
Sheryl	Well, not so much. At least you're with someone. If you're by yourself you should come in earlier.
Leanne	My mum waits up for me, she does. This is my mum . . . she waits up for me. Like she says, 'If you're going out tonight', she says, I'm not gonna wait up for

	you". 'All right then, I don't mind'. She waits up for me. Sick!
Sheryl	What was the question?
Stephen	Go on
Bimal	You said they should and they shouldn't, right. So when should they tell you?.
Stephen	Not all the time, but most of the time
Bimal	Yeh, when?
Stephen	All right. If you're going out to a disco or something. . . . If you're just going out with your mates then it's different isn't it. . . . . what time
Leanne	Yeh, but do you have arguments with your parents?
Stephen	Yeh, with my dad I do.

In this chapter, we have been less concerned with methods of investigation (except by implication) than with various accounts of the distinctiveness of classrooms as communicative settings. Normal forms of teacher-pupil interaction have been described at the levels of vocabulary, grammar, semantics, style or variety, and discourse. While researchers have certainly neglected unconventional classrooms, often because they are seen as beyond the scope of available methods for recording interaction, we have argued that a high level of generalization is possible about the patterning of communication. We have also indicated some structural similarities with other settings where 'knowledge' is unequally distributed, and where unequal communicative rights are created and sustained by its transmission to the 'ignorant'. How and where those rights are 'evident' in classroom talk, and how different research methods seek out and analyze the evidence, are our concern throughout the rest of the book.

3 Research Purposes, Practices and Problems

> Because educational facts are constituted in interaction, we need to study interaction in educational contexts (Mehan, 1979a, p. 6).

The argument that the facts of greatest value for the study of education are those constituted in classroom interaction, and that they are most readily displayed in classroom talk, provides a persuasive reason for regarding classroom research as 'basic' research and recorded language as its vital evidence. Indeed, as we noted earlier, Dell Hymes (1979) argues that classrooms offer an exceptionally useful and appropriate setting for basic work in sociolinguistics generally; the essential activities which take place there throw into relief both fundamental processes of verbal interaction, and the ways in which personal and cultural identities are realized in and through the resultant discourse.

Yet behind the logic and high promise of this perspective lies a bewildering variety of practical procedures and theoretical standpoints which compete for the researcher's attention. The range of methodologies is wide, and choosing among them is complicated by the knowledge that no single approach will serve all research purposes, or be applicable to any and every educational setting. Moreover, there are sharp differences of opinion about both the theoretical underpinnings and practical validity of every main option. And while a tolerant eclecticism may indicate that a combination of methods throws more light than a firm loyalty to one, some approaches are so incompatible one with another that combining them brings more problems than solutions. Yet principled choices must somehow be made.

In the previous chapter, we paid more attention to evidence than to the ways in which it was collected and interpreted. But in describing some familiar characteristics of classroom talk, we hoped not only to make them more noticeable and less taken for granted, but also to indicate some of the dilemmas which researchers face in deciding where to focus their attention and how to record the evidence relevant to their purposes. In this chapter, we review areas of decision which are common to all types of classroom research which use talk as evidence. Later chapters will detail the strengths and limitations, pedigree and typical applications, of each of the main research 'traditions'.

1   Choice of Approach

The first difficulty to face is a corollary of this diversity of methodological perspectives and procedures — the absence of any single conceptual framework or adequate shared vocabulary for describing classroom events and processes. We lack in other words a coherent meta-language, agreed ways of talking about classroom talk. Different disciplines have been drawn upon for specific purposes, often without reference to or even awareness of considerable epistemological differences and conflicts between them. Yet in the process of enquiry, and as methods of enquiry have been re-fined, there has been some convergence of interest. It has certainly not brought anything like a methodological consensus, nor does it promise one. Rather, areas of interdisciplinary interest have become clearer, while practitioners working within particular disciplines have become more self-conscious and reflective about the methods they employ and their relative effectiveness. This inter-disciplinary awareness is evident in several publications where the contributors display a wide range of academic allegiances but also find some common ground in issues and problems relating to verbal interaction in schools (French and Maclure, 1981; Delamont, 1984; Dillon, 1988). Our point is not to suggest any marked blurring of the edges of those allegiances, but rather to note that complementary insights are being developed and that particular studies are more likely to display awareness of how they compare with possible alternatives.

A broadening of research perspectives is occurring within disciplines as well as across them. Two sociological collections on teaching and on pupil culture can be cited as illustrations (Hargreaves and Woods, 1984; Hammersley and Woods, 1984). The editors of the first acknowledge the strong anthropological orientation of much of the American work which they include. And while few of the contributors focus explicitly on the organization of classroom discourse for its bearing upon teaching and learning, many of the chapters are liberally documented with extracts from recorded lessons. In linguistics itself, Stubbs (1984) has argued that the revival of interest in methods of sampling and analyzing naturally-occurring speech has drawn attention firmly to those forms and functions of language which are characteristic of educational settings, and to comparisons and contrasts with the pre-school and out-of-school experience of children (Cazden *et al*, 1972; Labov, 1972a; Garnica and King, 1979; Green and Wallat, 1981; Mercer and Edwards, 1981).

Those are all American examples. In the UK, as we indicated in the opening chapter, classrooms have had an appeal for discourse analysts as settings in which the allocation of communicative roles would be relatively defined and stable, thereby making the structure of the talk more accessible to analysis (Burton, 1980; Coulthard, 1987). From that analysis have come terms like 'teaching exchange' and 'responding move' which may have uses outside their initial 'technical' context, and which can contribute to accounts of classrooms events which are both precise enough for those whose interests are more esoteric, and accessible to those whose interest in them is more professional and practical.

There remain, however, pronounced differences in approach, which are argued and defended on principle. We quoted earlier Wolcott's (1982) concern that 'ethnographic' concepts and methods were being claimed by studies which were not properly and rigorously ethnographic at all, and we go on to Stubbs' criticism of casual, uninformed use of linguistic data in classroom research. Delamont (1983) has warned that no easy rapprochement can be effected between systematic and ethnographic approaches to classroom interaction because they rest on opposed conceptions of the nature and objectives of research (but see Galton and Delamont, 1985). Mehan (1979a) distances his own approach, which he calls 'constitutive ethnography', from both the systematic tradition and the more loosely ethnographic case studies of classroom life which were becoming common by the late 1970s. It is therefore important for researchers to realize the implications for every stage of their work which arise from their chosen orientation. This will influence the choice and definition of topic. It will affect ways in which data are recorded, analyzed and interpreted, and in which outcomes are eventually conceived and reported. Any claim to absolute neutrality or objectivity would imply a failure to grasp the inescapability of all these inter-related choices. 'The researcher is a perceptual lens through which observations are made and interpreted, so the researcher profoundly affects what can be understood' (McCutcheon, 1981, p. 9). The metaphor is striking, and it emphasizes the dependence of what is observed on the instruments which are employed. Yet it does not go far enough. What has to be appreciated is the researcher's progressive commitment to whatever ensues from how topics and tasks are initially defined, through decisions about what are to count as data, to what those data are thought to signify. There is a view of reality implicit in each research perspective; no research is atheoretical, in the sense of being committed 'simply' to following the 'facts' wherever they lead without preconceptions about the kinds of facts relevant to the enquiry and how they are to be collected and analyzed.

It will be relevant at this point to return to Stubbs' (1981) insistence on a 'principled' approach to classroom language. In his view, researchers will only 'scratch the surface' of its characteristics unless they curb their random interests, and go far beyond picking and choosing as evidence 'any feature of language which appears intuitively to be interesting'. Too many of them lack credibility because of their unwillingness, or perhaps lack of the necessary linguistic knowledge, to undertake a close structural analysis of the talk they have recorded before drawing their conclusions.

They have rushed to judgment about its functions without paying sufficiently rigorous attention to its forms. While the best of them, like Douglas Barnes, may offer highly 'insightful observations', there is 'no method or guiding principle for those of us who are not so sensitive' (Stubbs, 1984, p. 220). Proper regard has to be paid to 'the organization of language as a system of communication'; research into classroom language is therefore seen as being under a double obligation — to be systematic in its own treatment of such systematic phemonena.

The argument for a 'principled' approach of this kind is persuasive, at least at the level of aspiration. It would be more persuasive in practice if there were more general agreement among linguists that discourse is susceptible to a similarly coherent analysis into a system of elements and rules as can be demonstrated (for example) at the level of syntax. In other words, even the pure analytical rigour which Stubbs advocates may not be immediately rewarding. Moreover, a range of work falling outside his criteria can still be seen to possess merits which can be undervalued from too strictly systematic a perspective. The achievements of the National Oracy Project can certainly be cited in support of the potential of non-specialist investigations. The many valuable insights emerging from that work were built upon a blend of teachers' insider-knowledge about their own classrooms and shared professional understanding tested out in the contexts of their own teacher groups. Such methods served very adequately the growing insights of those concerned, even if they may have been less well-adapted to providing more generalizable knowledge. Arguments within the Project understandably favoured non-specialist approaches. Johnson *et al*, (1992) note, for instance, that many of the teachers concerned, while attempting analysis of 'children's phonology, syntax, lexis, language use and so on . . . have not often found these detailed processes helpful' (p. 12). Ruling out more technically-demanding analyses, however, can have the effect of sacrificing some of the hard evidence which rebutting traditionalist opposition to pupil-talk also requires. The debate can be seen reflected in reviews of the first edition of this book, perceived by members of the Project (for example, Alan Howe, writing in *English in Education*, 22, 2; 1988) as essentially written for researchers not teachers, despite its authors' professed intentions to address a wide audience interested in classroom talk, teachers most certainly included. That recognizing the significance of teacher-pupil interaction may be accompanied by a rather cursory investigation of its patterning is also illustrated in Altrichter *et al*, 1993, pp. 138–46.

Barnes' 'insightful observations' have been especially influential through the immediacy of the recognition they have evoked in many teachers. His earlier, more 'intuitive' analyses of (for example) teachers' 'closed' and 'pseudo-open' questions, or the ways in which instructional language which is unnecessarily formal may shut pupils off from the knowledge being transmitted, matched the intuitions not only of the teachers who co-operated in his investigations but of a wide professional readership. They also made 'visible', and so available for reflection, aspects of classroom language which are easily taken for granted. We recall, in this context, Hugh Mehan's assertion that the highest compliment which a piece of classroom research can elicit from practitioners is — 'Ah yes, of course!'. But where Stubbs is right is in insisting on research being carried out from an explicit and consistent standpoint, being properly reflective about the assumptions and methods on which it rests, and displaying some aware-ness of the alternative methods which were NOT chosen.

Such principled research may reflect a single theoretical perspective, or the harmonious blending of different techniques chosen for their value in illuminating different aspects of the same topic. The former is more likely to gain from its consistency the appearance of rigour; a more eclectic approach may be more realistic where the phenomena being studied are highly complex and many-faceted. The former is associated more often with researchers at the 'pure' end of the research continuum. Thus while Sinclair and Coulthard (1975) stress the applicability of their structural description to most varieties of classroom, they see it mainly as a start towards a more general analysis of discourse (see also Coulthard, 1987; Burton, 1980, 1981). More strictly still, Brazil (1981) has argued that an explicitly purist conception of linguistics is required if the rules underlying discourse are ever to be established. As at the Chomskyan stage of syn-tactical analysis, there has to be a deliberate restriction of view and a deliberate avoidance of distractions. He would therefore eliminate from his analysis such non-linguistic factors as the speakers' intentions, as being too numerous and diffuse to be classified and which are in any case irrelevant to a speaker's preference for one linguistic form over any alternatives. While the first objection is a practical one, and might well be conceded wearily by a researcher who had attempted just such a classification, the second is a theoretically justified lack of interest which might not be avail-able to a researcher with a more 'educational' and applied interest in classroom interaction. Hammersley (1981), for example, maintains that attention to the speakers' intentions is necessary to exploring linguistic rule-breaking, which may be more significant than routine observance of rules in the determination of meaning.

The studies we cited in the previous chapter, and those which are explored methodologically in chapters 4–6, range widely along that often misleading continuum between the 'purest' and the most 'applied'. Through much of the rest of this book, we will be concerned implicitly and expli-citly with some of the questions which that diversity raises — for example, about how theoretically rigorous it is necessary to be to say anything 'useful' about the subtleties and complexities of classroom talk, about the power and scope of various methods of analysis, and about the knowledge (of linguistics, or of language in use) which should support those methods. Broadly, our own view is close to that expressed by Romaine (1984, p. 15) about the relatively 'pure' area of research into the language development of young children —

> In deciding to adopt one methodological strategy rather than another, there can be no question of choosing one method which will be universally the 'right' one. Methodology can be evaluated only within the context of some question which one wants to answer.

This is the case for eclectisicm summarized: appropriateness of instrument for a specific research task. In this light, it is no less principled than a consistent devotion to a single approach. It does not mean attempting to include the incompatible within the same study, but bringing together concepts and methods which can yield complementary insights into the 'same' phenomena, or can bring into view different aspects of classroom talk and its organization.

2   Recording and Transcribing

We have argued that choices of approach are inevitably related to purposes and procedures. They also necessarily involve theoretical, even philosophical, questions with echoes at every stage of the work. For classroom research which requires the collection and interpretation of linguistic data, there are further questions arising from the phenomenon of language itself to which the intending researcher must offer at least provisional answers. For example, how transparently does language carry meaning? In the organization of talk in particular settings, what are the critical 'indicators' which reveal what is 'happening'? Is other evidence needed to supplement the recorded talk? If so, what evidence should that be?

On some response to questions like these will depend a researcher's choice of recording method, or methods. For instance, an initial decision has to be made between the immediate coding of observed behaviour as it occurs, and the creation of an audio- or audio-visual record that can be replayed after the event, as many times and with whatever supplementary material (like field notes) as may be found necessary to make sense of that event. Simultaneous coding is carried out by observers trained to assign features of the interaction to pre-specified categories listed on an observation schedule. Such schedules proliferated in the 1960s and early 1970s so that they themselves needed to be catalogued and classified (Simon and Boyer, 1967, 1970, 1975; Galton, 1978b). Their original purposes and underlying assumptions are revealed in the title under which Simon and Boyer collated them — 'mirrors for behaviour'. That is, they were conceived as devices through which teachers might inspect themselves at work, profiting from the almost immediate feedback which they provided. They therefore have strong links historically with microteaching and other 'competency-based' teacher training programmes, though they have also been put to a wide range of research purposes which are explored in the chapter which follows.

The relevance of coding schedules to the present discussion consists in some of the assumptions which they embody — notably, the common assumption that those features of the interaction of teacher and taught which are relevant to the researcher's purposes are evident 'beneath' or 'within' the words exchanged, Utterances can therefore be adequately categorized as they occur in terms of their broadly defined functions. The resulting record then extends beyond who talked, how much, and to whom, to a listing of what was 'done' through what was said. The outcome is a great quantity of data about what 'really occurred' which can be computed like any other survey material. In short, the principle is that of looking 'through' talk, the words being treated as primarily conventional tokens of a shared culture which label an objective reality (McIntyre and McLeod, 1978).

By contrast, those who prefer to make recordings for retrospective analysis tend to the view that interaction is constructed both through the participants' interpretation of many factors not easily accessible to an outsider, and in ways which are influenced by the structure of the discourse itself. Those participants draw on background knowledge of which the observer may be unaware, they respond to the constraints of particular types of discourse at various stages in the lesson, and they regularly reinterpret the meaning of what was said in the light of what was then said after it, or make provisional interpretations while waiting for further 'evidence'. All these subtleties are seen as defying instant coding. Instead, they are judged to require patient scanning of a transcript, and also (because any transcript is itself selective) a willingness to return to the original recording to check or amplify details. Choice between instant coding and the various styles of retrospective analysis, then, reflects working assumptions about interaction and the transparency of talk, and about the kinds of data needed if the researcher is to capture more than the most unambiguously observable phenomena (who talked, most, and to whom).

There are wide disagreements, however, about what constitutes an adequate transcript on which to base some analysis of the complexities of the talk or to validate claims made at the reporting stage. The initial record cannot be all-embracing, yet its form will guide or predispose the directions which analysis can take. The final report must provide evidence in support of whatever conclusions are drawn, and allow the reader some scope for judging these against at least sample sections of the record. Researchers vary in their practices from the minimally helpful to the complicatedly tedious. In general, the guiding principle is still to suit the type and quantity of the data to the kind and depth of analysis intended.

That guiding principle may be difficult to follow in practice. Literal transcriptions of classroom talk which faithfully record all the words can be lifeless, and can also be uniformative about some of the meanings being exchanged. This is more likely where the transcription is not the teacher-managed, public talk of whole-class instruction, but the often hectic, over-lapping talk of (e.g.) group problem-solving, practical work, or discussion to which a play-script style of presentation would give a quite artificial tidiness. This is why Graddol (1992, pp. 183–184) uses parallel columns for each speaker so that overlapping turns, including sounds and gestures of agreement or disagreement, can be displayed.

Josie	Sara	Louise	Anne	Comment
Who's who's where where was the blood found outside somebody's flat (... who's flat that was)				J. looks round table. A. catches her eye and begins searching through cards
	Hold it what's this one for '*Mrs Jones had made an appointment with the bank manager to try to bo(.)*'			S. reads from card
				S. looks up from card
		Borrow		
What's it say	to go and			J's question addressed to S.
	see if he could go into business			J. and S. talk to each other. L. looks on.
mmh				A. still leafing through cards.
	I don't think it would have been him then that killed him		[touches L. on arm]	A. pulls out card.
who	if he was going to the bank manager			
Say that again	Mr Jones		(.....*Smith's garden*)	A. makes an aside to L.
				L. question towards A.
		hub		
got to keep his business going			(....*knife* ....)	A. aside to L. again L. takes A's card
	Yeah (he's going to) the bank manager	Anne's Anne's got '*A knife with Mr Kelly's blood on it was found in Ethel Smith's garden*'		L. reads from card S. looks over L's shoulder
	That has got it's got Mr Scott's fingerprints on I			S. To L. points to table decisively J. sits back, hands on table.
Oh he's got (.....) It's the whole lot of them	*think*			L. looks towards J. A looks towards J. smiles. S. leafing through cards.

Such informal talk is also likely to rely more than whole-class exchanges on gesture, facial expression, and on how words are said. We note elsewhere the possibility that traditional teaching is so prominent in classroom research because it is easier to observe and record. Conversely, talk which may be educationally more interesting and is certainly less familiar, is both harder to pick up and requires higher quality recording if communicatively significant details of (e.g.) pitch and intonation are to be transcribable. Howe (1988, p. 65) notes how group talk which appeared rambling and shapeless at the time of hearing is revealed on close examination to have a strong shape and structure. But the structure may come from what is hardest to record. Thus Susan Pirie, whose initial research into her pupils' mathematical discussions was prompted by a suspicion that they were more coherent than was apparent from overhearing them, was compelled to notice that 'much interpretable meaning may be lost between the visual observation and the audio-tape, and still further loss can occur between the tape and its transcription'. What the transcript showed as fragmented, ambiguous discussion, 'full of hesitations, repetitions, irrelevancies and non-sequiturs' may have been for the participants efficient communication in which their utterances were supplemented and interpreted by 'body language and shared background understanding'. The following brief extract illustrates an apparent incoherence which seems not to bother the speakers at all. The girls (aged 15 and 16) have been trying to construct from identical rectangular pieces of paper the largest possible container for some popcorn they have cooked. 'Height' in their discussion seems to have several, different, referents each of which is apparently understood.

Ann	. . . so that has the bigger area and can hold more
Louise	Thank you. That's got a different height, hasn't it?
Harriet	It's got a one sixth of the height
Louise	Uhh? Oh yes
Ann	But the height wasn't the height
Louise	No, it was one sixth of the height. Because I divided the paper by six
Ann	No, but the height of that is not one sixth of that is it?
Harriet	Louise, did you cut them along the length?
Ann	That isn't a long
Louise	Yes I cut them that way, the longest way. (Pirie, 1991, p. 281)

That extract is easy to read, if not to understand, because several channels of communication which the children were probably using are not marked at all. Yet including them may so clutter the text as to make it almost unreadable, and ignores the fact that spoken language is not planned and performed to be written down. Thus Halliday comments that even the most 'sympathetic' transcribing — that is, the most attentive to details of intonation, pitch and so on — is unlikely to make informal spoken language look coherent because speech and writing are not different ways of doing the same thing. Thus normal speech includes all the hesitations, false starts, errors, redraftings and periods of silent thought which are usually deleted before the final version of a written text is presented (Halliday, 1989, p. 76).

His advice is therefore to include in the transcript whatever features are necessary to the researcher's purposes. An important example arises from his reference to 'periods of silent thought'. Pauses are likely to be more frequent in discussion, and in other forms of exploratory talk, where meanings are being jointly constructed as the talk proceeds rather than transmitted 'ready-made'. They indicate speakers who are thinking aloud, and who are enabled to do so by the willingness of other participants not to seize on a hesitation as an opportunity to take the turn over. A prominent characteristic of normal, whole-class, interaction is its very fast pace. The silence which follows a teacher's question is usually very short indeed; if no answer is forthcoming, the question will be reformulated or a quick prompt given, and any hesitation by the pupil nominated or permitted to attempt an answer is likely to lead to the turn being swiftly re-allocated. Such pace is not easily compatible with reflection, which is why unsanctioned hesitations have been treated as such a significant indicator of more 'open' learning, and why some classroom research has produced strong recommendations that teachers should learn to pause more often, and for longer, before they intervene (Dillon, 1988; Rowe, 1986; Tobin, 1986).

Often a relatively simple format will be revealing. Consider, for example, the following extract from an audio-recording made in the reception class of an English infants school (Hester, 1985). Here the class of speaker (teacher or pupil), their words, and the overlaps (the onset of which is marked in each case by a square bracket) convey a great deal of information which enables the reader to appreciate the nature of the event. The traditional punctuation, and the sign (=) linking utterances which carry on from one line to another are valuable too, while line-numbering makes reference easy.

```
1   T    And how many did you catch in your jar? How =
2        many's that?
3   Ps   Three.
4   T    Three. He caught one, two, three ⌈and that little . . .
5   P                                     ⌊Guess what. I put =
6        = them in my jar and when I got them home and =
7        = put them in a dish they died ⌈without the water =
8        = in the sea                    |
9                                        ⌊Oh, they died! I =
10       = expect they would rather have been in the pond or =
```

```
11          = river, don't you? Maybe they didn't like being =
12          = in a little jar?
13   P      I had a ⌈little fish that died.
14   T             ⌊Maybe they didn't have enough to eat.
15   P      So I flushed him down the toilet.
16   T      Oh, did you? Oh well, maybe you can go =
17          = and get some more another day. Let's =
18   T      = see if ⌈you can remember that little song =
19   P             ⌊flushed him with a little one as well
20   T      = about ⌈the fish.
21   P             ⌊I can.
22   T      Ready?
23   T/Ps   (Song: One, two, three, four, five, once I caught . . . )
```

The conventions of lay-out and notation employed in this case are for the most part those common in conversational analysis, though by usual standards they are somewhat simplified. Indeed, it might be asked whether the information they provide is sufficient. Although single pupil-speakers (P) can be distinguished from those talking at the same time (Ps), marking the individual names might also be necessary. It would be crucial in a study focusing on particular children and their linguistic development or more general interactional competence. It would certainly be useful to have confirmation that the speaker at lines 13, 15 and 19 is the same child, and that the speaker at 21 is another child, since very different inferences would be drawn about the interaction if that were not the case. Has the teacher several eager conversationalists to cope with, or just two? That answer would be important in, for example, a study of how teachers distribute attention, or of the relative interactional dominance of boys and girls in this setting. For most purposes, too, a number of longer passages would be needed. As the extract stands, we can believe we are witnessing a teacher accommodating the anecdotes which are offered as she pursues her own agenda and perhaps contributes to her charges' socialization into the pupil role. But many questions will remain.

There is an important source of meaning to which the participants in talk pay attention but which is missing from the extract just discussed. We refer to details of pausing and intonation. Both may be highly significant in assessing the illocutionary force of an utterance, and such features as a speaker's deference or tentativeness. Both may thus form a crucial basis for the interpretations that are now thought largely to determine the coherence of discourse. In the following extract, taken from French and French (1984b), figures indicate the length of pauses in seconds and tenths of seconds — for example (1.5) — while a full-stop in parentheses marks a pause that is noticeable but too brief to measure — i.e. (.). Other conventions used here are again ones customarily used in conversation analysis (see Stubbs, 1983b, p. 229). Included are single brackets for speech about which the transcriber is uncertain; the space between them is left empty if the words are totally unclear, or marked with asterisks for whatever syllables are heard. Double brackets surround descriptions of relevant activities taking place during or around the talk. A colon after a syllable (for example fif:ty) indicates a long drawn-out delivery of the word. The extract is of the talk following a question addressed generally to the class — 'Anybody get up earlier than eight o'clock?' At the start of the extract, Tom is described as sitting with his hand raised.

1	T	what time do you get up Tom?
2		(0.7)
3	Tom	half past four.
4	T	what?
5	Tom	half past four.
6	T	(what do you get up at that time for?)
7	Ps	((exclamations etc.))
8	Tom	(no:) I've got to feed the a-animals and (clean all the aviary).
9	T	what?
10	Tom	I've got to clean the (aviary) and feed all the animals and (.) all that.
12	T	what animals?
13	Ps	⌈all the animals. ((various pupils call out —
		⌊he's got a difficult to distinguish individuals))
14		(hamster)
15	T	(I think) half past four perhaps is a little bit early I mean.
16		that's half way through the night Tom.
17		(1.9)
18	T	what animals have you got?
19	Tom	erm =
20	T	= you've got your parakeet.
21	Tom	two cats (.) two dogs (.) hams-no hamster (.) two rabbits.
22	Wayne	birds.
23	Tom	erm (1.0) parrot (1.0) that's all (.) I've got about (0.5) two rabbits (.) (I've) got about (.) fifty three birds something like that.
24		like that.
25	T	what (.) have you got them in an aviary have you (.)
26		(have you got them in the garden)?
27	Tom	yeah.

(French and French, 1984, pp. 128–129)

Note that the (=) sign here functions differently, marking what the writers call 'latched speech' — speech where there is no pause between speakers.

Conversational analysis demonstrates a consistent concern for pausing, often according it an important role in providing cues for would-be speakers who wish to enter the talk. In our final example of this type of transcription, however, pausing is treated more like verbal punctuation which separates utterances within a given speaker's continuing turn; and it is this kind of demarcation which is reflected in the numbering (left-hand column). Measurable pauses are still shown in brackets, but dashes (—) denote very short ones. Prolonged sounds are represented by sets of colons (for example, s:::city), and overlaps by marking // at the onset and] at their close. A striking additional feature here is the attempt to capture certain details of pronunciation, such as — 'y'd be wrong', or 'eighdeen'. Though the recording was made in a geography lesson in Canberra (Australia), these items are not included for the sake of local colour. The researchers who note them (McHoul and Watson, 1984) do so in order to highlight what they regard as one aspect of the significant 'echoing' by speakers of 'their own and each others' forms of talk in plainly visible ways (see, for example, the Teacher at 3 and 10). In the topic of this lesson, CBD stands for 'central business district') —

1 T   Perhaps a court house is likely to be centred very close t'the
          CBD then again there're other types of public buildings
               (0.7)
2 T   Ee gee
               (0.3)
3 T   E:r fire station — which possibly should be — located in the
          suburbs — so y'd be wrong if y'had all y'public buildings in the
          CBD — y'd probably be wrong if y' had e::::::r a great dispersal
          of y'public buildings
4 Lois   The university would also be away fom the s:::city centre (a bit)
          too
5 T   Why's that Lois?
6 L   Oh th's just more space out there I s'pose
               (1.0)
7 L   Ahm
               (3.4)
8 L   Ah wouldn't be too far away but it wouldn't be right in among
          all the court houses n'
               (0.2)
9 L   churches 'n things like tha//t]
10 T   M:] well actually you are showing good foresight because in y'
          next reading — eighdeen nie'y to nine'een hun'red you'll find
          th't there is a relocation of the university
               (0.4)
11 T   the reason being the high value of land in the inner city area
               (McHoul and Watson, 1984, pp. 282–3)

In the three extracts so far discussed in this section, the only intonational clues provided are the question marks, which stand out the more because of the absence of other forms of punctuation. Much more technical detail is usually given by linguists interested in the complex relationship between meanings and forms, and particularly in marking the rhythms and tunes of spoken discourse which interact with text to convey precision and nuance. Noting the close links between rhythm and intonation, Halliday (1989), for instance, marks both. As in the extract which follows, his basic unit is the foot, a group of syllables beginning with an accentuation, and enclosed by a single slash (/). This in turn belongs to a tone group, defined as a 'meaningful segment of the discourse . . . one quantum of the message, the way the speaker is organising it as he goes along' (p. 53). Each tone group begins and ends with a double slash (//), and its 'tonic nucleus' is given in bold type; at the same time, it is characterised by one of five tones, marked at the beginning as follows:

Tone 1   (falling)   \
Tone 2   (rising)   /
Tone 3   (low rise)   _/
Tone 4   (fall-rise)   /\/
Tone 5   (rise-fall)   \/\

Some combinations of tone are also possible — for example, 13 (fall followed by low-rise) — within a tone-group. Brief silences have also to be accounted for as part of the rhythm: as it were, a verbal comma (shown as ∧), except that such a 'silent beat' may occur at the start of a foot or tone-group, as well as in the middle. It is thus possible, if painstakingly slow at first, for a reader to reconstruct with some accuracy the tones of each speaker's contribution to the discourse. Here, Halliday's much-recorded son, Nigel (aged 6.3), is speaking with his father about the Rainhill trials for the Liverpool-Manchester railway in 1829.

N: //1 what is there / in the / water that / makes you / **sink** //2 ∧ in a / **marsh** //

F: //1 **nothing** it's //4 just / ordinary / **water** //1 ∧ you / **always** / sink in / water //

N: //1 ∧ but / why / can't you / **swim** in the / water //

F: //1 **oh I** //1 **see** //1 ∧ be/cause it / isn't / **deep** e/nough //1 ∧ it's / all mixed / up with / mud and / **weeds** //

N: //1 ∧ but / why / can't you / hold / **on** in the / marsh //1 ∧ to the / bits of / **land** //

F: //1 ∧ well you / **could** //4 ∧ if you were /sinking / in too / **far** //1 ∧ but the / bits of / land /sometimes /sink in / **too** //

N: //2 ∧ but / was / Rainhill / still joined / on to / **England** //2 ∧ by a / bit of / land / far /far a/**way** //

F: //1 **oh** yes //1 Rainhill is / **near** the / marsh //1 near Chat / **Moss** //1 ∧ and / Chat / Moss is / all / part of / **England** //1 ∧ it has / England / all / **round** //

N: //4 ˬ so the / trains / **could** have gone //1 **round** a //1 long
long / **way** //1 ˬ but it would have / been too / **far** //

F: //1 **yes** //1 **right** they //4 **could** have gone / round but it would
have //1 been too / **far** //

N: //1 ˬ because / Rocket was the / fastest / train in the / **world**
//1 ˬ it was the / **only** / train . . . //1 ˬ because in / England
were the / only / trains in the / **world** //1 ˬ they / only / had
/ trains in / **England** be/cause they //1 thought it / would have
/ been too / **frightening** //1 ˬ because the / other / countries
/ thought the / trains would have / terrible / **accidents** and they
would have //1 been too / **fast** / ˬ //1 how / fast did the / Rocket
/ **go** //

F: //1 twenty-nine / miles an / **hour** //

N: //1 ˬ that's / just a/bout / **one** / mile an / hour for //4 **these**
/ days //4 ˬ but for / **those** / days //5 **wow** // ˬ it was . . .
(p. 89)

Technically, such prosodic marking is of interest because it reveals, in
Halliday's view, the significance of points in the intonational flow where
there are abrupt and highly significant changes in pitch — usually at the
most prominent place in the tone-group. Knowledge of this phenemenon
makes interpretation much more reliable. Seen in another light as well,
however, this adult-child exchange well illustrates what Dillon (for example,
1988) makes clear and we discuss at length elsewhere: namely, that such
exchanges are most evidently thoughtful and mind-engaging for the child
when the child rather than the adult does the questioning!

A simpler device, but one quite adequate to its purpose, is adopted by
Cazden (1988) in her account of 'sharing time' in her (US) elementary
school's combined first-, second- and third-grade class. These speech-events,
which consisted of short, personal narratives about recent occurrences,
were notable for providing pupils with the 'only opportunity during official
classroom air time for children to create their own oral contexts: to give
more than a short answer to the teacher's questions, and to speak on a self-
chosen topic that does not have to meet criteria of relevance to previous
discourse' (p. 8). Nevertheless, the events are characterized by certain 'for-
mulaic' features, one of which — a rising intonation pattern — would
seem to indicate the children's awareness of the danger of being interrupted and their determination to keep the floor. Cazden simply marks the
relevant passages with a rising arrow. One sample-extract, again organized
by tone-groups, is given, as follows:

Well when I slep' over my mother's /
the cãt /
in the middle of the night she w-- /
went under the covẽrs /
(p. 9).

As in a previous study by Cazden and Michaels, this simple technique is sufficient for identifying the stylized tone contours which may be evident in particular routine classroom activities, and which are used (for example) to mark the opening and closing of exchanges, or the nomination of a next speaker (Michaels 1984). It can also show how teacher and pupils, or pupils from different cultural backgrounds, may draw differently on their repertoire of communicative skills.

In the chapters which follow, we shall have much more to say about relationships between talk and macro-factors associated with (for example) social class and ethnic origin. It is worth noting here, however, that in one kind of research project the collection of such background information in anticipation of its possible relevance is clearly justified. We refer to longitudinal studies of language development. Our next extract is taken from such a source — the Bristol study directed by Gordon Wells which recorded young children in their homes and at intervals during their first years of pre-school and more formal schooling (see for example, Wells 1979; Wells *et al*, 1981; Wells and Wells 1984). At the stage which provides our example, the children being recorded were of pre-school age. For each child, the collected transcripts were preceded by systematic notes of a general kind, while each individual sample contained more detailed contextual information. The transcript conventions include the familiar asterisks for undecipherable syllables. Utterances, or parts of utterances, about which there is doubt, are enclosed in angular brackets < >. Pauses are shown in seconds, or by dots (. . .) where they are very short. The symbol (v) indicates that the preceding word was used as a vocative (a call on a person by name). The target child's utterances are listed on the left, with any necessary commentary in square brackets on the right.

1 Preliminary notes:

Code No.: So7CF8	Name: KERRIE
Date of Birth: 8.7.70	Date of Recording: 9.10.73
Age: 3 years 3 months	Recording No. 1

Father's occupation: Driver	Education: Minimal
Mother's occupation: Factory worker	Education: Minimal

Position in family: Second out of two

Siblings:	Name	Sex	Date of Birth	Age
	Lisa	F	29.5.68	5 years

Type of accommodation: Semi-detached Council house
Area: Council estate

Names of other people present during the day's recording:

Name	Identification
Mother	M
Mother's Friend	Fr
Lisa	L

Notes relevant to this recording:
    Kerrie not well on day of recording

2 *Transcript:*
Name: KERRIE.   D. of B.: 8.7.70.   D. of R.: 9.10.73.   Recording No. 1

SAMPLE No. 5	Participants:	Kerrie, Mother and her friend
	Location:	Lounge
Time: 10.43 am.	Activity:	Talking. Kerrie is telling Mother's friend about the little girl with the burnt face.

Go * get face *burnt*

        Fr.: *Yes*
           Yes
           Did you see it?
           Horrible in it?
           . . .

< And some > matches

        Fr.: Yes

I didn't play matches

        Fr.: You don't
           No
           You don't want a burnt face
             like that girl do you?
           . . 7 . .

Sometimes I allowed to * —
   make fags * — make fags
   sometimes

        Fr: Make fags?

Yes

        Fr.: *Yeh*
           That's all right
           . . .
           But you're not allowed to use
             matches are you?

No (whisper)

        Fr.: No
           . . 6 . .
        Fr.: You're in a better mood   Mother's friend says Kerrie
           today aren't you   is in a better mood and
           Kerrie(v)?   discovers it is because she
                             is going to visit her Nan's
                             house later on]

I'm going up my < Nan's >
   house later on

        Fr.: Later on?
           . . .

(University of Bristol 1975)

This extract is presented in a form which does not include complexities of intonational coding (for details of which, see Wells, 1975). It nevertheless clearly reflects the researchers' purposes and theoretical orientation. Exploration of language development at home and at school clearly required the collection of a great deal of a naturally occurring talk, recorded over time and in both settings. The home-based recordings were obtained by using radio-microphones worn for the whole day, and a time-switched recorder operating with the subjects' consent but without their knowing when it was on. The transcription includes details of timing and location; given the emphasis throughout the research on 'learning through interaction', the interplay has to be presented from both 'sides', the child's and his or her interlocutor's — hence the two-column lay-out of the text, with a third column to carry the contextual commentary.

In the extract we have quoted, the brief commentary may seem to add little to the reader's understanding beyond what is already inferable from the text. Yet its presence bears witness to a general problem in transcriptions treated as data. To what extent is it possible to let the words speak for themselves, where so much that is meant may not be directly stated? In this example, Kerrie does not actually say that her better mood is due to her forthcoming visit to her 'Nan's house'; yet if there is any coherent link between that utterance and the utterance which precedes it, what else could Kerrie mean? The gloss on it may simply be the product of the transcriber playing safe. In general, it would surely be wise either to provide maximal clues through fairly elaborate notation of intonation, or to provide some sort of systematic coding that can be relied upon in ways that a transcriber's intuitive running commentary cannot. The latter is the stance adopted by the discourse analysts referred to in chapter 1 and to be discussed more fully in chapter 6. At this stage, we simply invite the reader to consider two brief transcripts from recordings made in an English primary classroom with ten-year old pupils, before and after the mid-morning break (P. Smith, 1982). It is coded using an adapted form of the system developed by Sinclair and Coulthard. The reader should attempt to judge the general 'tone' of the two encounters between Michelle and her teacher, and assess the value of the coding as evidence for whatever opinion which has been formed. (see over, p. 73)

				Acts		*Moves*	*Exchanges*
TS1	T	Good Grief Michelle	1	directive	T	frame	boundary
		what's that monstrosity	2	elicitation	T	elicit	eliciting
	Michelle	Oh	3	marker			
		I can't do it . . . I'm no good at using a compass	4	reply	P	response	
	T	Rubbish	5	comment	T	feedback	
		with a bit of care and concentration . . .	6	directive	T	initiate	directing
	Michelle	But it's loose	7	reply	P	response	
		the thing just slides when I use it	8	comment			
	T	Seems all right	9	comment	T	feedback	
		it's just you	10	aside		initiate	directing
	Michelle	I'm no good at it	11	comment	P	response	
	T	It's easy	12	comment	T	feedback	
		I could train a chimpanzee to do this	13	aside			

				Acts		Moves	Exchanges
TS2	Michelle	Mr. — Mr. —	1	bid	P	frame	boundary
		I've botched it again	2	starter	P	inform	informing
	T	What	3	prompt	T	elicit	
		Oh Michelle	4	marker	T	inform	
		I've shown you twice	5	comment			
	Michelle	But . . . the compass	6	starter	P	response	
	T	The compass is no worse than anybody else's . . .	7	informative	T	inform	informing
		Look	8	marker	T	direct	directing
		use this one . . . it's tighter	9	directive			
		Don't make a mess this time	10	directive			
	Michelle	No Mr. —	11	reply	P	response	

How good-humoured, then, are these 'transactions'? The first is initiated by the teacher, but consists of more (and fuller) responses from Michelle than would probably be consistent with any but a fairly light tone. How else could the teacher say such potentially wounding things without Michelle turning a hair? Is it fanciful to see her initiation of the second passage as a memory of the tone of the previous encounter an hour or so earlier? By the end of it, however, she has had recourse to a respectful form of address, apparently as a result of sharper and more extensive reactions by the teacher to her initiative. The question remains about the certainty of those inferences, given the evidence of the coding. In this respect, the impact of the two marker-acts in TS2 is significant. Their presence before a comment or directive appears to give those acts a character which others of their type did not have in TS1. Is it to that type of evidence that one can look for the objective grounding of an analysis?

It might still be concluded that for all its technical complexity, the coding is less than fully sufficient; indeed, it may seem less helpful than other kinds of non-verbal or paralinguistic information. It is in making judgments about the interactional 'tone' of an encounter that one realizes how much is communicated and interpreted on the basis of posture, gesture, facial expression, eye-contact (or the lack of it), and of the rapidity, volume, timbre and intonation of a speaker's voice. Any account which lacks such evidence will from time to time appear short-suited. The researcher's highly problematical task remains therefore that of devising ways of capturing, and displaying for analysis in the first place, enough evidence from the relevant channels of communication for the observer's interpretations to approach the reliability of those originally made by the participants and upon which they acted.

In this section, we have considered ways in which linguistic data are created by recording and transcription. In later chapters, we return to these issues from the perspective of several main research traditions. An apparently mundane but critical point must be noted here. We refer to the sheer hard labour of creating an accurately transcribed version of an audio-record. At each stage, decisions have to be made with serious consequences for future work, and every hour's recording may require fifteen hours or more of transcribing (Edwards and Furlong, 1985; Barnes and Todd, 1977; Westgate *et al*, 1985). Short cuts are tempting, but remove information which may be valuable later, and any failure to be systematic (for example, in logging footage numbers on the recorder), or any taking of short-cuts, is dearly paid for later.

3 Reality Observed

In this section, we turn to two related problem areas — the theoretical notions of what constitutes a reality to be observed, and the disturbance of that reality by activities of the observer.

We have already demonstrated the dependence of particular kinds of data on styles of recording and transcription, as well as on the researcher's general theoretical orientation. We have also noted how investigations can be framed and focused by technical limitations, so that (for example) the prominence ascribed to centrally-controlled interaction may owe something to the difficulties of gaining access to more 'informal' styles of teaching and to 'unofficial' classroom talk. Generally, any research can be said to carry with it an implicit view of what is to be treated as significant, of a 'reality' to be studied. Thus a basic difference is evident between concentration on observable (or 'surface') behaviour, and on what may underlie that behaviour and give it shape. The dilemma has loud philosophical echoes: a positivist stance towards a directly observable reality, as against a view which seeks to encompass those complex and less accessible dimensions which some consider to be the defining characteristics of human affairs. Are such opposing views ever reconcilable? Turning in one direction or the other has long marked both argument and practice in the social sciences. In linguistics, the contrasts have been heightened by the sociolinguistic emphasis on language as social action, requiring reference beyond the 'purely' linguistic data to its social and cultural correlates (Halliday, 1978; Hymes, 1977).

Consider, for example, a range of purposes in classroom research. If the researcher intends to observe the distribution of a teacher's individually targeted speech around the classroom, the relevant questions would be — 'How much? And to whom?', rather than 'Why?'. The significant reality would be immediately visible. But where the structure and sequencing of discourse in specific settings is the focus of attention, then meanings are involved which are not directly accessible from the surface features of vocabulary and syntax. Significant reality for such research may be said to lie, at least partly, behind both words and actions. Harder still to discern are the sociocultural values and assumptions which belong to a reality extending far beyond the observed setting but which may be playing a crucial role within it. What appears, then, to divide researchers who take any account of classroom talk is not just whether they attempt to integrate it with other kinds of data, but the degree to which an intersubjective reality is acknowledged as being either important or accessible — that is, a reality of mind as well as of action, saturated with cultural and social knowledge as well as with more personal connotations, and not merely displayed but endlessly formed (and reformed, and modified) in events like those under observation.

Abstractions of this kind cry out for an example. In their largely ethnographic study, Erickson and Mohatt (1982) were interested in what they termed 'implicit culture in the classroom', particularly in so far as it helped to explain the mutual misunderstandings of teachers and the Indian pupils in their classrooms. The setting for their study was a school in Northern Canada, within which children from a local Indian reservation were to be integrated. It was therefore intended as a further contribution to resolving the problems posed by the 'silent Indian child' in mainstream schools, investigation of which had gained impetus from the work of Susan Philips (1972, 1983). The data gathered by Erickson and Mohatt were drawn from video-recordings, first-hand observation and field notes, and 'viewing sessions' in which video-tapes of lessons were discussed in an 'open-ended manner' by researchers and teachers together. The eventual 'fine-grained' analysis of selected sections of the video-record could thus draw upon shared perspectives on what constituted the reality under discussion. Another pertinent feature of the methods adopted was that the recordings were made, not by the researchers themselves, but by a member of the local community whom they had trained in the necessary techniques and who knew both the local culture and the individual teacher and children. His presence in the classroom was thought unlikely to be seen as that of an outsider, and so unlikely to provoke untypical displays or interaction. By working from the inside, and using the skills of an insider, the researchers claimed to have at least potential access to those differences in cultural perception which were thought to cause communicative difficulties. It should be noted that there were difficulties at the level of discourse, and so much less 'visible' than differences in the forms of speech employed by teachers and pupils (Ainsworth, 1984).

The researchers' determination to integrate cultural understandings with the particular interactions they were observing calls for a brief elaboration of the notion of context we outlined in chapter 1. Their procedures operationalize a concept of context very different from that of a set of given 'background' factors vaguely considered relevant to the talk. On the contrary, it is very much a 'foreground view' of context (Erickson and Schultz, 1981). From this perspective, situational and cultural knowledge are considered as being 'alive' in the interaction, not as inert data drawn upon for subsequent interpretation of events. And while such 'foreground-ing' is indispensible in studies of evidently 'intercultural' classrooms, all classrooms can be considered as settings in which pupils work as quasi-ethnographers trying to crack the teacher's code (Green, 1983). Accordingly, much would be lost in any study which maintained a rigid distinction between the 'performance' of teacher and pupils, and so-called 'back-ground' features.

Research often seeks to penetrate beneath 'surface' features of be-haviour and interaction to the rules which generate it, as we show in detail in the chapter which follows. But for those researchers who are determined to get beneath that surface and to crack the participants' codes, there are many pitfalls in the way. An obvious one is ignorance of the shared history of a class and its teacher. Walker and Adelman (1976) were among the first to demonstrate the impenetrability of an 'in-joke' which owed its meaning to a previous, unobserved lesson and to previous unobserved recapitu-lations. Researchers sensitive to, or intrigued by, such interactional ambigu-ities have devised ingenious strategies for penetrating the hidden layers of classroom reality. Some have subjected the discourse itself, or the turn-taking structures, to detailed analysis; others have sought to immerse them-selves for long periods, as participant- or involved-observers, in the settings they studied.

A third option, compatible with either of the others, is that usually termed 'triangulation'. The concept has its philosophical basis in phe-nomenology. Reality is seen as residing, not in any would-be objective account separable from the participants, but rather in their respective perceptions. Researchers are therefore interested in the three-dimensional picture composed from the varying angles of actors and observer. Some see a valid account as having to fall within the area of overlap between the various views; others simply juxtapose complementary narratives without attempting to reconcile them. As a practical procedure, then, triangulation involves the 'taking back' to the participants of a provisional account pre-pared by the observer (for examples, see Adelman, 1981; Hale and Edwards, 1981; and, for an unusual application to photographic rather than verbal evidence, Walker and Wiedel, 1985). Significantly different versions of what 'happened' may then be revealed. Where the procedure is carried out at some distance in time from the events recorded, there may be problems of memory over what may anyway have scarcely seemed significant at the time. While memory may then be prompted by replaying the rele-vant audio- or video-recording, there are also dangers of defensive re-interpretations of what 'really' happened or was 'really' meant. More important still, triangulation occurs when the subsequent direction and destination of the talk is known, whereas the talk itself proceeded on a basis of at least some uncertainty about its outcomes and some reliance on provisional and revisable interpretations as it proceeded. Critics of the method (for example, Barnes and Todd, 1977, p. 18) therefore consider it no more valid, and no fairer to the participants' views, than the methods used by perceptive observers working from recordings, transcripts and field notes.

All observation of naturally-occurring talk, and indeed all classroom research, shares a further common problem. This is usually referred to as the 'observer's paradox', and has to do with the effects of observational activity on the phemonena observed. We discussed it briefly in the preceding chapter, in relation to the over-frequent ignoring of immediate situational constraints in studies of linguistic or communicative competence. The concept was formulated in linguistics by Labov (1972b) as the need 'to observe how people speak when they are not being observed'. If a solution were to be found in eavesdropping, then ethical objections might themselves prove insuperable. Yet we know that observers and their recording devices are likely to be obtrusive, and that people who know they are being overheard may well talk more, or talk less, or just talk differently.

Some of the effects in classrooms are well documented. Samph (1976), for example, found that under observation, teachers' verbal behaviour came more closely to resemble both that of their own ideal teacher and that which they believed a visitor might expect of them; this tendency was most marked when formal teaching styles were being observed. There are also the distortions which Wragg (1984) identifies as resulting from teachers' simple irritation at being watched and having their every move recorded in a setting which they are likely to regard as their territory. Observed teachers tend also to adopt a style of teaching which is thought to fit an observer's expectations and which may in consequence distort normality in the direction of teacher-performance. Similarly, Blease (1983) reports children tending to play to the gallery when observers are present. Recording equipment too carries a similar double-bind to that ensnaring its operators. The more elaborate it becomes in order to meet requirements of technical quality, the heavier the metaphorical shadow it casts over the events being recorded. By the converse logic, the researcher may turn to 'low-technology' approaches, and rely on what can be achieved by a discreet observer armed with little move than pen and paper (King, 1978; Evans, 1985). But since such low-technology is unlikely to be sufficient in investigations of classroom talk, how are the inherent difficulties to be reconciled with claims for the superiority of 'naturalistic' research over that conducted in explicitly contrived settings (there is a useful discussion of these issues in Wells, 1981). Also, to what extent can interference be minimized, or its residual effects assessed?

One remedial strategy often used is to allow the researcher's presence to become, over time, so familiar a feature of the setting that observer and equipment are 'hardly noticed'. There is little consensus, however, about how long this familiarization process is likely to take, and 'measuring' the extent and duration of the disturbance is likely to remain an imprecise art highly dependent on the shared intuitions of those involved about how 'normal' they feel things to be. It is also likely to be influenced by the credentials and credibility which those being observed are prepared to accord their observer. Milroy's (1980) ingenuity in gaining access to un-inhibited vernacular speech in Belfast communities may hold lessons for classroom research. Her success was founded on establishing an accept-able role within the groups she recorded, as someone who was not 'one of them' but was a 'friend of a friend' who had a professional interest in their talk. As such, she was treated as visitor with a right to be there.

Similar intentions led Westgate (1985) to blur his research role in a comprehensive school by at first simply sharing the teaching of classes who were later to be recorded with their usual teachers. His research interest was explained to all from the start, but over the seven weeks which preceded the recorded sequence of lessons he became 'part of the de-partment'. A further advantage claimed for this arrangement derived from what might be called 'reciprocal vulnerability'. By the time recordings were made, the 'observer' and each of the teachers involved had built up a shared experience of teaching in front of each other. Nervousness on both sides had given way to involvement in the project, and an openness had been achieved not only towards being observed but also towards the is-sues to be explored once the recordings and their analysis began. Discussion of research purposes doubtless had some effect on the teaching recorded, if only because of the teachers' greater self-consciousness about aspects of their teaching. Yet the pupils, when asked, reported the recorded lessons as not being noticeably unusual or special, while many features of class-room practice identified while researcher and teachers were exploring the recordings together came as a distinct surprise, both pleasant and unpleasant, to all those involved in the analysis.

Other common strategies for minimizing distortion are to record whole sequences of lessons, or compare recordings made at different stages in the research to see whether any differences are apparent. Ethnographic studies especially are often based on data-gathering over far longer periods of time. Heath's (1982) account of culturally-differentiated responses to teachers' questioning, for example, is derived from five years' of field-work, and revealed aspects of discontinuity between the purposes and organization of talk at home and school which would almost certainly not have been visible to a researcher less familiar to those she observed, or less familiar with their lives. As in all research, purposes and methods have to be framed by what is possible, and gains in quantity and quality of data balanced against the costs in time and other resources.

4 Reality Reported

The procedures and problems so far discussed in relation to recording and transcription have their counterparts at the reporting stage too. Two issues concern us particularly. The first has to do with the the relationship be-tween the account being offered and the evidence which is displayed to support and illustrate it. The second centres on the extent to which any particular study, and the insights to which it makes claim, can be justifiably presented as having a more generalized relevance.

There is as much variation in procedures for selecting and using evidence in reporting research as at any earlier stage in the investigation. This is true both of the quantity and nature of the evidence displayed. Predictably, studies based on systematic classroom observation mostly rely on straightforward summary findings in numerical or tabular form, the original talk being entirely contained in the categories used to capture those features pre-selected as significant. For research recording the actual words used, the problems of grounding accounts in evidence are more interesting; they also reflect a greater divergence of practice. For instance, discourse analysis requires first, that the entire corpus of recorded talk be systematically categorized, partly to evaluate the category scheme being used or developed, and partly to reveal its role in giving coherence to the talk. That is, a built-in assurance is offered about the adequacy of the system to account for all that was recorded in the given setting. Recurring patterns within the categorized discourse then provide the basis for selecting passages which will illustrate simultaneously the scheme itself and nature of the events.

Both conversational analysis and ethnography tend to distribute their analytical attention more unevenly across the data, with differing implications for their reports. From the former standpoint, for example, McHoul and Watson (1984) offer twenty pages of dense argument about four 'data fragments', totalling together no more than twenty-three transcribed utterances (half of which we quoted earlier in this chapter). It is, moreover, upon selected details within these fragments that the minute analysis and argument are constructed. Ethnographic diversity is considerable, especially in the reliance placed on transcripts. There is, however, a common tendency to delay 'judgment on what is significant to study . . . until the orienting phase of the field-study has been completed' (Spindler, 1982, p. 6). Such an open-minded stance delays the identification of patterns for report, and imposes few restrictions on the nature or quantity of evidence used in illustration. A single quoted utterance from an interview may be judged to encapsulate a significant point, while at another stage the argument may seem to require the citing of lengthy transcript sequences.

Given that some selection within the data is necessary for illustrating an analysis (which may itself have focused upon selected data), what criteria can the reader use to judge how convincingly the case is being made, and how compellingly its logic points in the direction suggested? Mehan (1979a) includes among his own criteria for a properly rigorous 'constitutive ethnography' an insistence on the exhaustive testing of all the recorded data against emerging hypotheses before an account can be offered. He also argues that the original recordings and transcripts remain available for possible re-analysis. In these ways, the 'final' account would be both well and truly 'warranted' and open to challenge. Taken literally, Mehan's criteria would present many practical difficulties — not least for the publishers of research! Yet the underlying spirit of his advice can provide a principled guide to practice. Where short extracts are cited in the text, the longer transcripts in which they are embedded can often be displayed in appendix form, so that some check can be made on (for example) how representative they are. Some studies have recognized this issue by publishing separately the full corpus of transcripts on which they have based their analysis; Gordon Wells' project is a notable example. Where the issue is not even recognized, there must be scepticism about whether the evidence quoted is not merely a convenient rather than a representative sample of the whole body of data collected.

The notion of representativeness also raises questions about the typicality of the setting which has been observed, and so of the generalizability of any conclusions about the interactions recorded. It may seem relatively easy to provide sufficient factual detail about setting and participants for the reader to make some judgment of its typicality. Much more difficult are the questions about the validity of procedures, and about inter-researcher reliability in particular. One line of argument is to suggest that solutions can only lie in broadening the number and variety of settings studied, even at the cost of adhering to data which is relatively unambiguous and accessible. Another is to exploit qualities and strengths associated with case studies. This second strategy reflects the view that indepth studies of particular settings carry more intuitive conviction, enable more penetrating questions to be asked about them, can develop observational and analytical methods which can then be applied (with suitable modifications) to other 'cases', and are especially valuable in generating hypotheses for others to follow up.

In illustration of this last point, consider the corrective offered to a hitherto generally held belief by an analysis of a single lesson involving pupils aged ten and eleven (French and French, 1984). The researchers explored the gender imbalance in teacher-pupil exchanges which has often been reported, and which their initial count of the teacher's interactions with boys and with girls seemed to confirm. Further work on the recording indicated, however, that the overall predominance of boys was the product of a few notably active individuals, and that some of the girls participated considerably more often than many of the boys. At a deeper level, the interactional basis of the study allowed some exploration of why particular boys sought or attracted so much of the teacher's interactional attention.

Gender differences in classroom talk, more fully documented now than when we wrote the first edition (for example, Kelly, 1988; Swann, 1992), raise important methodological questions about where the most educationally significant imbalances occur and so (to return in this particular research area to the general point made earlier) to the kind of recording and transcription necessary to make them evident. A main conclusion from this research — that the relative dominance of boys is constructed and sustained by the mutually reinforcing actions of teachers, boys and girls — raises questions about whether particular classroom contexts may enhance the inequalities. For example, it is suggested that whole-class discussions may be too public, and so more inhibiting, for girls. Thus Mary Bousted's (1989) investigation of her own classroom revealed not only that what she had thought of as whole-class discussion was 'in fact small-group discussion with the teacher's participation', but that the small cast of contributors consisted of five of the ten boys and none of the twelve girls. But there is also evidence that girls risk being crowded out in some activities involving small, mixed groups where the curriculum area is perceived as more of a male domain, hence the studies focussed on science, mathematics and computing (Culley, 1988; Hoyles and Sutherland, 1989; Morse and Handley, 1985; Randell 1987; Rennie and Parker, 1987; Underwood *et al*, 1990; Singh, 1993).

In discussion, investigations, problem-solving and other forms of collaborative learning, pupils' usual preference is for single-sex groups and teachers may need persuasive powers to engineer anything different. If they did so to improve the quality of the talk, they might cite evidence that girls give fewer directives, make more requests, offer more supportive talk, interrupt less often, and refer more often to what has been said before. The teacher might then have to question whether the presence of girls was working more to the benefit of boys. In a small-scale but intriguing study, Cheshire and Jenkins analyzed mixed-group discussions which were part of the oracy assessment for GCSE. They concluded that the girls were more co-operative 'talk partners', because they were better listeners and so more able to build on the contributions of others. They seemed better at drawing other speakers into the discussion, and were much less likely to close it down. But these researchers also concluded that girls were not given full credit for those qualities. The teachers involved 'seemed to expect the girls to play a sustaining role' and penalized them where they did not, while their supportive role seemed sometimes to be at the expense of their own contributions (Cheshire and Jenkins, 1991; Jenkins and Cheshire, 1990). The critical methodological point illustrated by this and other studies is that made earlier — namely, that literal and plain transcription of the words and their presentation in play-script form would be unlikely to reveal the subtler differences in participation. To establish (for example) that girls tend to receive fewer 'difficult' questions, to ask fewer questions them-selves, and to receive less teacher feed-back, or that shouting out and other interruptions are more likely to be tolerated from boys — these are imbalances which are relatively easy to quantify. But those facilitating and supportive 'background' contributions to group talk which are also more likely to be made by girls ('uh huh', 'yeh', 'right', and so on) may not be noticed at all unless the transcriber is careful and the quality of recording good, yet they may be highly beneficial to the cohesiveness of the group and the coherence of its discussion. Jenkins and Cheshire (1990) comment that such responses tend to mark attentive listening rather than agreement or disagreement, but may be misinterpreted by males as signs of agreement so that any ensuing disagreement may be taken as evidence that females do not know their own minds! There may well be the dilemma too of having to choose between sounding 'feminine' and sounding competent, especially in subjects like physical science and computing which may be seen as a male preserve.

In this chapter, we have reviewed some of the methodological choices reflected in recording, transcribing, analyzing and reporting classroom talk. We began by noting the absence of a common metalanguage or conceptual structure for such work, and we have discussed consequent implications for each of its main phases. In the rest of this book, we consider three broad orientations to the investigation of classroom talk, from the least to the most linguistically based, noting some of the differences between and within them. We discuss for each their theoretical roots, their empirical priorities, and the kinds of question which they seemed equipped to answer.

4   Coding Classroom Interaction

The first large-scale entry by researchers into classrooms was made by observers briefly trained in the fluent use of schedules and category systems. It was argued that to record interaction in such crowded and busy settings without knowing what to look for was to risk confusion and waste time. What it was necessary to notice had to be marked out in advance according to the researcher's purposes in being there. A relevant observation schedule would then make it possible to sift out these significant items from an otherwise overwhelming stream of talk and action. As we noted earlier, such studies proliferated so rapidly that it became possible to compile large collections of research 'instruments' from which those wishing to observe teacher-pupil interaction directly could find something to borrow or to adapt (Simon and Boyer, 1967, 1970, 1975; Galton, 1978b).

1   Systematic Classroom Observation: Purposes and Methods

The label commonly applied to this style of research means no more than that observation is contained within some predetermined system of categories. Indeed, from other research perspectives, the approach has often seemed seriously unsystematic. But alternatives to it were slow to develop. Certainly during the 1960s, it flourished without serious competition. At that time, ethnographic studies of schools were rare, no branch of social science had displayed a strong interest in classroom language, and sociolinguistic research in any kind of setting had hardly begun.

Some theoretical stimulus for classroom-based research was found in behaviourist psychology, and in a more general 'scientific' commitment to recording objectively what 'really' occurred. The main stimulus, however, was the lack of any detailed knowledge about how classroom interaction was organized. Accurate description, sufficient in range and variety to permit generalization, was to be the basis from which to identify effective teaching, explain what made it so, and build eventually an adequate theory of instruction. As Medley and Mitzel (1963) argued in an influential paper, it was high time that the training of teachers passed beyond the stage at which 'witch-doctors' passed on to their acolytes 'a treasured store of traditions'; it should become grounded instead in properly scientific accounts of those teacher actions which could be shown to have positive effects on their pupils' learning.

It was also time to make available to teachers, whose practices seemed so largely a matter of professional instinct and improvisation, methods by which they could make their behaviour (especially their verbal behaviour) less routine and more reflective. The emphasis was not on prescribing exactly what good teachers should do, but on enabling teachers themselves to record what happened in their own lessons, compare that record with their intentions, identify any changes they themselves wished to make, and then monitor their success in making them (Amidon and Hunter, 1967; Flanders, 1970, 1976; Wragg, 1974). In the context of a strong commitment to the self-improvement of teachers, it was natural for researchers to extol methods of observation which were reliable, easily learned, cheap to apply, and capable of producing data so quickly that it could be fed back so as to influence subsequent action.

Most observation schedules concentrated on verbal interaction, treating it for practical purposes as a sufficient sample of everything that was going on. Many gave particular attention to the teacher's talk, partly because there was likely to be so much more of it, but mainly because of the assumption that it was what the teacher said, and did by saying, that determined the course of classroom events. Most were explicitly designed for (or were in practice limited to) traditional forms of teacher-centred instruction which produced a single (and public) 'mainstream' of communication which it seemed feasible to chart without feeling that promising side-waters were being left unexplored. The most widely used schedules required the observer to decide immediately on the interactional function of what was being said, the words thereby disappearing into categories from which they could never be recalled but which could be readily counted, grouped and analyzed. This was certainly the most economical way to survey a large number of classrooms and lessons. It also provided the quickest 'action replays' for teachers who might then decide to play the next game rather differently. Some schedules were intended to 'cover' the interaction, the observer having to enter whatever was being said in one of the categories at each prescribed 'moment in time' (for once, that cliché is appropriate). Three- and five-second intervals were common arbitrary moments. Others allowed respite when nothing relevant was occurring, the focus of attention being solely on (for example) teachers' questions, and the proportion of them which could be coded as 'broader', 'higher-order' or 'reasoning' kind.

The examples which follow illustrate the main strategy, though not the range of tactical variations within it. We have avoided the best-known system because Flanders' original ten 'verbal interaction categories' are now so familiar that they are often treated as though they represent the whole approach, without reference even to his own later modifications of them.

The first example treats both teacher and pupil talk in terms of initiation and response, and makes a basic distinction between types of teacher-question which appears in more elaborated form in several of the schedules to be discussed later.

Verbal Interaction Category System (adapted from Amidon and Hunter, 1967)

1	teacher-initiated talk:	presents information or opinion
2		gives directions
3		asks narrow question — answer short, predictable
4		asks broad question
5	Teacher-response talk:	accepts ideas, behaviour, feeling
6		rejects ideas, behaviour, feeling
7	Pupil-response talk:	responds to teacher predictably/unpredictably
8		responds to another pupil
9	Pupil-initiated talk:	initiates talk to teacher
10		initiates talk to another pupil
11	Silence	
Z	Confusion (can be set alongside other categories)	

In our second example, much more space is created for recording pupils' talk by working on the 'reciprocity principle' that for every teacher verbal behaviour that can 'either be observed or theoretically conceived, there exists a corresponding student verbal behaviour'. The same categories are therefore used for each (Ober *et al*, 1971). Acts are coded as 'warming' or 'cooling' the climate of the classroom (making it more or less formal); accepting; amplifying another's contribution; eliciting; responding; initiating; directing; and correcting. Throughout the presentation and justification of this category system runs the confidence that the observer 'can understand what he sees because he observes with both a purpose and a means for observing'. Accuracy and consistency are thereby secured by training in the appropriate techniques of such purposeful observation.

Much more ambitious are the 'equivalent talk categories', used by the same researchers to investigate teaching styles; these 'simply make possible the examination of teaching strategy in terms of sequence and levels of thinking' (Ober *et al*, 1971, p. 93). The following ten categories are claimed to create that possibility —

Categories for coding 'sequences and levels of thinking'

1   Presents information
2   Asks question eliciting restricted thinking

3   Asks question eliciting expanded thinking
4   Responds, restricted thinking
5   Responds, expanded thinking
6   Reacts to maintain level of participation — for example, invitation to continue talking to amplify, clarify or summarize ideas at the same or a lower level
7   Reacts to extend level of participation — for example, by requesting further information
8   Reacts by terminating level of participation — for example, by indicating that a thought sequence is complete
9   Structures learning activities — comments that organize learning activities, give assignment
10 Pause or silence

The schedules we have cited are intended to 'cover' the interactions observed as far as it is necessary to do so for the researcher's particular purposes. They reflect the usual confidence that the categories provide a 'mirror' through which the behaviours relevant to those purposes can be clearly seen.

By the mid-1970s, energetic attempts were being made to undermine the claims by systematic researchers that they could record objectively relevant features of classroom reality. The critics identified as weaknesses of the method what its practitioners regarded as being among its strengths — the deliberately detached outsider's view, the insistence on knowing what to look for, and the consequent restricted focusing on what lay within the observer's frame of reference. They emphasized instead the danger that such carefully prepared researchers were more likely to exemplify their preconceptions than to gain access to how the participants themselves organized and interpreted their interaction. They also rejected as unwarranted the optimism that data obtained by coding classroom talk could be used as direct evidence of what teacher and pupils had done and meant (Hamilton and Delamont, 1974; Coulthard, 1974; Stubbs, 1975; Walker and Adelman, 1975a; Furlong and Edwards, 1977; Long, 1980). We elaborate these criticisms later in the chapter.

It is worth noting first, however, some facts about classroom communication which systematic observation was capable of revealing or confirming when its aims did not exceed its grasp. For as McIntyre (1980) argues in a notably balanced review of its achievements and deficiencies, it has often been blamed for ignoring aspects of classroom life (such as the more personal meanings exchanged by teacher and pupils) with which it never claimed to be concerned (see also Croll, 1986, chapter 7).

Our first cluster of brief examples is chosen because the objects of enquiry appear, at least initially, to be open to some form of coding; indeed, they may seem to depend on data in the quantity which only coding makes possible if the necessary generalizations are to be firmly grounded. We summarize the findings so as to make evident the kinds of observation on which they are based.

In traditional whole-class teaching, teachers did most of the talking, decided who else was to talk, and normally evaluated what pupils were required or permitted to say. Those who were rated as being 'good' by their colleagues talked rather less, as did teachers of younger children and of certain subjects (for example, English and social studies, compared with mathematics or science); but the differences were less significant than the similarities (Gage, 1978; Wragg, 1973). Teachers asked very large numbers of questions, most of which elicited factual and brief answers rather than any extended display of reasoning (Hargie, 1978). This tendency persisted even where more 'open' forms of questioning were indicated by the innovative curriculum being transmitted (Eggleston *et al*, 1976). In whole-class teaching, most communication occurred within a 'central action zone', leaving considerable areas relatively safe for those pupils not wishing to participate in the official business of the lesson (Adams and Biddle, 1970).

In more informally organized classrooms, and in laboratory-based teaching, the action was often more dispersed. Those teachers who moved away from the traditional 'front-of-stage' location interacted more often, and less impersonally, with individual pupils (Turner, 1982; Reid, 1980). But such individualized encounters tended to be very brief, and to be concerned largely with the routine management of classroom tasks, though there was also likely to be both more pupil-pupil interaction and more pupil-initiated interaction with the teacher (Galton and Simon, 1980). On the other hand, pupils spent more time engaged on academic tasks where social interaction between them was limited by the teacher (Rosenshine and Berliner, 1978; Bennett, 1978). In mixed classes, teachers gave more attention, praise and blame to boys, and received more initiatives from them (Good and Brophy, 1978, pp. 19–32; Simpson and Erickson, 1983). In inner-city schools, teachers were less accepting of pupils' behaviour and more critical of pupils' errors than in suburban schools, so intensifying the control aspects of classroom relationships (Leacock, 1969). Teachers' responses to misbehaviour were more effective in ending it when they followed swiftly, and when any extended disciplinary encounter was shifted away from the public arena (Wragg, 1984, pp. 34–44). In mixed-ability classes where the teacher had adopted a more individualized mode of instruction, most of the public talk was disciplinary and managerial, and most instructional talk was private; less able pupils were more likely to seek, and less able to avoid, the teacher's attention than in traditionally-organized classrooms, though the resulting instructional encounters were typically frequent but short (Evans, 1985).

With doubts about the solidity of the evidence temporarily suspended, it might be claimed that the mixed-bag of findings which we have cited could have been produced by coding the amount of classroom talk, its distribution, and even (in broad terms) its functions. For example —

> How much of the talk was contained within a central communication system, in which whatever was being said was supposed to be heard by all?
>
> How much of it was produced by the teacher, and how much of it was directly instructional?
>
> How much of the instructional talk was exposition, how much questioning, and how factual were the questions?
>
> How many pupils were called upon or volunteered to answer questions?
>
> Which pupils were they, and where were they located?
>
> How many pupils were involved in any kind of direct interaction with the teacher, and how often was the initiative theirs?
>
> How much 'unofficial' talk was there, which pupils were most actively involved in it, and where were they located?

These are all questions for which an appropriate category system could provide some answers. But those answers might still not take researchers far towards an understanding of the complexities and subtleties of classroom communication.

We now consider, in greater detail, some ambitious and extensive studies which have relied heavily on the capacity of standardized observation schedules to record the same facts in a large number of settings so as to make generalizations about them. That they are all British is not a display of academic chauvinism on our part. American research of this kind has turned rather sharply away from interaction analysis and towards investigating the time pupils spend undistracted 'on-task' and 'academically-engaged' and not involved in distracting interaction (for example, in Rosenshine and Berliner, 1978; Doyle, 1983). A main message of this research has been (in the words of a British exemplar) that 'high achievers work harder and interact less' (Bennett, 1976, p. 114).

Our first example is an investigation of the 'intellectual transactions' generated in Nuffield-science teaching. This was teaching explicitly intended to provide pupils with unusually extensive opportunities for active learning — for posing and solving problems, and for gaining some sense of being a scientist. Observation of a hundred teachers and over three hundred lessons was therefore focused closely on the quality of those transactions. Other aspects of classroom interaction were ignored (Eggleston *et al*, 1976; Eggleston, 1983; see also Hacker *et al*, 1979).

Science-teaching observation schedule (Eggleston *et al*, 1976, pp. 34–9)

1 Teacher Talk

> Teacher asks questions (or invites comments) which are answered by:

a1   recalling facts or principles
a2   applying facts and principles to problem solving
a3   making hypotheses or speculation
a4   designing experiments
a5   direct observation
a6   interpretation of observed or recorded data
a7   making inferences from observations or data

Teacher makes statements
b1   of fact and principle
b2   of problems
b3   of hypothesis or speculation
b4   of experimental procedure

Teacher directs pupils to sources of information for purpose of:
c1   acquiring or confirming facts or principles
c2   identifying or solving problems
c3   making inferences, formulating or testing hypotheses
c4   seeking guidance on experimental procedure

2   Pupil Talk

Pupils seek information or consult for purpose of:
d1   acquiring or confirming facts or principles
d2   identifying or solving problems
d3   making inferences, formulating or testing hypotheses
d4   seeking guidance on experimental procedure

Pupils refer to teacher for purpose of:
e1   acquiring or confirming facts or principles
e2   seeking guidance when identifying or solving problems
e3   seeking guidance when making inferences, formulating or testing
     hypotheses
e4   seeking guidance on experimental procedure

Within this highly 'intellectual' frame of reference, three types of teaching
styles were identified from the frequency of scores recorded in each category. Quite against the logic of the Nuffield approach, there was a marked
predominance of 'fact-acquirers' — teachers who gave out a great deal of
information, asked mainly factual questions, and set little practical work.
The 'problem-solvers' certainly posed more questions requiring inference
and speculation, but largely managed and controlled themselves the search
for solutions. The small minority of 'pupil-centred enquirers' were closer to
the Nuffield objectives on those occasions when they involved pupils in
forming and testing hypotheses. But the evidence overall showed a strikingly

few entries in the more challenging transactional categories — for example, a3–a6, c3–c4, d3–4 and e3–4. It may be useful for the reader at this point to try out the coding scheme on two brief extracts from science lessons, partly to see how many of the categories seem to be necessary to do so, and partly to explore whether either extract could be identified as being at a 'higher' level than the other on the basis of such an analysis.

In the first example, the teacher is asking a first-year mixed ability class in a secondary school to describe ice-cubes which he has taken from the refrigerator:-

T   Now describe them to me please. Go on, imagine you are trying to describe an ice cube to someone who has never seen one before. There are plenty there (holding them up). Right.
P   Well, it's frozen like water.
T   Yes, anything else? That's one thing. It's frozen like water.
P   It's cold.
T   It's cold. Anything else, Mr Ridings?
P   It's not quite see-through.
T   It's not quite see-through, no. Most people seem to think that if you've got ice you can see right through it. If I hold all these ice-cubes up there, ah, you can't . . . ?
P   You can't see a thing.
T   You can't see a thing. That's rather interesting, isn't it, you can't see through it. Most people seem to think we can. But why can't you see through it? Alison.
P   Well, there's sort of like little air bubbles in it.
T   Smashing. Lovely. Yes. Little air bubbles trapped inside. How did they get there? How did the air bubbles get inside?
P   When the water freezes, it traps them.
T   Yes, when the water freezes it traps them. So they aren't put in afterwards are they? It's as the water is freezing.

In the second example, the teacher is encouraging a fifth-year class of pupils revising for O-level and CSE to examine two graphs showing the changes in sugar and starch content of apples.

T   Look at the graph and ask yourself questions.
P1   Why do they begin to fall again?
T   Yes, that's a question which needs answering. Is there another question? (Pause) . . . Do both graphs begin to fall at the same time?
P2   No, the starch begins to fall before the sugar.
P3   It's more than that, the sugar rises until all the starch has gone and then it begins to fall.
T   Yes, that's a good observation — give me two good questions to answer if you can.

P2   Two questions, sir?
P3   Yes. Why does the sugar rise after the starch has stopped, and
        why does the sugar begin to fall?
(Both extracts are taken from Carre, 1981, pp. 33 and 44)

Examining the 'cognitive level' of the tasks which pupils are set has
long been a preoccupation in classroom research. Doing so in brief transcribed extracts may not seem too difficult. Doing so by coding whole
sequences of interaction as they occur will be formidably difficult where
the range of those tasks is wide, which of course is what the researcher-
as-educationist would hope. Yet instant categorizing may seem essential
where a large-scale survey of teaching methods is required. In the Teacher
Education Project directed by Ted Wragg, the choice of research methods
was deliberately eclectic. It included both case studies of mixed-ability
teaching (Sands and Kerry, 1982) and transcript analysis of 'good explanatory
lessons' (Brown and Armstrong, 1984). Yet while observation of 'over one
thousand lessons' still only 'scratched the surface of the vast and complex
matter of studying and nurturing skilful teaching' (Wragg, 1984, preface),
it could only have been done at all by relying heavily on coding systems.
The system most relevant to our purposes here was designed to produce
'cognitive maps' of lessons across the curriculum, all involving mixed-
ability classes.
    'Armed' with the seventeen categories which follow, and after 'a little
practice', it is supposedly possible to — 'Sit in on lessons and obtain an
impressively full account of those features of the lesson which indicated
the quality of thought demanded by the teacher or produced by the pupil'
(Kerry, 1982, p. 84).

Categories for coding verbal transactions

Teacher talk —
T0   management, demonstration, administration
T1   data level   ('This particular creature I've got in my hand was
                                called an ammonite')
T2   concept level   ('The path that the planet takes around the sun
                                is called its orbit')
T3   abstract level   ('So the Chinese thought there were these two
                                forces, Ying and Yang, to control the universe')

Teacher questions —
Q0   management level   ('Are you paying attention?')
Q1   recall level   ('What did we say an orbit was?')
Q2   comprehension   ('How can we understand that, can anybody help
                            us? These two forces that control the universe?')
Q3   application level   ('So who do you think made up these stories of
                            Ying and Yang — men or women?')

Q4   analysis level   ('Why do you think these remains of the ammo-
                              nite are like stone, then? It's quite heavy.')
Q5   synthesis level   ('What can these stories about the universe tell
                              us about the people of those days?')
Q6   evaluation level   ('So what have we learned from these myths?
                              Anybody say it before I say it?')
C   contacts with pupils — brief and of no learning significance.

Pupil responses
R0   management level
R1   data level   ('What's the shell for?' 'Protection')
R2   concept level   ('If I die tomorrow and float to the bottom of the
                              sea — don't cheer — and if you were a scientist
                              coming along in a couple of million years and
                              you looked at my fossil, what would you find?'
                              'The skeleton.')
R3   abstract level   ('God sent out two forces — what does that mean?
                              How can we get to that?'
                              'Two powers.')
RW incorrect answers.
(Source: Kerry, 1982, p. 84; possible transcript illustrations of the categories
are taken from the Humanities teaching reported in Edwards and Furlong,
1978).

The intention in this system for coding verbal transactions is that — 'Each
statement, question, oral response, task or written response could be graded
for the quality of thought which it evidenced' (Kerry, 1982, p. 84). There
is a confidence in the firmness of that evidence which we do not share,
especially in relation to the treatment of pupils' answers as direct reflections of the 'level' of their understanding when those answers may be
produced more by 'reading' the clues provided by the teacher in the course
of the interaction than by comprehending what we might call 'the logic of
the argument'. We return to this point when we consider in the following
chapter various approaches to analyzing question-answer sequences. But
as it stands, Kerry's evidence supports that from other studies in indicating
the rarity of 'high level' tasks — those we might reasonably expect to find
coded in categories T2, T3; Q3, Q4, Q5, Q6; and R2 and R3.

The ORACLE Project was also directed explicitly at the improvement
of professional practice, this time at the primary stage, by providing detailed
descriptions against which teachers could compare their own methods.
There was the further academic objective of bringing evidence to bear on
old arguments about the relative prevalence, characteristics, and merits of
'traditional' and 'progressive' forms of teaching so that classrooms could at
last be described 'in terms of reality rather than rhetoric'. For both purposes, the quality of description needed was high. Ways had to be found

of identifying and analyzing 'patterns of interaction' which were 'reliable and valid (in the technical sense), and . . . discriminate effectively between classrooms of different types in terms of teaching tactics or approaches' (Galton and Simon, 1980, pp. 7–9, 23).

While some effort was made to cross the gulf between systematic and ethnographic styles of observation by using both for different but complementary purposes (Galton and Delamont, 1985), the main weight of fact-finding fell on the two observation schedules first devised and tried out by Deanne Boydell (Boydell, 1975). These consisted of a separate Teacher Record and Pupil Record. Whereas Flanders (for example) had included both teacher and pupil behaviour within the same category system, and also concentrated on interactions centred on the teacher, the modes of instruction common in many primary schools mean that for most of a normal lesson, most pupils will not be interacting directly with the teacher at all.

The Pupil Record therefore provides over fifty categories for noting an individual (or 'target') pupil's activities, interactions and locations, during sequences of five 25-second intervals. As in all forms of instant coding, these have to be 'low-inference' measures — that is, the observer has to feel confident that what is being recorded is sufficiently 'obvious' not to require interpretation, or merely provisional judgments of its significance in the interaction. Many of the judgments which have to be made seem straightforward enough. For example —

Is the target-pupil moving around or still?
Is the child inside or outside its 'base area'?
Is the child interacting verbally, or non-verbally, with the teacher, or with another pupil, or with several other pupils?
Is she or he, at this moment, the direct focus of the teacher's attention; or 'interested' in the teacher's interaction with another pupil or group of pupils;
or one of an audience comprising the whole class and expected to attend to what the teacher is saying;
or working;
or 'resting'; or socializing?

It is not difficult to see how frequency scores compiled from such measures enabled the research team to construct their four types of pupil — the attention seekers, the intermittent workers, the solitary workers and the quiet collaborators (Galton and Simon, 1980, pp. 144–8; Galton and Willcocks, 1983, pp. 29–41). More generally, such data also enabled them to confront 'rhetoric with reality' by reporting high levels of pupil task-involvement, so contradicting the persistent conservative folklore about the decline in habits of work brought about by 'progressivism'. The data further indicated that even where pupils were rarely taught as classes, they were much more likely to work as individuals in groups than they were to work collaboratively as groups, and that didactic forms of instruction persisted within apparently progressive forms of classroom management. Indeed, 'enquiry activities' were more closely associated with whole-class teaching than with more individualized modes of instruction.

It is at this point that the conclusions seem most clearly to outrun the evidence for them, because that evidence depends more heavily on inference than the practice of instant coding requires. For example, difficult observational decisions may well be necessary about whether a pupil's work is indeed being praised or criticized; whether that pupil has 'successfully begun', 'responded co-operatively to', 'sustained', or 'ignored' contact with another pupil; whether he or she is 'fully involved and co-operating in' an approved task, or is 'partially' or 'totally' distracted from the serious business of classroom work.

Similar doubts arise about the Teacher Record, which displays the familiar confidence of systematic researchers in being able to judge, not only whether a teacher's statements and questions are about tasks, supervision of tasks, or more general classroom routines, but also whether they stated or asked for 'facts' or 'ideas' and whether the 'ideas or solutions' asked for were 'open' or 'closed'. In principle, it may seem obvious enough that a successful 'progressive' teacher should be seen regularly 'stimulating independent enquiry by pupils'. But how such stimulation is manifested in practice needs much more detailed description than it receives here. Thus the final composite profile of such a teacher remains at a frustratingly high level of generality, not because it is summarizing earlier, more precise accounts, but because the information on which it is based is itself too removed from the fine details of interaction (Galton and Simon, 1980, p. 199). That successful 'progressive' teacher may give more 'feedback' than less successful (and less progressive) colleagues, but what kinds of feedback, and with what effects on subsequent interaction? She may 'interact more often' with individual pupils, but what kinds of encounters are they? She may make 'above average use of higher-order interactions', such as those initiated by 'more open-ended types of questioning', but how immediately evident (as we argued earlier) is the 'quality' or 'level' of the pupil contributions which are elicited?

It is the 'quality' of pupils' learning which is the focus of Neville Bennett's recent research (Bennett *et al*, 1984; Bennett and Dunne, 1990). His earlier, much publicized, work on teaching styles was not grounded in direct observation at all, and its results were frequently misrepresented as 'demonstrating' the superiority of 'traditional' methods (Bennett, 1976). A subsequent investigation of how learning was organized in 'open-plan' primary schools involved the use of three observation schedules, recording how space was used, and sampling pupils' behaviour and interactions at set intervals of time (Bennett *et al*, 1980, pp. 55–6). In research reflecting an American-style interest in pupils' work-rate, it was nevertheless recognized that decisions were often difficult about whether a pupil was or was not 'involved' in some academic task, especially where involvement took the form of 'listening' to the teacher or another pupils. Yet the researchers seem more sanguine about the problems, which seem no milder, of deciding whether teacher-pupil exchanges should be counted as 'interventions' or 'consultations', and whether exchanges between pupils are 'positive or negative in character' (*op. cit.* pp. 119–24).

In Bennett's more recent research, radio-microphones were used to record all the talk of one group of pupils in a sample of the lessons which were observed (dummy microphones being used to conceal from both pupils and teacher which group was actually being recorded). This talk was then transcribed, and a category system derived from analyzing it rather than being imposed on it. In this part of the study, therefore, the method moves away from the systematic tradition and towards the approaches which we explore in the chapter which follows.

After charting how the talk was distributed between the pupils, and how much of it was task-related, more subtle analysis focused on its 'purpose and quality', and on the 'nature' of any explanations by the teacher which were part of it. The first stage made it possible to show without much difficulty that (for example) the target pupils talked and listened to one another three times more than they talked and listened to the teacher, and that talk with the teacher was initiated three times as often by her as by them. But qualitative distinctions were again made between 'lower-order' exchanges which sought or gave relevant facts, and those which 'enhanced' the task in hand by seeking or offering explanations. Although there is more justification for such judgments in that analysis is carried out retrospectively and extends over whole stretches of interaction, the assumption is still being made (at least for practical research purposes) that the interactional and pedagogical significance of what is said can be readily identified and readily displayed.

We illustrate this criticism by considering what is perhaps the most important finding contained in the study. In classrooms commonly marked by an explicit commitment by the teacher to individualized and 'active' forms of learning, most teacher talk was indeed directed at individual pupils. But most of it was initiated by the teacher, took place at her desk, was typically brief, and was often interrupted by her perceived need to correct, advise or reprove other pupils. Encounters often intended to be 'diagnostic' — that is, directed as exploring the level of the pupil's knowledge, skill or understanding — appeared in practice to be too directly 'instructional', to be more oriented to providing or checking right answers. Identifying this as a weakness, the researchers then sought to provide solutions. Yet their attempt to devise a training programme to develop the 'formidable array of skills' needed by teachers to conduct successful diagnostic 'interviews' in the normal course of their lessons would surely have benefited from much closer analysis of the structural differences between such encounters and those dominated by the further transmission or checking of facts. Thus a lengthy transcript is used to report an exchange in which, while having 'the trappings of the Socractic method', only displayed in the teacher's questioning 'a series of winks and nudges to put the child right'. That verdict is set out as being self-evident in the commentary which follows the transcript (Bennett *et al*, 1984, pp. 207–9). We are not arguing against that judgment, but against the 'leap' towards it without any intermediate stage of analyzing how the talk is organized as discourse, and how the teacher's instructional intentions are 'evident' in the text.

In all the projects which we have reviewed in this section, the advantages of observing large number of teachers had to be balanced against the advantages of more prolonged and detailed, but also much less extensive, observation and analysis. From the various perspectives to which we turn in the following chapters, the disadvantages of pre-coded category systems can be summarized in an objection formulated within one of the most sharply contrasted alternatives, that of ethnomethodology. It is the objection to 'simplifying and reducing the social world to manageable proportions yet still wanting to generalize about it in terms of the detail which it has had to jettison,' (Payne and Cuff, 1982, p. 6).

2 Systematic Classroom Observation: Assumptions and Limitations

As a preliminary to examining alternative approaches, we want now to outline some of the 'simplifications and reductions' to which critics of systematic classroom observation most often refer. But we emphasize again that all research methods have to simplify and reduce 'reality'. All observation is selective, all forms of recording partial. All researchers have to make simplifying assumptions about that part of the social world which they seek to investigate if they are to gather data at all. These basic facts of research life were emphasized in the previous chapter, and we have tried in the present one to bring out what systematic researchers sought to gain by their particular methods of reducing classroom interaction to 'manageable proportions'. We want now to identify some of the assumptions about talk in general, or at least about talk in classrooms, which have to be made (whether explicitly or implicitly) if category-systems are to be used with any confidence in their capacity to capture significant patterns of interaction. They are assumptions which necessarily limit their scope.

First, the researcher has either to assume that what is said will be sufficiently explicit to be accessible from the words alone, or that it will be said in forms sufficiently typical of classrooms (or classrooms of that kind) that general knowledge of the setting will be enough to remove surface ambiguities.

Now as we have shown, linguistically-oriented researchers with a general, academic interest in discourse analysis have sometimes chosen classrooms as an appropriate empirical setting because of the relatively overt structure of roles and purposes which they believe simplifies the task of interpreting the meaning and function of what is said. But whatever recourse they have to 'context' is complementary to close scrutiny of recorded utterances and to what is made evident in each sequence of the text. Most of the systematic studies we have cited relied on recognizing the 'force' and effect of what was said as they heard it. Even where teacher and pupils are strangers to one another, and might be expected to take particular care to make themselves clear, a surprising amount is still taken for granted, so that even their first encounters may be much less verbally explicit than the researcher expects. We illustrate this point in the next chapter. Where the relationships of teacher and pupils are already well-established, however, the transitory observer risks being either baffled by much of what is said because its meanings depend so heavily on the participants' past encounters and their consequent stock of shared knowledge, or (which is worse) 'seeing' and recording events which the participants themselves would not recognize as having occurred at all.

These risks have been located most firmly in relatively 'informal' classrooms, where the relatively public meanings generated by a staple diet of whole-class exchanges may be outnumbered by the more private encounters between teacher and individual pupils (Walker and Adelman, 1975; Stenhouse, 1975, pp. 148–51). But it should be recognized too that even in traditionally 'formal' classrooms, a great deal of the talk is implicit or oblique. We referred to this fact in the previous chapter when questioning Bernstein's claims about the predominance there of speech regulated by elaborated codes — that is, speech in which 'principles and operations' are made verbally explicit. Empirical studies have highlighted how economically teachers often indicate the rule that has been broken, the culprit, and the restitution expected, all without referring directly either to the rule or the particular offence against it (Hargreaves *et al*, 1975). Indeed, given the hectic pace of classroom events, it is hard to see how the teacher could often take the time to spell out the rationale for a rule, or to 'justify his or her authority' (to borrow the phrasing of one of Flanders' ten categories). There are good managerial reasons why teachers avoid making their authority too obtrusive by various mitigating devices — for example, by formulating commands as apparently polite requests ('Would you please turn to your books, page fifty'), or as questions ('Are you getting on with you work?'), or as general statements which mark a trouble-spot without naming the perpetrator ('I can't hear what John is saying', 'Someone is being very silly'). These are all familiar classroom devices, even when the pupils are very young, and their function is normally identified by pupils without difficulty (King, 1978, pp. 50–6). But they are not verbally explicit.

It can still be argued, of course, that they exemplify those general rules and conventions regulating classroom communication which enable teachers to cope with varieties of pupil, pupils to cope with varieties of teacher, and researchers experienced in classroom observation to cope with the various interactions of both. We have already pursued this argument ourselves when considering how far classrooms constitute a distinct setting in which 'normal' patterns of communication, and the ways in which those patterns are achieved, are matters of common knowledge among the participants. As Croll (1986) argues when defending systematic observers against the charge of ignoring participants' meanings, their coding of behaviour into categories like 'teacher praises' or 'teacher asks a question' does not depend on claiming privileged insight into the minds of teacher and pupils, but on their access to conventional ways of assigning meanings to words and acts in the accomplishing of communication.

That access is limited in multi-cultural classrooms to the extent that different sets of conventions co-exist or come into recognized or unrecognized conflict. We consider that limitation in the chapter which follows. Yet there are also dangers in assuming too easily that the particular encounters being observed are typical of their kind, and classrooms have an 'obstinate familiarity' which can lull observers into a false confidence in their capacity to understand what is going on. It may then be necessary to 'make the familiar strange', for example by observing less 'mainstream' settings (Erickson and Mohatt, 1982), and so replace that premature confidence with the hard work needed to disentangle what the participants themselves seem to be assuming to organize their talk as they do (Delamont, 1981; Spindler, 1982). Systematic researchers know their schedules are reliable in that similarly trained observers watching the same interactions will record the same facts about them; the common frame of reference provided by 'knowing what to look for' will provide solutions for most of the uncertainties which arise. But from a very different research perspective, trained observation of a classroom event is not enough; 'it is also necessary to be aware of its history, to be alert to its possible outcomes, and above all to be sensitive to the thoughts and intentions that guide its participants' (Hamilton, 1977). We illustrate this contrast with an important aspect of classroom interaction which is often regarded as being peculiarly inaccessible to systematic observation.

Many category systems include humorous remarks which are judged to have 'warmed' or 'informalized' the classroom climate. Now jokes, consciously performed as such, are indeed likely to be marked as distinct communicative units. Many teachers, and some pupils, 'tell jokes' to lighten the otherwise serious business of instruction and provide light relief. But a great deal of classroom humour takes the form of repartee, whether between teacher and class or between teacher and individual pupils who seem almost to have been granted, or have claimed, a jester's license (A. Hargreaves, 1979; Pollard, 1984b). Repartee trades on common knowledge, not only of particular events in past encounters which are referred to obliquely, but also of the conventions which mark off permissible humour from humour which has 'gone too far' (Walker and Adelman, 1976). The real example which follows illustrates the subtle line which can often distinguish cohesive from divisive humour, as it also does that 'ritualizing' of insults which removes any offence as long as implicitly agreed limits are not overstepped. The teacher is checking a pupil's work at his desk, but the interaction is clearly in full public view. We suggest that to interpret it as evidence of the teacher's relationship with his class, it would be necessary to know how often such verbal duelling occurred, at what stages of lessons, and how far they constituted breaks from otherwise orderly, 'working' transactions. In short, the observer would need extensive knowledge of a teacher interacting with a class, and coding only a brief sequence from the 'outside' would not be practical.

T	Mmm, well, do you know Tracey, it hurts me to say it, but for you — it's not a bad piece of work.
Tracey	Gee, thanks.
T	No, I mean, just think, if you really got stuck in — you know, really tried — you could be almost average.
Tracey	Who'd want to be like you anyway?
Pupils	Come off it, sir, she'd never make average.
Tracey	Hey, if I was average, bird-brains, I'd be top of this class.
T	(Laughing) If you were average, you wouldn't be in this class.
Pupils	(Laughing) Nice one, Porky, nice one.
Tracey	You must be a not-average teacher then, having us.
T	Dead right, I'm not average.
Tracey	That's what I said.
T	(Laughing) Right — one to you.
Tracey	You can't count either.

(Quoted in T. O'Connor, 'Classroom Humour', unpublished BPhil. dissertation, Newcastle University, 1983).

A second major criticism, to be stated briefly at this stage, is directed against the neglect not only of the wider contexts of the interaction being observed (including the history of those relationships), but also of the immediate sequences in which the 'acts' recorded are located. In particular, it is argued that the function of an utterance is often unidentifiable without reference to what came next. We illustrate this criticism briefly by considering what has been a main object of enquiry in all research traditions.

The frequency with which teachers ask questions ensured them a prominent place in most observation schedules as salient evidence of teaching style and the level of pupils' thinking. We quoted several examples earlier in the chapter. The evidence produced from such observation indicated that most of the questions were factual, their sheer number eliciting mainly brief recalls of already provided information because the pace of interrogation left little or no room for thinking aloud. It has therefore been readily assumed that the way to raise the cognitive level of the answers is to ask 'better' — that is, more demanding, more 'open-ended' — questions. But that expectation of a direct causal (or stimulus-response) relationship itself assumes that the question which the teacher intends is the question which the pupil perceives (Dillon, 1982a, 1982b, 1988). The problem which pupils often face is also a problem for the researcher recording the interaction. For pupils' past experience of that teacher, or perhaps more generally in that subject, may suggest that the kind of answer which the question seems to require is not the kind of answer which the teacher really wants. And what the teacher really wants may become apparent, not when the question is asked, but when the teacher responds to the answer. For given the high probability in classrooms that answers will be immediately acknowledged, corrected and otherwise evaluated by the teacher, the pupil's attention is likely to be thrown forward to what the teacher says next. A question which is potentially 'open' may be closed down by the teacher's refusal to accept alternatives to the answer needed for that part of the lesson to progress. Peter Ustinov's radio reminiscences of his school-days include caricatured examples of a pervasive tendency in two brief sequences —

T   Who is the greatest composer?
P   Beethoven.
T   Wrong, Bach.
T   Name me one Russian composer.
P   Tchaikovsky.
T   Wrong, Rimsky-Korsakov.

It is the pervasiveness of that tendency to ask what Barnes *et al*, (1969) called 'pseudo-open' questions which constitutes a serious objection to any coding scheme, however sophisticated its appearance, which categorizes questions as they are asked — for example, as eliciting recall or inference or speculation or opinion (Eggleston *et al*, 1976). While Hargie's (1978) review of studies of questioning mainly in the systematic tradition makes predictable reference to the importance of 'thought-provoking questions', none of those studies seems to have followed sequences through to the thoughts provoked. Hargie's own suggestions for further research extend no further than advising teachers to wait longer than they normally do before rushing in to either redirect their question to another pupil or answer it themselves.

In both the chapters which follow, we examine alternative ways of analyzing classroom questions which retain that sense of sequence which their interpretation will often require. We do so in the context of a more general examination of contrasting research perspectives, and the methods of recording and analysis which these seem to indicate and justify.

5 Interpreting Classroom Communication: Turns, Sequences and Meanings

The 'interpretive' label has been used to cover a wide range of classroom studies, from the loosest to the most rigorous kinds of ethnography, and from discursive commentaries on how teachers control the transmission of knowledge to detailed structural analyses of how turn-taking is organized. This range of approaches will be illustrated in the present chapter, in rough sequence from the more general and intuitive to the formally systematic. Our starting point, however, is with some of the basic assumptions about social interaction which lead those making them in different methodological directions from those described in the previous chapter.

1 Learning the 'Language'

From any broadly interpretive perspective, orderly interaction is seen as being achieved and maintained through the meanings which the participants express in and assign to their words and actions. Where their interaction is frequent enough to appear routine, the familiar setting provides 'a frame of understandings shared and enforced' within which to interpret what is happening (Speier, 1973, p. 34). And since so much will then be taken for granted as a 'silent language' underlying and supporting what is put into words, any researcher wishing to understand how the interaction is organized and what it 'means' to those involved will have to take the time and the trouble to enter that 'frame of understandings' or risk seriously misreading events.

In 'informal' classrooms where relatively less interaction is so centred on the teacher as to become common knowledge, pre-constructed observation schedules are likely to appear evidently unusable because there will be too many 'frames' for them to contain (Walker and Adelman, 1975a). They will be 'fatally flawed' in multicultural classrooms where their working assumptions about how things are done with words differ markedly from those of the pupils being observed (Saville-Troike, 1982, p. 132;

Ainsworth, 1984). But interpretive objections to pre-coded observation schedules are more fundamental and pervasive than these examples might imply.

It is argued that in any classroom, teacher and pupils will treat much of what is said as an index to more extensive background meanings, some of which they bring from 'outside' while others have accumulated in the course of their own interaction. In doing so, they assume that others will be filling-in from the same stock of relevant background knowledge. Researchers working in the interpretive tradition are obliged to be aware of the danger of imposing an outsider's view of what is happening — of reading-in to what they observe meanings drawn from a significantly different frame of reference, thereby recording events which the participants themselves would not recognize.

Their awareness of that danger often leads to prolonged observation of the same teacher and pupils, often through some 'natural cycle' of classroom encounters. While this is certainly no guarantee that the 'silent language' of that classroom will be learned, fleeting visits ensure that it will not. Indeed, there is a special danger in classroom observation to which we have already referred. So much seems superficially familiar that the observer may categorize it prematurely as being typical of classrooms (or classrooms of that kind), without going through the hard work of systematically and self-consciously making sense of it. This hard work should involve treating any patterns perceived in the interaction as provisional until checked against more and more data until a sufficiently close 'fit' is established (for a full account of that laborious but necessary process, see Corsaro, 1981). The data itself will normally include recordings and transcriptions of what was said so that it is possible to analyze and re-analyze the interactional significance of any utterance in the sequence in which it occurred. It also makes available, as we discussed in chapter 3, an apparently potent way of displaying evidence on which the researcher's eventual conclusions about the interaction are based. To one researcher strongly influenced by ethnomethodology, it seemed at the time when he was beginning his research that 'transcripts of natural talk' were the only adequate form of data (Hammersley, 1984, p. 46).

While a main stimulus to recording such talk certainly came from ethnomethodologists' particular interest in everyday conversation, any talk is 'natural' which conforms to the normal constraints which participants perceive as applying to communication in that setting (Romaine, 1984, pp. 15–23). Thus teachers and pupils regularly rely on their sense of what forms of interaction are appropriate to their relationship to organize the interaction which actually occurs. But it remains a critical methodological assumption of interpretive researchers that such patterning cannot be assumed to be obvious — not to the observer, nor to the participants themselves. They will need frequent, reassuring evidence that they are indeed interpreting what is happening in similar ways. Talk is the main source of such reassurance. So what information, both explicit and implicit, do they need to provide and receive in order to sustain orderly, coherent interaction? And how much of that information does the researcher need, and be able to decode, to make sense of that interaction?

These questions have special relevance for investigations of talk between teacher and pupils who are encountering one another for the first time. For if it is a main hazard in classroom observation that the meaning of utterances will often depend on past encounters which the observer has not shared, then there are good practical reasons for observing relationships (and the rules which govern them) being talked into existence — that is, before they become a taken-for-granted backcloth to the interaction. There is also an important theoretical reason for doing so. Interpretive researchers have often criticized 'normative' portrayals of interaction as occurring in situations where the rules are already there to be followed, and the following of them 'explains' why the interaction took the course it did (Hammersley, 1981). From their own perspective, situations and relationships are defined and redefined in the act of speaking. Through what they say themselves, and how they evidently respond to the speech of others, they display, reproduce or renegotiate their sense of what constitutes normal interaction in that context.

In an early, intensive investigation of this process, a researcher (Smith) recorded how an American elementary school teacher (Geoffrey) stated, reiterated and enforced the rules which he intended to regulate relationships with his class until they became so 'grooved-in' that references to those rules could become progressively more indirect and implicit, thereby 'softening the tone' of the teacher's control through the creation of a 'silent language' understood and accepted by all (Smith and Geoffrey, 1968). Stephen Ball (1980) places a similar emphasis on the relative clarity with which the 'negotiation of social parameters' is exposed to view in the initial encounters of teacher and pupils. Both rules and rule-breaking are then defined much more explicitly than when relationships have 'settled down', and thereby become accessible to the researcher who is also trying to 'learn the rules'. Ball then interprets the 'exploratory mucking about' by some pupils after the first 'honeymoon' lessons, not as subversive but as a search for evidence — evidence about what it takes to be a competent pupil in that classroom or, of course, to be competently troublesome so that nonconformity to the rules will be interpreted as displaying intent rather than ignorance. Some other recent accounts have also presented pupils almost as participant-observers in such early encounters, concerned either to establish a stable framework for future interaction, or to test the teacher's capacity to define clearly and then defend the intended rules (Pollard, 1984a; Beynon and Atkinson, 1984; see also Davies, 1983; Delamont, 1983; Measor and Woods, 1984, pp. 46–50; Edwards and Mercer, 1987; Woods, 1990).

At the end of chapter 1, we described teacher-pupil relationships as being normally high in power and low in solidarity, so that much of the talk between them constitutes the working-out of a power-relationship. In all the studies we have just cited, the new relationships being contructed involved pupils already experienced in classroom life. Was the knowledge they needed to cope with those relationships substantial, or a fragment to be added to old knowledge about teacher-pupil relationships in their normal forms, and to even more general knowledge about how talk is organized in relationships which are unequal and impersonal?

These questions arose for one of us in research which included recording the first humanities lessons experienced by new pupils in a comprehensive school with a reputation for being innovative. When negotiating access to the school, Edwards and Furlong (1978, p. 75) made explicit both a general interest in how teachers 'trying to move away from traditional teacher-pupil relationships . . . use talk to define with their pupils what school-work is and what the learner's role is to be', and also a particular interest in those first 'settling-in' lessons when teachers 'will have to be more explicit than usual about what they mean when they ask questions, give instructions, or evaluate answers'. When recording the lessons, we hoped to identify 'both the explicit guidelines, and what pupils and teachers seemed to be taking for granted about their relationship'.

As it emerged, the analysis surprised us. For while the teachers certainly talked at length about (for example) how pupils were to locate resource materials, 'get down to work', and avoid too much 'chatter', they also relied heavily on knowledge which the pupils were assumed to have already about the normal range of activities and interactions appropriate to classrooms. Initially detailed instructions were given so that pupils could later fill-in exactly what was meant by such abbreviated directives as — 'settle down', or 'get yourselves sorted'. Such 'grooving-in' was sometimes made quite explicit. For example, a teacher said —

> T   OK . . . in future, when you come into this lesson, you come in, you put your bag on the floor by your place, and then quickly go and get a booklet yourself, and you'll find that it works. You might think there'll be sixty kids charging over there at the same time, but it doesn't happen. You'll find that you'll be able to come in, walk quietly over to the trolley there, get the booklet you need, go back to your place, and you'll be ready to start work . . . Are you listening? (Further elaboration of the instructions then followed)

Careful attention was also given to the essential practical distinction between 'working noise' and mere 'chatter' in classrooms where the central place of resource-based learning meant that pupils would have conversational partners readily available. Pupils therefore had to learn how much

First, by conveying something of the presence of particular teachers and pupils in their recorded encounters, such accounts (at their best) had something of the immediacy of travellers' tales, allowing teachers rare glimpses of fellow professionals at work. There is a valuable early example in the contrasts described by Massialas and Zevin (1967) between (traditional) 'didactic' teaching, and more 'dialectical' alternatives. Lengthy transcript examples 'show' more dialectically-inclined teachers 'legitimizing creative discussion' by talking less themselves, evaluating fewer of their pupils' contributions, and prompting questions directed at other pupils rather than at a single, authoritative source of information. The analysis by Barnes (1969) of 'open, closed and pseudo-open' questions was widely cited, not only for its depressing speculations about the preponderance of 'closed' varieties, but also for the many verbatim examples from many areas of the curriculum.

Secondly, they were travellers' tales from a land so familiar that some of its most prominent features were rarely noticed at all. Where teachers found reading Barnes' account a 'crucifying experience', it was because they saw reflected the dominance they exerted in their own classrooms (Torbe and Medway, 1981, pp. 5–6). In this respect, practitioners of the 'language in education' approach to classroom research resemble more theoretically-oriented ethnographers in their wish to make routine practices, and the assumptions underlying them, more noticeable.

Especially noticeable has been the extent of teacher domination, over the knowledge being transmitted and therefore over communication. For what was regularly displayed in such case studies was the sharp contrast between 'progressive' recommendations, of the kind we cited early in the book, and 'traditional' practices. From the sidelines came prescriptions for pupils to be more regularly involved in problem-solving, and in sustained discussion of their own ideas. From classrooms came accounts of teachers' neglect or discarding of pupils' knowledge, their focusing of attention on themselves as the source of clues to and judgments on right answers, and of the very limited communicative space available for pupil initiatives or pupils' elaboration of their ideas (Barnes, 1976; Hammersley, 1977; Edwards and Furlong, 1978; Wade and Wood, 1980; Dillon and Searle, 1981; Young, 1984; Evans, 1985; MacLure *et al*, 1988). Pupils' subordinate communicative roles were especially evident where the teacher's concern for correctness in detail seemed to leave little or no room to negotiate meanings. Westgate *et al* (1985) describe such heavy constraints in their account of modern language teaching strategies where the teacher is preoccupied with lexical accuracy. Hale and Edwards (1981) describe the routine classroom activity of 'hearing children read' as one in which pupils' close attention to the teacher's evaluative responses made possible some notably condensed and implicit imputations of error. In such encounters, the teacher's expertise was so salient for both participants that a child's attention was often drawn to an error without any direct reference to the word at fault. The teacher would (for example) repeat the last acceptable word, echo an incorrect word with some intonational marker of incorrectness, or simply indicate that an error had been committed somewhere —

    P By the time they were . . .
    T Read it.
    P By the time they had talked a lot.
    (Hale and Edwards, 1981, p. 119)

Both examples are presented as having some particular features of their own, but also as representing heightened forms of practices evident throughout the curriculum. Summing up both his own findings and the results of other studies broadly in the ethnographic tradition, Young (1984) refers to a process of 'indoctrination' being pervasively evident in classrooms. That term, more commonly used as a contradiction of 'true' education, is defended as the appropriate description of interaction through which teachers regularly and routinely channel pupils' ideas 'towards a viewpoint held by the teacher but unstated at the beginning of the lesson' (p. 230). As guardian of the sole criteria of 'truth', a teacher will then discard, close down or reinterpret a pupil's contribution to 'discussion' unless or until it can be confirmed as lying within that teacher's frame of reference. The resulting 'indoctrination' has to be seen as 'an ordinary, natural and unrecognized outcome of teaching, even "good" or "competent" teaching', and pupils acquiesce in it through the acceptance of correspondingly subordinate parts (p. 225).

So far, we have remained deliberately at the level of fairly general description. But if the transmission of knowledge is to be shown as generating distinctive and predictable patterns of communication, then it is likely that description will need to be much more specific, especially if the intention is to recognize the 'natural and unrecognized'. Where is that patterning most evident? The practical value of that question lies in its potential not only for drawing attention to taken-for-granted practices, but also for identifying on a surer basis than intuition those classrooms where something other than 'indoctrination' is taking place.

We noted earlier the tendency of case-study researchers to let transcript evidence 'speak for itself', and have indicated some of the reasons why. The tendency has been very marked among those teachers who have been stimulated to record language in their own classrooms as a reinforcement of their practical judgment, and as a guide to innovation (Martin, 1984). For unless a researcher's theoretical position demands the timing of every pause, or the noting of every hesitation and repetition, the recording of talk can be done without expensive equipment or much technical and linguistic expertise. Its transcription can bring back a strong sense of the original events, and can convey to outsiders some sense of them too. If the transcript seems 'evidently' to show the teacher's close control over the meanings being exchanged (especially where this contradicts the expectations of the teacher-researcher, or the outside observer), or to show an unusually high level of pupil contributions, then it is tempting to leave those transcripts to 'do their work' unsupported by the hard labour of detailed analysis. There is then a distinct danger that much of the hard labour already undertaken will be largely wasted, because critical items of evidence about the quality of the talk are much less obvious than the brief commentary on it implies. Thus for all the good intentions behind the reporting of often lively 'learning episodes' by the Talk Workshop Group (1982) or in Barr *et al* (1982), there is neither a background of theory nor a clearly explicated set of methods which other teachers could use to draw well-grounded conclusions about their own teaching through comparisons with the accounts which are offered. Similarly, in another example of a teacher doing his own research, Robert Hull's (1985) conclusion that the comprehensive school teachers he observed were much more 'directional' than appeared on the surface is not warranted by any systematic analysis of what was going on 'beneath' the surface. His arguments — for example, that the existence of a predefined conclusion to the sequence renders question-answer sequences essentially 'trivial', and that pupils' contributions are 'shaped by the retroactive effect of the resumé-to-be' (p. 136) — are both lucidly presented and copiously illustrated. But they are not 'warranted' by any kind of structural analysis of the extracts transcribed which could reveal the detailed strategies by which teachers 'get through' the knowledge they wish to transmit, and in doing so leave pupils' knowledge 'unconscripted'.

Similar examples of essentially unanalyzed reporting can be found in research into classroom 'discussion', and especially into the comparative qualities of talk which is teacher-led and unsupervised (Berrill, 1990; Howe, 1988). Salmon and Claire (1984) define 'collaborative learning' as occurring in classrooms where there has been a shift away from the indoctrinational assumptions described by Young to some 'interplay of frames of reference' and some emphasis on creating 'common ground and mutual understanding' (p. 6). Their account of its occurrence in the classrooms of five comprehensive school teachers is rich in contextual detail, and may well be found intuitively acceptable, yet it offers only generalized descriptions (unsupported even by transcripts) of how such talk is marked by — 'thinking aloud, acknowledging uncertainty, formulating tentative ideas, comparing interpretations, and negotiating differences' (p. 3). Kerry (1981) takes a more practical approach to identifying the skills which teachers may need to facilitate 'genuine' discussions in their classrooms, rather than the slightly tempered versions of teacher-exposition which are much more common. In doing so, he asks a series of clearly empirical questions, the answers to which might immediately seem not too hard to find. For example,

Does the teacher ask so many of the questions that pupils' questions are crowded out?

> Does the teacher's reformulation of pupils' ideas seem to prevent them clarifying those ideas for themselves?
>
> Do such teacher-responses as 'Good' or 'Interesting' function to limit the expression of alternative ideas by being seen as rewarding right answers?

Those questions imply some of that sensitivity to the function of particular utterances in a sequence of utterances which mark the more theoretical approaches we discuss later, but they also seem to imply that such functional identification is a fairly staightforward matter.

Pinnell's (1984) account of competent participation in group discussion takes us much further towards detailed structural analysis, though her practical purpose is to indicate a range of skills — for example, those of getting and keeping the floor, signalling intentions, being appropriately explicit oneself, extending and clarifying the remarks of others — which are sufficiently complex to make it essential for teachers committed to 'real' discussion to provide explicit training in their use. Where such discussion is unsupervised by the teacher, then the communicative options available to pupils are potentially much wider. For the research we have cited in this chapter points strongly to the conclusion that in normal forms of classroom interaction, it is the teacher who does most of the communicative and semantic work. Where the teacher temporarily relinquishes that dominant role, then conditions may be created for the kinds of talk which the Bullock Committee associated with groups in which children 'can stretch their language to accommodate their own second thoughts and the opinions of others', free from the usual constraints to play safe and look for right answers. Such talk was more likely to be 'tentative, discursive, inexplicit and uncertain of direction' (Bullock Report, p. 146). How that tentativeness was displayed and recognized was the main concern of Barnes and Todd (1977), their initial attempt to find its intonational and lexical markers being rapidly abandoned for a more comprehensive analysis of how pupils simultaneously 'framed' both the form and content of their talk so as to maintain (when things were going well) both the cohesiveness of their relationships and the coherence of their utterances. We discuss their work more fully in the following chapter because of its strong linguistic roots.

Other researchers have also examined what happens in pupil talk in the absence of a single claimed and conceded position of authority, and described in varying detail how meanings are negotiated rather than imposed, and how the talk is organized without bids for at least temporary leadership being made so explicitly as to cause offence and bring resistance (Talk Workshop Group, 1982; Halligan, 1988; Phillips, 1985). Corden (1992) has provided a valuable model of teachers re-defining their authority and giving expression to it in a variety of roles. Each such role represents an attempt to respond to pupils' learning needs in ways which recognize their existing knowledge and experience. His eight 'snapshot' transcripts show teachers: responding to children's expertise, also as a working group member, and as a neutral chairperson; scaffolding learning; responding as a source of information, then as an equal, as a learning partner, and 'with minimal intervention' (p. 182). Through such interactions, Corden suggests, 'teachers can not only extend children's existing knowledge in ways that increase understanding, but also teach them how to learn' (p. 184).

Others have focussed on what happens when pupils are set explicit talk-tasks, and particularly on the effects which pupils' own expectations can have on the course of that talk. Phillips (1992) points to the need for teachers to make their purposes in requiring talking as clear as possible, but also for pupils to reflect on these too, with their teacher's help. Similarly, Westgate and Corden (1993) compare discussions from two English lessons, only one of which was deemed 'successful', although the participants were the same four boys, with the same teacher, and no explanation for the different outcomes seemed to flow from the tasks themselves. Pupils' consistent prior experience of classroom talk is suggested as the most influential factor and as a frequent source of difficulty when pupils are required to behave in new ways: 'a cumulation of apparently normal contexts can be seen to cast a shadow of inhibition forward onto later and differently intended talk' (p. 119). Quite explicit re-assurance may be needed if pupils are to overcome such 'historical dimensions' of their present contexts: in particular, that the talk is to be valued as a process, without 'right answers' which will be assessed. And risks have to be run; not least in respect of talk which goes beyond its brief. Phillips (1988) warns against valuing exclusively so-called 'on-task' talk, if only because genuinely exploratory talk is bound to lead in unpredictable directions.

We now return to classroom settings where the focusing and framing of talk is predominantly the responsibility of the teacher and is 'evidently' so in the recorded data. Throughout this section, we have drawn attention to some of the practical limitations of research into classroom talk which may be 'insightful' but is also theoretically 'unprincipled' and unsystematic. Having drawn these criticisms from sociolinguistic, ethnographic and ethnomethodological sources, we turn now to some methods of analysis which these approaches have indicated. In doing so, we make no attempt to pin theoretical labels on all the studies which are cited. There is too much eclecticism for that, at least outside the more self-absorbed sectors of ethnomethodology. Instead, we have grouped studies according to their main focus of investigation, and their main mode of analysis.

3 The Methodical Management of Turns and Topics

In 'well-ordered' classrooms, teachers normally tell pupils when to talk, what to talk about and how well they talked. Those facts of classroom life are common knowledge, and the implications for pupils' talk of being produced within such constraints shape the prescriptions for alternative, less asymmetrical forms of communication to which we referred in the previous section. But even the most basic facts of classroom communication may need to be better 'documented', in the sense of being tied more tightly to detailed evidence of their existence.

One approach, initiated in sociolinguistics, was to draw attention to a limited set of teacher-dominated *participant structures* normally evident in classrooms. The terms refers to the arrangement of speakers and listeners (including their physical positioning) in communicative networks, to the 'constellations of mutual rights and obligations' which guide their actual participation in those networks, and to the various situationally-appropriate discourse conventions through which those rights and obligations are created and sustained (Gumperz, 1981). Susan Philips' account of those structures was an influential contribution to understanding the problems posed by the 'silent Indian child' in classrooms designed to assimilate them into mainstream American culture (Philips, 1972, 1983). In communicative settings outside their classrooms, the Warm Springs children whom she studied were unaccustomed to clear-cut distinctions between an authorized performer and an audience, and to being required to talk or listen on demand. They were therefore least 'at home' in classrooms where the teachers frequently 'lectured', asked numerous direct questions, and centred communication on themselves. In such classrooms, they were unwilling to talk on the teacher's terms, and indeed became increasingly unwilling to talk at all. They were most 'at home' in classrooms where they were able to do much of their work in small groups with no obvious leader, and where they could initiate contacts with the teacher as they perceived the need to do so. The most common participant structures in traditionally-organized classrooms — teacher talking to a silent audience, or talking or listening to an individual pupil with other pupils as audience — had no direct parallels in the community outside. The least common structures in those classrooms — pupils working together with the teacher as 'consultant' rather than 'performer' — displayed the greatest continuity with their communicative experience outside. Later research in another Indian community also indicated that systematically altering the incidence of critical participant structures was a necessary part of a more culturally-responsive pedagogy, as was the more general avoidance by teachers of forms of control and of questioning which were too overt in their 'spotlighting' of individual pupils (Erickson and Mohatt, 1982).

The structures identified by Philips as predominating in traditionally-organized classrooms can be linked readily with the routine classroom activities of teacher-exposition, teacher-questioning, teacher-led 'discussion', and teacher-supervised seat-work. As we shall see, discourse conventions mark their boundaries, and mark transitions from one activity to another. More specific and routinized classroom activities, such as 'story time' or 'hearing children read', have highly conventionalized and economical opening and closing moves, together with particular rules and procedures guiding their organization (Cuff and Hustler, 1981; Michaels, 1984; Hale and Edwards, 1981; Cazden, 1988; Christie, 1990). But these particularities exist on a base of participant structures firmly centred on the teacher. There is normally a formalized allocation of speaking and listening roles. Teachers expect both appropriate silence and appropriate willingness to talk, and they manage interaction so as to produce pupil participation which is both 'orderly' and 'relevant'. We want now to look more closely at how the orderliness is achieved.

One of the most rigorous alternatives to the discursive commentaries on classroom communication which we examined earlier has its empirical roots in the investigation of ordinary conversation. Its theoretical roots lie in the intention of making more noticeable the 'methodical practices' through which 'competent' members of a culture, or a group within it, 'bring off' the routine encounters of their everyday lives. The researcher's task is then to make these 'ethno-methods', which are normally taken for granted, into objects of intensive enquiry (Garfinkel, 1974; Speier, 1973; Hustler and Payne, 1985).

In the study of conversation, that task meant identifying the rules which account economically, and yet comprehensively, for how orderly talk is achieved and maintained across the contributions of several speakers. For example, the following 'problems' have to be solved if the talk is to be 'reasonably' orderly in form and coherent in content —

How are smooth transitions managed from one speaker or topic to the next?

How are turns at speaking bid for, claimed, conceded, taken and completed?

How do the participants avoid disruptively overlapping turns and disruptive interruptions while also avoiding awkward silences?

What are a current speaker's rights (and obligations) in relation to the next or 'upcoming' turn?

In what ways does that speaker indicate that the current turn is ending, nominate the next speaker or open the floor for competitive bids?

How do potential next speakers indicate their availability or eagerness to take over?

How are mistimed entries distinguished from intended interruptions?

How are particular topics introduced, talked through, and talked out?

These are all 'problems' in a strictly technical sense of that word — that is, they have to be solved if the talk is to be orderly in form and coherent in content. But the participants themselves are unlikely to be aware of them as problems, or to consciously plan for their solution, unless things go wrong and 'repair work' is needed. Indeed, poring over them may well leave the analyst temporarily unfit to take part in conversation, since by definition it makes explicit and 'problematical' what is normally 'managed' without the management being noticed at all.

The essential definitional marker of conversation, as we noted in chapter 2, is that it is 'talk between equals'. Its management is a corporate responsibility, no participant having any predetermined special rights or special obligations which allow the others to (metaphorically or literally) sit back and leave someone else to solve the problems to which we have referred. Conversation is therefore described as being managed both collectively and 'locally' — that is, as it goes along. Now while the main focus of their work has been such talk between equals, ethnomethodologists do not deny the plain facts of inequality in social life. They insist, however, that these can only be incorporated into the analysis where they are evident in the structuring of the talk — where there are clear 'warrants' for them in the recorded text (Edwards, A. 1981; French and Local, 1983).

We now consider some applications of conversational analysis to the study of classroom talk. At least implicit in that application is the possibility that more 'open', untraditional patterns of communication may be recognized in the extent to which they move towards the conversational end of the continuum of speech systems. The point is not that classroom talk 'should' resemble conversation, since most of the time for practical purposes it cannot, but that institutionalized talk (such as talk for instructional purposes) shows a heightened use of procedures which have their 'base' in ordinary conversation and are more clearly understood through comparison with it. This form of contrastive analysis may also provide a way of identifying and displaying occasions when the patterning of communication is 'really' different.

To return to an example cited briefly in chapter 2, McHoul places normal instructional talk towards the formal end of the continuum which runs from the most locally-managed (conversational) to the most sharply defined and pre-allocated of turn-taking systems. He does so because teachers' rights to begin and end the encounters, ask the questions and evaluate the answers, allocate all those turns at speaking which they do not claim themselves and determine their length, provide a framework within which both they and their pupils normally operate. As we have seen, encouragement of more 'real' discussion and of more opportunities for small-group talk unmanaged by the teacher, reflects the value placed on pupils taking responsibility themselves for sustaining orderly turn-taking and coherent (though *not* necessarily consensual) exchanges of ideas.

We explore in the following chapter why such conversational opportunities have been advocated so strongly from other research perspectives, and are concerned here only with some of those structural features which display differences from more conventionally teacher-controlled forms of talk. In the following examples, no special rights or single 'manager' are evident in the texts, though they seem orderly in turn-taking and in topic. As elsewhere in this section, we have chosen to illustrate analytical points made in conversational analysis with transcripts produced mainly by researchers working in other traditions. We do so for simplicity's sake, the insistence of conversational analysts on including in their transcriptions any information which might be useful in its elucidation producing texts which are exceptionally difficult to read (as may be recalled from the examples given in chapter 3).

In the first example, a group of four children have been asked to design a vehicle to travel across snow and ice which the Netsilik Eskimo might be able to build from materials available to them. All four were 'reluctant talkers' in ordinary class-lessons.

Mark	We, first we have to know what body — what —
Bryan	Yeah, well, we could make the tent the — body, can't we? Turn the tent upside down —
Mark	So you want the body — let's get the body down then (i.e. draw it on a transparency, as the teacher had asked them to do)
Bryan	Mmm
Mark	Which way — how do you want the body — like —
Bryan	Just made out that tent leather
Mark	Let's say that could be — not like a tent — like that (emphasized)— what about the body — there — that's how you want the body done
Bryan	Mmm
Mark	That —
Bryan	And then we could use —
Karen	Use one of the bones for handlebars
Bryan	Bones — for handles — hold on to the handles . . .
Bryony	What are you going to do for the base?
Bryan	The base. We can —
Bryony	We could use the —
Bryan	We could use the antlers
Bryony	What as?
Karen	You could use the fish as the sled
Bryan	Yeah, fish
Mark	What, the fish um skins, go underneath like —
Bryony	No, you could have the moss — put the moss and put the fish on top so It'd be softer with the —
Bryan	Yeah
Mark	You want the moss
Bryan	The moss, then some fish skins underneath the moss. The moss goes right round underneath it . . .

(from Enright, 1982, pp. 25–6)

What seems interesting in this extract is the way the children some-times allow their utterances not so much to be interrupted as to be com-pleted by another child; they seem to take the floor only to start things off. Added to the frequency with which they explicitly agree with or implicitly accept another's substantive contribution, it gives to the extract as a whole an appearance of both fluency and coherence which conversational analysts would want to dissect item by item to see how those characteristics were achieved.

The second extract has particular interest because it is is taken from a discussion in which the participants' communicative skills were being assessed as part of the their GCSE language examination, and because the contributions in a mixed group seem collaborative rather than competitive.

Peter	With Thy [a recently arrived fellow pupil], I mean every-one had friends so no one was bothered to try and be friendly with him
Becky	And he didn't push himself into a group. Cos if you say. . . . .
Peter	You don't need to, if you're not really bothered
Becky	If you keep on talking to people, and stuff like that, and you gradually make friends then it's . . . but if you just cut yourself off because you haven't joined in a couple of lessons
Ruth	Because they all look happy and that
Becky	Yeah
Peter	Another thing is if you push yourself into a group they might resent it
Becky	Yeah, because they might think you're a bit pushy and that
Suzie	That's right
Becky	It depends on how you put yourself over
Peter	If you don't join in with anything you can't be friends with everyone
Becky	If you put yourself over in the class. Some kids come in the class and, I don't know, someone who really fits in with everyone else and puts on a flashy accent and just gets into the group straight away . . . Whether they join in or not or what the class do or not. Others, they just . . . don't know, depends on the age and the . . .

(from Jenkins and Cheshire, 1990, p. 278).

Both these examples are of groups of conversational size; the number of potential speakers is not so large that the waiting for turns becomes so irksome or the competition for them so hectic that sub-groups form. Where there is both a central communication system and a 'crowd' expected to attend to whatever is being said, then local turn-by-turn management of the talk is likely to veer between the difficult and the impossible. The teacher's third turn in the extract which follows illustrates this neatly; the group is discussing how townspeople in the Middle Ages could defend themselves against barons running amok.

DL   We could build our own private army
NM   We need money
T   We'll, we have got money
NM   We'll we need food
T   We've got food at the moment but supplies may dry up if we . . . (confusion of voices)
NM   We could get people working for us
AW   But who's going to train them, though
T   Now gentlemen . . .
DL   We could have just a handful of already trained soldiers and . . . train them
PS   But that would be no good
DL   Why not?
NM   But suppose . . . when we . . .
DL   But then we'll have chance then, innit, if we buy our soldiers, right . . .
(Burgess, T. 1984, p. 20)

In even more crowded whole-class conditions, the teacher either allocates turns or invites bids for the next turn according to rules which he or she has taken great trouble to establish and defend. As a secondary teacher known to the authors explained — 'If they don't seem to have twigged what is expected of them, I stop and say — "Look, there's only one rule to obey in my classes. Can anybody tell me what it is?" I can usually get them to tell me, but if they can't, I tell them: "Only one person is allowed to talk at any one time, whether it's one of you or me".' The comment sums up our present perspective concisely. From it, even the high frequency and long duration of the teacher's own turns are less significant than the right to determine what other turns, and whose other turns, are admitted into the speech system. Where the current speaker is the teacher, the next speaker is likely to be a pupil either nominated directly by that teacher or chosen from among the contenders for the floor; where the current speaker is a pupil, the next speaker is either the teacher (responding to or evaluating the contribution) or a pupil selected by the teacher. Only the teacher is normally able to 'direct speakership in any creative way' (McHoul, 1978). In the following extract, that pre-allocated system is evident in the explicit control over turn-taking exercised by the teacher, and in the teacher-taking-every-other-turn format which is so characteristic of class-teaching. The extract is from a humanities lesson on fossils in a comprehensive school.

T   It's quite heavy, it weighs about a pound or so. It's — I won't
     tell you how a fossil happened yet — you'll be learning about
     that later, but why isn't the erm — why don't we find the
     remains of the creature inside here? Why don't we find —
     Ssh! — yes?
P   Would have rotted away.
T   Would have rotted away. Why didn't the shell rot away?
PP   (Mumbled answers, among which can be identified — 'Too
     hard')
T   Yes Edgar — yes?
P   It's too hard.
T   It's too hard — good. If I die tomorrow, and if I float to the
     bottom of the sea — don't cheer! — um, if I float to the
     bottom of the sea, what parts — if you were a scientist and
     you came along in a couple of million years, and you looked
     at my fossil, what parts of my body would you find?
PP   (Murmurs)
T   SSh! Just a minute, put your hands up please. Heather?
P   The skeleton.
T   The bones in other words.
P   Your watch.
T   Although a watch would rust away. What other parts would
     you find. Yes?
(from a recording made by Edwards and Furlong (1978), but not
included in that book)

In Mehan's (1979a) exhaustive account of nine lessons in an American elementary school, these normal forms of turn-allocation and turn-taking accounted for 88 per cent of all the turn-transitions recorded. For all practical purposes, the rest could be accounted for as either 'sanctioned violations' — breaches of the rules which the teacher explicitly or implicitly reproved — or violations unsanctioned either because they were not noticed, or tactically unnoticed, or because their useful contribution to the lesson's substantive agenda outweighed their procedural irregularity (for example, where the lesson had become bogged down, or where the contribution introduced 'news' which the teacher was willing to sponsor). What Mehan called a pupil 'initiative' was an unsolicited bid to speak which the teacher (for whatever reason) accepted. We might call it a conversational intervention in an otherwise unconversational speech system. Such initiatives were conspicuously more frequent later in the school year, when pupils had become more skilled in finding 'the seams in an essentially teacher-controlled discourse' (Mehan, 1979a, p. 139).

We end this section by considering two types of turn to which conversational analysts pay particular attention, and which in most classrooms are monopolized by the teacher. The first relates to the organization of interaction, and the second leads into the following dicussion of how teachers organize meanings through the 'essential teaching exchange' (Young, 1984) of question-answer-evaluation.

Opening a conversation will be experienced as a more than 'technical' problem where it risks rebuff — a refusal on the part of others to make more than token acknowledgment of the initiative. It is a major professional preoccupation of teachers, because 'getting attention' and 'getting the lesson started' so often require arduous and stressful communicative work (Wragg and Wood, 1984).

Ideally, the teacher — '. . . should only have to ask you once to be quiet, and then everybody should be hushed straightaway' (Edwards and Furlong, 1978, p. 96). Realistically, something resembling the following is more likely. It comes not from the opening of a lesson, but from the point of return to a central communication system after a period of practical work in the laboratory; the problems for the teacher are very much the same. Walker and Adelman (1975b, pp. 40–1) illustrate their transcript with line drawings of the teacher's studied waiting for everyone's attention. The whole episode lasted 74 seconds.

> T Can you sit down in your seats please (6 second pause)
> We're waiting for some people at the back (20 second pause)
> Oh look you two boys — do you really want me to start getting angry about it? (2 second pause)
> We're still waiting for you people at the back (6 second pause)
> Right, now. Now you're all sitting down could you all look this way please (10 second pause)
> Thank you. Now then. Someone asked me a very good question.
> They said why can't we just carry on mucking around with all these things. Why do we have to write it all down. . . .

Several ethnomethodologists have focused microscopically on the routine practices through which whole lessons are 'opened', from the first 'Er, come on, settle down', to the concluding 'Right, now what were we talking about last time?' (Payne, 1976). They have also looked at how teachers talk collections of pupils into being as a 'class to be taught', so that what is said is heard by the 'class as a whole' and can justify references to what 'we' were 'talking about last time', and at how deftly and swiftly a latecomer is both reproved and incorporated into the class (Payne and Hustler, 1980; Payne, 1982). This second example retains the transcript conventions of the original, which in this case is easily readable —

> T E:r — come o:n settle down — no one's sitting down till we're all ready
> (pause circa 7.00 seconds) (General background noises)
> T Stand up straight — bags down

> (pause circa 8.00 seconds) (General background noises getting quieter)
> T Down I said.
> (pause circa 5.00 seconds) (General background noises getting quieter still)
> T Right quietly sit down
> (pause circa 9.00 seconds) (General background noise)
> P (   )
> T (   ) Right now then what were we talkin about last time —
> yes
> P (Sir) the Vikings how the — were going to raid — Wessex
> T How they were going to raid Wessex yes . . .
> (From Payne, 1976, cited and discussed in Hustler and Payne, 1985, pp. 278–83)

The finely detailed analysis which conversational analysts carry out on such brief transcripts is claimed to be necessary because the technicalities being identified are the 'technicalities of the trade' — part of the largely unnoticed repertoire of professional skills (Anderson, 1982).

Central in that repertoire are all the 'formulating utterances' through which teachers provide a running commentary on what is being done and said in their lessons. We have emphasized in this chapter how much routine interaction depends on the participants' assumption that each is defining the situation, and assigning situationally-appropriate meanings, in similar or at least congruent ways. On occasions when understanding clearly breaks down, or meaning is ambiguous or uncertain, then speakers will display their need to check that they are indeed following what is going on — either by summarizing what they understand to have happened, or by questioning the definitions of others. In other words, the form or content of the talk will become an object of explicit attention, something to be overtly talked about. But the expression or meeting of that need may come from any participant.

In classrooms, as Stubbs (1976) indicated from a sociolinguistic perspective, formulations are both unusually frequent and monopolized by the teacher. It is central to the teacher's task to define what is happening and going to happen, and make their definitions stick. So they say things like — I'm not going to stand any more of that', or 'You are being very silly', or 'Are you trying to be funny', or 'You remember last lesson when we . . .', or 'Right, put your pens down, what I want you to do now is to . . .'. And since they are so often bringing information (or 'news') to rather unwilling and (by definition) inexpert listeners, they have regularly to mark the boundaries between what pupils know already and the new knowledge belonging to that school subject (McHoul and Watson, 1984), monitor its reception, identify and repair breakdowns in understanding, and exhibit for the class those meanings which should by now be shared.

In conversation, such formulations are not only likely to be shared around, they are also liable to be contested or rejected as inaccurate characterizations of the talk. In classrooms, however, there is normally a single 'authorized' source of definitive statements about what is happening and what is meant. From this perspective, therefore, markers (amongst others) of relatively 'open' classroom discussion would be the extent to which the teacher's formulations of facts and ideas are questioned and responsibility for checking and summarizing the meanings being constructed is sometimes taken over by the pupils. The following examples illustrate, in deliberate contrast, the usual and unusual distribution of formulations.

In the first extract, the teacher is summarizing (or trying to get pupils to 'say it for him') what a series of lessons about early myths have 'really' been about —

T   Right, do you notice what we've done? We started off saying we're going to look at ideas about the world, how people long ago explained the world. But what else — and this is very important — what else have we also done?

P   Saw how men looked at women.

T   We saw how men looked at women — you're nearly there. What exactly do you mean? Can you say — go on, tell us a bit more, go on.

P   How he doesn't like her, and how he thinks she's weak.

T   Yeah (tentatively) So we've also looked then — can anybody else before I say it, anybody else have any ideas? He's on the right track there. He said that we've also looked at how men looked at women. What else have we looked at here?

P   God.

T   No, not to do with God. . . .

P   How they lived?

T   How they lived! In other words, the ideas they had about themselves and how they lived. So from a story from long ago, we've used that story to work out how people thought about themselves, how they lived . . . (interruption) Let's get on because this is very important, because all the time you're in humanities you'll be doing this, you'll be looking at what people have said about themselves long ago, and trying to work out how they lived, and we call that something that you look for EVIDENCE.

(form Edwards and Furlong, 1978, pp. 125–6)

In this second extract, an obviously well-practised group of older (American) high school students are experiencing 'dialectical' teaching, in which the responsibility for developing generalizations about the political functions of secret societies is clearly being handed over by their teacher —

Janet	Our rule seems to hold pretty good (the rule formulated earlier by Debbie as — 'oppressive governments cause secret societies to grow up' and then suggested in predictive form by Steve that — 'we should find secret societies where there are oppressive governments') If we reverse it we do seem to have some trouble but that's because the proof is so hard to find. It's easier to work after the fact, after something has already happened.
Lauren	I just thought of a new problem. Maybe we're all being too agreeable with our own rule. We didn't consider Ku Klux Klan. We studied it, and we have their oath, but where do they fit into our rule?
Teacher	Ah! That's a very good question.
Janet P.	They thought that the American Government in Washington was being oppressive to the white people of the South, so they formed their organization to protect their rights.
Teacher	I like your choice of words.
Janet P.	What does that mean?
Teacher	What do you think it means?
Steve	Oh! I think I see what you're getting at. Janet said that the Ku Klux Klan thought the US government was bad. But was it? For whom? It wasn't bad for the Negroes in the South.
Debbie	No, it was giving the Negroes their rights for the first time. The KKK was oppressing the Negroes . . .

(Massialas and Zevin, 1967, pp. 45–6)

Teachers' control over the topics of classroom communication, and over what is treated as being relevant for curriculum purposes, is pervasively evident in formulations of what it is which has been learned, is being learned, and is to be learned. In the final section of this chapter, we consider how that control is exercised and displayed in those questioning sequences which are so distinctive a feature of classroom talk, and which have been investigated from so many research perspectives.

4 The 'Essential' Teaching Exchange

The task of the ethnographer is to discover and explicate those 'rules for contextually-appropriate behaviour' of which the words and actions recorded are a manifestation (Saville-Troike, 1982, p. 107). 'Ethnography of communication', like conversational analysis with which it overlaps, focuses on those rules which regulate the exchange of meanings in particular contexts, and which assign functions to forms. If classrooms indeed represent a 'unique communicative context' (Wilkinson, 1982), then the task is to discover those rules which most economically account for its distinctive patterning.

For many researchers, the 'essential teaching exchange' is that sequence of moves describable as 'question-answer-comment/evaluation' or in more abstract form, 'initiation-response-evaluation/feedback (IRE, or IRF). The frequency of those exchanges, and the overwhelming tendency of teachers to make the first and third moves, is 'essentially' what makes classrooms so distinctive (Young, 1984, p. 223; Mehan, 1979b; Burton, 1980 pp. 141–5; Romaine, 1984, pp. 170–84; Cazden, 1988, pp. 29–41). The sequence establishes a pedagogical frame of reference which is renewed with every 'third (evaluative) turn'.

Having earlier made various organizational comparisons between conversational talk and talk in classrooms, we now extend comparison to the structure of questioning. Analyzing two-party conversations in which events are being reported, Labov (1972b) suggests a 'single invariant rule' to cover them which is derived from the extent of their shared knowledge. The events being reported are either known to A, to B, or to both. If A makes a statement about a B-event (that is, an event known only to B), then it is normally 'heard' as a request for confirmation, since A cannot provide information which only B possesses. But if A makes repeated and unmitigated statements about B-events, then these statements are 'heard' as appropriate only if B recognizes A's claim to being in some way an 'authority'. Now while classroom talk can be described as a two-party conversation in so far as pupils are treated as a 'single subordinate participant' in the allocation of turns, it is certainly not conducted normally on a basis of shared knowledge. Its outstanding characteristic, as we have already discussed at length, is one participant's claim to all the knowledge relevant to the business in hand. As a consequence of that claim, which is normally conceded by pupils, teachers routinely ask questions to which they already know the 'only' answer, or at least know the limits within which an acceptable answer must fall (Mehan, 1979b). In a 'real' question, the questioner displays ignorance of a matter to which he or she presumes the answerer to be knowledgeable. In such a context, information is likely to be offered and acknowledged. Most instructional questions, on the other hand, are typically the property of only one party to the exchange; they require a response displaying knowledge and are 'acknowledged' evaluatively: i.e. as right/wrong. If they are acknowledged by an expression of agreement or disagreement, then, as Dillon (1990) suggests, the context is not one of teacher-led recitation-teaching but a discussion.

Conversational analysts stress the importance of 'paired' utterances in the organization of talk. 'Summons and response', and 'request and acknowledgment', are examples of 'adjacency pairs' — the second part being contingent upon the first through being constrained by it, a 'failure' to produce the second part constituting a noticeable event requiring explanation or repair. Even more obviously, questions 'require' an answer, in the sense that a refusal to provide one will be, in most cultures, a noticeable event unless the missing answer is acceptably replaced by some expression of regret at being unable to provide one (the qualifying phrase is necessary because of evidence, referred to later, that there are some cultures where a question may, quite legitimately, be ignored). In conversation, the normal sequence is —

Question — Answer
Answer — Acknowledgment

While politeness is likely to indicate some acknowledgment that the 'news' has been received, the answer cannot be evaluated unless the question was a device to elicit an admission of ignorance from the other which the questioner (who 'knew all along') may now feel entitled to change into a 'state of knowledge'. While such known-answer questions are not infrequent in conversation, they are strikingly frequent in classrooms. Most teachers' questions are 'closed' or 'pseudo-open' — that is, they are asked from a position of knowledge, and are intended to find out whether the pupil questioned knows what the questioner clearly knows already. There is therefore a marked predominance of the IRE sequences mentioned earlier, which can be seen either as in three-parts or as two adjacent pairs —

Question — Answer
Answer — Evaluation (or Feedback)

The point can be put more formally. In conversation, questions are 'oriented to what lies ahead', while answers 'look back to what has just been said', and will be inspected for their relevance to the enquiries which called them forth (Goffman, 1981, pp. 5–8). In classrooms, pupils' answers will certainly be inspected in this way. Indeed, a striking feature of teachers' questioning is the care with which they listen for answers, or elements within answers, which can be usefully built into their own developing exposition (Hargreaves, 1984). Even the briefest answers can then be treated as 'relevant' to the purposes of the lesson, and 'heard' and 'made up' into something usable. Reciprocally, pupils' answers are commonly oriented to what lies ahead — to the teacher's immediate verdict on their adequacy, and to any evidence which the teacher's evaluative response may provide about what a more adequate answer might look like if they are unfortunate enough to have the question remain focused on them. The process which we have described is so common in classrooms that it is doubtful whether pupils need those formal-linguistic markers of 'test' questions which some analysts have proposed. It is illustrated in the sequence which follows, taken from an infants' class

T   Matthew, what do you think hedges are useful for?
M   Corn. (quietly)
T   Can't hear you, Matthew.
M   Corn.
T   Hedges are useful for corn? No. Karen?
K   So the things can't get out.
T   So the things can't get out (3 second pause) Stop the animals getting into the cornfield to eat all the corn wouldn't it?
PP   Yes.
T   And if you've got cows in the field it would stop the cows from getting out . . .
     What about animals like rabbits, squirrels, hedgehogs, insects, butterflies. What are hedges useful for for those animals?
C   Birds.
T   Birds can use the hedges. . . . What's the hedge used for?
C   The birds can make homes in.
T   Yes. Good.
C   I know.
T   The birds can make homes in the hedges. What else?
C   Nests.
T   Nests. Yes . . .
(from MacLure and French, 1980, p. 86)

Apparent in this extract, as in many others we have cited, is the routine way in which teachers discard answers which they judge to be irrelevant, insufficient, or simply wrong, and reallocate the question to someone else to answer. In conversation, turns are often interrupted in error (when an intending next speaker mistimes a bid to speak next), or are legitimately interrupted in order to request clarification of what the current speaker is saying, or to express interest or agreement, or to indicate disagreement as a preliminary to bidding for the floor next time. In all these cases, the current speaker will normally resume the interrupted turn. In classrooms, however, pupils' turns are highly vulnerable to interruption and sudden termination, for the reasons already suggested. Most of their contributions to the lesson proper are in answer to the teacher's questions, and are unlikely to be allowed to stand or 'run on' if they fail to fit within the teacher's frame of reference. And teachers are extremely skilful in throwing doubt indirectly or obliquely on an answer they have elicited (for example, by simply repeating it with a sceptical or disbelieving intonation) so as to indicate that the floor is still open to more substantively successful bids.

Our account should not be taken, however, as assigning pupils a merely passive role. The zeal and skill with which teachers pursue 'right' answers is so familiar to their pupils that it makes available to them ways of getting the teacher to do the work. For they have ways of making the teacher talk — for example, by offering token answers or wild guesses which the teacher chooses to 'hear' as genuine attempts to solve the problem which deserve some additional signposts which may lead towards finding a correct or more acceptable answer (Edwards and Furlong, 1978, chapter 6; MacLure and French, 1980; Edwards and Mercer, 1987; Hargreaves, 1984). The following sequence could almost have been scripted to illustrate this point, so clearly does it show not only the hazarding of guesses to a question whose purpose is evidently obscure to those to whom it is asked (unsurprisingly, since the sequence of lessons is about Tristan da Cuhna), but also an unusually explicit request for the criteria on which an answer acceptable to the teacher should be based:-

T　But what is it that makes a housing shortage in some parts of Britain?

P　The bricks?

T　No.

T　The land?

P　No (there follows a prolonged exchange in which the pupil tests out various answers relating to the making of houses)

T　Look, forget about the houses and think about those wh're going to live in them.

P　The people who build them.

T　The people who build houses are going to live in them? In this country?
　　We're on about this country now, remember.

P　Oh, in this country — oh, we get people who build them.

T　But why is that in some places there are not enough houses for the number of people in that place?

P　There are not a lot of workers?

T　No.

P　They've got vandalism?

T　No — don't think about it from — you're thinking about it from one end, the houses.

P　Which end do you want us to think from?

T　I want you to think of it from the other end, which is the number of people.

P　Yes, 'cos there's a lot of people — too many people after one house.

T　Right. . . . (Edwards and Furlong, 1978, p. 30)

We have already moved towards answering a further question about classroom questioning which has been addressed from the perspective being discussed here. Since the competence of both pupils and teachers is manifested so routinely in the production of 'right' answers to the teacher's questions, how do teachers make eventual right answers more likely — even when producing them may involve whole series of questions through which negative evaluations of the answers function as 'continuation turns' and the sequence is only completed when a positive evaluation can at last be given (Mehan, 1979b)? We have commented briefly on the skill with which pupils can elicit and make use of cues as to what a 'right' answer might be like. Teachers are no less skilful in providing them. But they have other strategies too. In the terms used and well documented by French and MacLure, they frequently 'Preformulate' questions — that is, they provide advance warning that a question is imminent, and some pointers to knowledge (perhaps from a previous lesson) relevant to answering it. If the question is answered irrelevantly or incorrectly, they are likely to 'Reformulate' the question — whether by simplifying it, or by building into its restatement some of the information needed for an answer — and to go on doing so until an acceptable answer is achieved (French and MacLure, 1979; 1981b). If the objective is still to leave room for the pupil to demonstrate competence (if only at discovering the teacher's answer), then the reformulations will not be too precisely informative. But if the lesson is going too slowly, then enough may be done by the teacher to make it almost impossible for the pupil not to answer (as in the extract quoted above). The answer may then be taken as evidence of an academically knowledgeable child, where close analysis of the sequence shows a pupil with the skills needed to identify and move into the teacher's frame of reference. We conclude this discussion with a rare example of a teacher digressing from his immediate frame of reference. A group of pupils had been heating various materials, and one of them produced the unelicited question — 'Where did the black coating come from?' — to which the teacher responded with a request for 'ideas':-

T   Let's think of all the items involved. What were they?
P1   Flame . . . foil.
T   Yes . . . what else was there? What else could it have been?
P2   The tongs.
T   The tongs, alright, let's put that down . . . maybe the tongs . . . let's put that down as a possibility. It may be unlikely, but it's still a possibility until we're proved that something else was responsible.
P3   The air.
T   Yes, the air. What else is in the vicinity? Have we got all the various agencies involved?
P   Gas?
T   It may have come from the natural gas . . . let's put that down. It may have. It's a possibility. Now — who would like to summarize what these possibilities are for causing the black coating on the tube?
P1   The copper coating, flame, tongs, gas, air . . .
T   Right, now how do we find out which was responsible?

P4　By an experiment?

T　Right, we need to design another experiment after half term.
　What should we do?

P5　We could scrape off the coating — and work out why —

T　We could so — we could analyze it . . . Good, right now, who
　found it weighed more after it had been heated?

(from Hull, 1985, pp. 141–2)

It is an interesting question to ask about this extract whether the 'fact' of
the digression is 'evident' in any of the features we have discussed in this
section, in a text which seems organizationally to be firmly centred on the
teacher.

Teacher control over the organization of turns and the formulation of
meanings has been the main theme of this chapter, in which we have tried
to show different methods of identifying how reciprocal assumptions of
teacher-knowledge and pupil-ignorance are evident in the structures of
classroom talk. Those methods have shown not only how much talking
teachers commonly do, but how they monopolize those 'turns' and 'moves'
through which the communicative initiative is secured and maintained.

We now return to the notion of 'normally competent interaction in
classrooms' in those normal classrooms where 'one participant has acknowledged responsibility for the direction of the discourse' (Sinclair and
Coulthard, 1975, p. 5), touching on two aspects of it which refer directly
to the typical question-answer sequences which we have already described
and which also lead to the fuller discussion of home-school continuities
and contrasts in the chapter which follows.

We have suggested at several points that the relative ease with which
even young children recognize and act on the main rules structuring
classroom discourse may be explained by their already extensive experience of playing subordinate parts in their encounters with adults. Some
studies have shown them shifting immediately to more functionally limited
forms of talk when an adult joins a previously 'unsupervised' conversational
group. The adult is left to take the initiative, ask the questions, interpret
what they 'really mean', the topics, and generally make the running (Cook-
Gumperz and Corsaro, 1977; Corsaro, 1979; also, for older children, Phillips,
1985). Most directly relevant to their future in classrooms is their experience of adults in a didactic role, providing information and checking
that it has been accurately received. At least in mainstream settings in
industrial societies, there is a high frequency of questions, and especially
of known-answer questions, in adult-child conversation. They have been
described as 'the first clearly conversational obligation to which children
are sensitive' (Cherry, 1979; see also Mehan, 1979b). It is the obligation
to perform what they know to someone who is testing whether they
know it.

In all these respects, then, children may be well prepared for the most salient communicative demands made on them in classrooms. Indeed, the inequalities and the obligations may well increase. For some important recent research, based on recordings of talk in both settings, has indicated a wider functional range in children's talk at home than at school (Heath, 1982; MacLure and French, 1981; Wells and Montgomery, 1981; Tizard and Hughes, 1984). This reflects, not on the competence of teachers, but on those most salient facts of classroom life to which we have referred repeatedly — the need to manage 'crowds', and the perceived need to transmit knowledge and to do so in a short time. Even harassed mothers are likely to have more time than teachers for prolonged exchanges with an individual child. They are also able more naturally to embed talk in activities of immediate relevance to the child, and to engage in collaborative recollections of past experiences, and collaborative planning of future action. Tizard and Hughes (1984) were surely right to stress children's extensive acquisition of knowledge 'simply by being around their mothers, talking, arguing and endlessly asking questions' (p. 249). In such contexts they are able to take initiatives and shape conversations in ways which become difficult when they go to school. Early-years classrooms do nevertheless often provide pupils with a range of talk-partners other than teachers. Nursery nurses, for instance, have been found to interact with pupils in more supportive, mother-like style, and to bring into the talk events or information from home (Westgate and Hughes, 1989).

It was mainly with reference to these features of mother-child talk (in both middle-class and working-class homes) that Tizard and Hughes (1984) explained the much higher proportions of questions from children, of extended sequences of question-and-answer initiated by the child, and of 'passages of intellectual search' through which the child seeks to explore some part of its world. The different patterning of communication was vividly illustrated in their comparison of story-telling in both settings, a particularly telling comparison since both mothers and teachers regularly used such occasions to extend the child's practical knowledge of matters arising from the narrative. In the sessions recorded in nine homes, the children asked 78 questions and their mothers asked 61. Of the 66 questions asked during story-time in eight nursery classrooms, 63 were asked by the teachers. In this and in other ways, contrasts were sometimes so sharp that it was hard for the researchers to remember that they were recording the same children.

As we argue more fully in the following chapter, generalizations about communicative continuities and contrasts between homes and classrooms are confounded by the diversity within the two kinds of settings, notwithstanding Gordon Wells' conclusion that all the homes in which he and his team made recordings were more 'enabling' contexts for children's language development than were some of the classrooms (Wells and Wells, 1984). Our concern at this point is still with generalizations, though at a different level. They are generalizations about the continuities and changes experienced by children from different cultural backgrounds when they enter classrooms which are organized communicatively as though they were monocultural. The achievements of sociolinguistics have perhaps been most impressive theoretically, and most obviously relevant to the process of schooling, in showing that an apparently 'common' language is no guarantee of shared expectations of, and skills in, its use. In seeking to identify the rules by which participants in classroom interaction devise situationally-appropriate performances and interpret meanings, such research has drawn attention to the various definitions of how language is (and should be) organized which can co-exist unnoticed within the 'same' situation.

The central anthropological obligation to avoid 'disembedding' interactions from their wider cultural settings was a major influence on such 'ethnographies of communication' (Hymes, 1977; Green and Wallat, 1981). They drew attention to different rules for organizing discourse, and to the implicit models of learning which these express. We cited earlier Philips' account of different perceptions of participant rights and obligations, in the course of which research she found reason to doubt the 'universality' of some of those basic rules of turn-taking which conversational analysts were then seeking to identify. In her Warm Springs recordings, she noted a generally slower conversational pace than in mainstream cultural settings, with greater tolerance for silences, fewer interruptions, a more even distribution of turns around the available participants, and less direction by a 'current speaker' over who should speak next (Philips, 1983). Of especial relevance to our own concern with classroom questioning was the analysis of question-answer sequences in a community where direct questions were disliked (especially in public settings where ignorance was thereby put on display), and where it was considered permissable not to offer an answer at all in circumstances where to do so was inconvenient or possibly disadvantageous to the person questioned (Philips, 1972; Erickson and Mohatt, 1982).

These studies were carried out in settings at a considerable distance from the cultural 'mainstream'. Johnson's (1979) observations in sixty classrooms in three southern American states suggested that such communicative patterns as the 'discussion cycle' of Solicit-Respond-React (or, in the terms used earlier, I-R-E) were so frequent and persistent that the rules governing them seemed to be shared by the roughly equal numbers of black and white teachers and pupils involved. In other words, the situational constraints and regularities were so strong that they overrode differences which the participants may have experienced in other important settings in their lives. Investigating the common practice of 'sharing-time' in four American elementary classrooms (regular opportunities for children to talk about their own experiences), Cazden and Michaels certainly found a classroom event so routinized that the children clearly (and concensually) recognized its distinctive stylistic features — for example, the tone contours used by the temporary child-leaders to open proceedings and to nominate other speakers. But there were also significant differences in the preferred strategies of black and white speakers for structuring their narratives (Michaels, 1984). Gumperz (1981) found a notable example of ethnic differences in 'contextualizing conventions' in black pupils' practice of saying 'I can't do this' when what they wanted was company rather than academic aid. And Kochman (1981) found a 'black mode' of participation in classroom discussion which displayed a cultural preference for vigorous argument as a way of testing views, a preference which led them to compete much more forcefully for turns than their white contemporaries and to be much more active in initiating disagreements (see also Evans, 1988). Thus, while classrooms do represent children's first experience of linguistic and socio-linguistic diversity, discontinuities from home experience appear in large measure to relate to specific functions of language. It is best not to see children's verbal adaptation to school therefore as a matter to do with possession or lack of a generalized mastery of language but one, rather, of familiarity with the genres of language use which are particularly valued in classrooms (Wells, 1987). As Cazden (1988) has noted, in her account of 'sharing time', it is possible for ethnic differences in narrative style simply to be interpreted by teachers as evidence of low-ability, and for the importance of such language within the home culture to be disregarded.

We conclude this chapter with a particularly impressive example of the ethnographic approach to classroom communication, based on many years' observations in home, neighbourhood and school settings in two working-class communities (Heath, 1982, 1983, especially pp. 103–12). We take from it the sharp, and carefully-drawn contrast between the types of question which black children were given the opportunities to answer, and expected to answer, as they moved to and fro between home and school. At home, there was an overwhelming predominance of questions about whole objects, and about events and their causes and effects; there were rarely questions about what things were 'called' and they were even more rarely test-questions to which 'right' answers were expected. In school, they frequently found themselves being asked for 'labels, attributes and discrete features of objects and events, in isolation from the context', and then having their answers precisely evaluated (1982, p. 105). In effect, they were 'foreign' questions. Yet their failure to give the right answers, or even to answer at all, could have a significant bearing on their teacher's expectations of them, and so on their subsequent progress at school. The problem as defined by many teachers was that — 'They don't seem able to answer even the simplest questions'. Shirley Heath's evidence supported strongly the alternative explanation of that failure which a black parent offered to justify her child's persistent silence in the classroom — 'Nobody play by the rules he know'. It was an essential part of her research to enlarge the teachers' awareness of such damaging discontinuities in the rules of those language games which the children had to play so often and in such different forms.

6   Analyses of Classroom Discourse

In this chapter, we come to those approaches to classroom talk which show the most directly linguistic orientation. Common to all the studies reviewed here is, first, a sense of talk as centrally involved in social action and, secondly, a distinctive concern for the structure of spoken discourse as influential in the shaping of events. This is talk considered less as a mirror to be looked *through* than as medium to be looked *at*, because of its role in constituting events. From this perspective, analysis of discourse structure also captures the structure of the events to which the discourse inherently belongs. Not all the researchers whom we group in this way agree on the extent to which systematic analysis is possible at this level. Nor do they agree on the extent to which features of other levels (notably intonation) can be integrated with those of discourse. Latterly, too, the apparently convergent concerns of 'basic' linguistic and educational researchers using classroom settings, to which we referred to in chapters 1 and 3, have tended once more to separate. Those bent on further refinement in the analysis of discourse have explored other settings (for example, Coulthard, 1987); those with an educational focus (for example, Cazden, 1988; McCarthy, 1991) have applied theoretical constructs of discourse analysis to pedagogy with little or no modification of the constructs themselves. Nevertheless, it is useful to identify a continuing and common *linguistic* orientation towards classroom talk, embracing as it does a range of purposes, theoretical arguments and substantive issues.

1   A Linguistic View

A useful starting point for distinguishing this general orientation is to contrast the concerns of discourse analysis, as Coulthard (1977) does, with those of Flanders when 'analyzing teacher behaviour' or Barnes' early exploration of the language of the classroom (Flanders, 1970, Barnes *et al*, 1969). In Flanders' observational scheme, to 'initiate' means — 'to make the first move, to lead, to begin, to introduce an idea or concept for the first time, to express one's will'. Now none of these actions is specifically linguistic. Each relates to a type of interaction, and each can be realized in a variety of linguistic forms. Each focuses upon behaviour involving or giving rise to language rather than upon language itself, on control of the topic or setting rather than on the structure of the discourse. There is no linguistic analysis of the behaviour at all. To give another example, any teacher utterance, 'of whatever grammatical form or illocutionary force, which is based on something a pupil has said is regarded as a response' (Coulthard, 1977, p. 96). The precise form of the utterance is not treated as significant, nor are its distinctive meanings and overtones. Coulthard directs similar criticism at Barnes, many of whose examples (in Flanders' terms) simply show the teacher failing to produce responding behaviour at crucial points. From a linguistic perspective, there are such serious dangers in neglecting either the sequencing and patterning of the discourse, or the function of particular utterances in the building-up of meanings, that any analysis using talk as evidence of classroom processes should pay the closest attention to its structure.

It must be said at once that this very idea was central to Barnes' later investigation of small-group talk (Barnes and Todd, 1977). To illustrate the general orientation being introduced, and also because of its relevance to our earlier comments on research which leaves transcript evidence largely to 'speak for itself' in showing (for example) the level of collaborativeness in unsupervised pupils' talk, we quote part of a discussion between three thirteen-year old boys. They had been asked to use their knowledge of air-pressure to consider the question — 'What would happen to the spaceman if he stepped out into space without a space-suit on?'

This exchange has several relevant aspects. Despite its brevity, we can easily recognize in it some of the conversational characteristics of 'talk between equals'. Although Alec says less than the others, his is nevertheless an important contribution. Notable for its absence is any constraining adult voice, although the talk is purposeful and proceeds in awareness of adult-set objectives. The boys were also aware of an eventual wider audience of adults (the researchers who would hear their taped discussion), but at the time had charge both of the talk itself and the recording of it. An important feature here, and one typical of conversation, is the way in which a formal ambiguity (the reference to 'it') is accommodated before being collectively resolved. The openness of the talk in its direction and the way meanings are defined may be a precondition for the emergence of unanticipated ideas (for example, that offered by Barry at 41) which are potentially fruitful and available to all the group. In the interpretive commentary which they provide, the researchers demonstrate their attention to detail and cohesion in the discourse, and build a pedagogically significant account upon it. At the same time, they demonstrate an awareness of the need for caution in reinterpreting events from recordings and transcripts. That is, they recognize throughout, sometimes explicitly (as in the comment on 37), the potential ambiguity of words alone.

| 34 | Barry | It's like a diving,
diving-suit, isn't it? |

35	Graham	Yeah . . . it's full of air.	'It' seems here to refer to the space suit, but since being 'full of air' is a characteristic shared by the diving suit, there is a potential ambiguity present.
36	Barry	It's only full of air so he can breathe.	The reference here is entirely ambiguous As in normal conversation, however, the ambiguity does not in the least check the exchange.
37	Graham	No, it, it keeps, it stops the er . . .	Graham must be attributing a meaning to Barry's 'it' since he begins to contradict the statement, but whether he himself is referring to space suit or diving suit remains as indeterminate to us as to the other two boys (unless we look at his later attempt at 40).
38	Alec	There's so much pressure when he gets down.	Here we apply our knowledge retrospectively. 'When he gets down' must (we say) mean into the depths of the sea, so Alec (who here speaks for the first time) has identified the 'it' of the two preceding utterances as the diving suit.
39	Barry	Yeah.	Barry now adds his support to this identification that is now taking shape.
40	Graham	It stops, it stops it.	Graham has now abandoned 'it' = space suit, and tacitly accepts the alternative identification. He also introduces a second referent for 'it', and we use our tacit knowledge to identify this as the pressure in the depths of the sea.
41	Barry	I wonder how fish and all them survive down there then.	This tacit identification is used by Barry as a springboard for a venture into a new topic.

What these boys mean, how they interpret each other, and the linguistic evidence for such meanings and interpretations, are integrated in a perceptive and modest account (Barnes and Todd, 1977, pp. 97–8). Indeed, throughout their book, Barnes and Todd show a high level of sensitivity towards the task of 'reading' meanings from a purely verbal record (although the ethnomethodologists whose work we reviewed in the previous chapter would be sceptical about how far statements about what participants 'must' have meant are 'warranted' by the textual analysis). That general task is made all the more problematical for the analyst by the advantages which obliqueness and indeterminacy of meaning hold for the participants. Ambiguity does not impede talk. On the contrary, and over stretches of discourse much longer than the extract we quoted, its presence can seem positively functional. It can allow talk to proceed without the interminable wrangling that would ensue if every nuance had to be clarified. As we argued earlier, talk is not based upon literal precision step by step, but upon interpretation (often provisional or retrospective) of linguistic and other signals intimately related to context. The analyst's task is to infer what was meant from what was said. And in the studies considered in this chapter, discourse and its organization represent the best available evidence. Despite all the problems of recreating the relevant context, the linguistic record is held to be the necessary starting-point.

Differences within this orientation can be understood by reference to the general problems which our brief extract has illustrated. Some researchers ground their analyses in exhaustive and exclusive attention to the transcribed text. Others, more conscious of the untidiness that typifies talk and of all the uncertainties in their own understanding of it, offer their insights (like Barnes and Todd, 1977) with a preference for a less 'scientific', more literary approach towards the complex, irregular relationships between linguistic forms and their illocutionary force. From the range of work referred to, we hope to show what can be achieved at different levels of technicality, and at different levels of confidence in discourse as evidence.

The central problem, then, concerns the relationship between the forms of speech used and the work these perform in the discourse — and hence in interaction and learning. Different solutions to the problem yield very different analytical practices. These turn on the degree to which discourse is perceived as regularly patterned — that is, governed by rules with the power to predict form-function relationships. Are these relationships constant? Are given forms (for example, utterances including modals such as 'would' and 'might') reliably associated with a limited set of functions, such as the indication of provisionality and doubt? How constantly are interrogatives related to questioning? The more stable these relationships are, the more predictably they function as 'markers', the easier it will seem to 'read off' social and cognitive meanings from transcripts subjected to thorough structural analysis. The less stable they are, the analyst must either have recourse to some of the other strategies for reducing ambiguities described in the previous chapter, or simply accept the caution in interpretation which the data dictates.

Answers to this problem can of course lead away from a linguistic orientation. Levinson's conclusions (1983, p. 291) — that 'it is impossible to specify in advance what kinds of behavioural units carry major interactional acts', and that 'there is simply no form-to-force correlation' —

might well point towards the more sociological brands of sociolinguistics or towards ethnographies of communication. On the other hand, Stubbs' views that 'people do not talk as enigmatically as speech act theory implies', and that speakers often signal the organization and illocutionary force of their utterances in overt ways', would encourage greater confidence in the clarity with which cognitive and interpersonal strategies are displayed in the forms of discourse 'normal' to different contexts.

2 'Normal' Classroom Discourse

> With . . . many . . . problems inherent in conversation we decided to begin again with a more simple type of spoken discourse, one which has much more overt structure, where one participant has acknowledged responsibility for the direction of the discourse, for deciding who shall speak when, and for introducing topics. We also wanted a situation where all participants were genuinely trying to communicate and where potentially ambiguous utterances were likely to have one accepted meaning. We found the kind of situation in the classroom (Sinclair and Coulthard, 1975, p. 6).

In these terms, the authors of a key study of classroom discourse explained their choice of setting. The research team (from the English Department of Birmingham University) were not educationists but linguists. Their particular project was 'one stage in a continuing investigation of language function and the organization of linguistic units above the rank of clause'. Their work was primarily intended, not to throw light on strategies of teaching and learning, but to provide linguistics with an impetus and a preliminary model for the systematic study of discourse. Indeed, the group itself went on to work in less 'overtly' (or differently) structured settings (Coulthard and Montgomery, 1981). At the outset, however, classrooms were chosen as being likely to give rise to tidier, more visible, patterning. Even then, the researchers deliberately sought out a particular kind of classroom, where 'the teacher was at the front "teaching" and therefore likely to be exerting the maximum amount of control over the structure of the discourse' (Sinclair and Coulthard, 1975, p. 6). We referred in chapter 2 to the danger that researchers may reinforce too narrow a view of normality if they avoid the more unconventional classrooms as being too difficult for their available methods of recording or analysis. But here there were good theoretical grounds for the deliberate restriction of view. Our own concern is to describe and comment on the analytical scheme which was devised rather than to report the conclusions which led from it.

Like the schedules developed by systematic classroom observers, that scheme was intended to be usable in other classrooms, including classrooms significantly different in organization. Unlike them, of course, its categories were derived from retrospective analysis of recorded data, not brought in ready-made. Thus, while the classification scheme did reflect theory developed from (or grounded in) the problems of coping with all the data obtained from the six twenty-minute lessons recorded, it was recognized that its application elsewhere might well require its modification and expansion. It was unlike them too in the comprehensiveness of the coverage. There was to be no sampling; 'the whole of the data should be describable' and no item defeat the scheme's capacity to classify it.

A further contrast with systematic observation arises from the objective of providing a linguistic rather than a quantitative account, an objective which derives from that view of language as social action which we have already discussed at length. Emphasis upon speech acts is evident in the scheme, where 'act' describes the smallest unit identified. It is also evident in the explicit distinction made between the three important discourse acts of 'informative', 'elicitation' and 'directive', and the conventional notions of statement, question and command.

> 'While elicitations are always realized by questions, directives by commands, and informatives by statements, the relationship is not reciprocal: questions can realize many other acts . . . Statements, questions and commands are only informatives, elicitations and directives when they are initiating . . .' (*op. cit.*, p. 34).

The analysis is thus enabled to capture a measure of indirectness in the discourse. It does so by reference forwards or backwards in the sequence to which the given utterance belongs, and to the force attributed to it by other speakers, for example —

T   How many times have I told you that?
P   Sorry, sir (the response 'three' being inappropriate, and probably subversive enough in intent to elicit a response something like — 'Are you trying to be funny').

It might still be asked how such an analysis might distinguish between a tease and a reproof in such cases, or identify the severity of a reproof, especially where the participants themselves seem uncertain. (A nice example is cited where a pupil mistakes a genuine teacher-question — 'Why are you laughing?' — for a rebuke). In the original study, solutions would have been sought through replaying the critical sequence in the audiotape. More recent work refers to systematic analysis of intonation, a matter which 'sooner rather than later . . . is found to be quite crucial in determining what a teacher or pupil . . . does' (Sinclair and Brazil, 1982, p. 92).

A final difference from systematic observation consists in the preparedness to admit situational data to the analysis. Situation is first invoked to handle that frequent 'lack of fit' between discourse categories and grammatical categories which we have discussed. We also commented in earlier chapters that indirectness is a salient feature of classroom talk because of its function in softening the tone of teachers' control by (for example) giving commands the form of questions ('Are you listening?'), or requests ('Would you please listen to me?'), or statements ('Someone is being very silly'). Thus 'Can you shut the door?', 'The door is still open', 'Shut the door', and (even) 'The door', are all possible discourse directives even though only one is grammatically an imperative.

Situation is defined as including 'all relevant factors in the environment, social conventions and the shared experience of the participants' which serve to 'reclassify items as statement, question or command' where they appear not to be so grammatically (Sinclair and Coulthard, 1975, pp. 28 and 33). That definition is clearly vulnerable to the criticism of creating a conveniently unspecified dumping ground for anything thought relevant to explicating the talk. But it is complemented by a notion of 'tactics' to refer to the way in which, for instance, utterances may be redesignated by the speakers as the discourse proceeds. Then discourse function may only appear to be at odds with the grammatical forms until the whole sequence is scanned. In the following teacher-utterance, the (grammatical) interrogative and declarative which precede the final (discourse) elicitation are seen in the sequence to be tactically a 'starter' act:

T   What about this one? This, I think, is a super one. Isobel, can you think what it means?

The suggestion is that teachers often begin with a question-elicitation, but change their minds and relegate the initial item to a 'starter', as part of an opening move (embracing both starter and elicitation acts). There is clearly some common ground here with the analysis of the function of 'pre-formulations' in question sequences with which we ended the previous chapter.

Intuitively, such modifications in speaker-intention seem very likely to figure in teacher-talk. Equally likely, however, are sequences in which the use of starter acts is routine. For distinguishing these from ones involving a change of mind, a predominantly text-based approach may seem less intuitively reliable. Or again, how could even a sequence of text reveal instances where the teacher's initial utterance is deliberately indeterminate, a time-gaining gambit? We recall how Barnes and Todd indicated the retrospective resolution of ambiguity. A teacher may also begin ambiguously and then wait to see whether the first part of the utterance is indeed treated as a question, thereby allowing its function to be defined by the other participants. Such negotiation of meaning is not reflected in Sinclair and Coulthard's scheme. Indeed, as we have seen, their choice of traditional transmission teaching was largely designed to preclude it.

It has been taken up by Burton (1980), however, who recognizes in her deliberate choice of less formal contexts features of talk which challenge or even defy analysis by what she calls 'collaborative-consensus' schemes of the kind now under discussion. Early analyses of discourse do assume 'all participants . . . genuinely trying to communicate' by the rules of the teacher's game. Yet that assumption is certainly counter-intuitive, and is challenged by a great deal of classroom research (for example, Woods, 1990; Pollard, 1984b). Pupils do not just 'avoid initiating', as Sinclair and Coulthard suggest; they are more often engaged in their own strategies, sometimes complying just enough to avoid trouble, sometimes initiating by 'testing out' the teacher, or pursuing their own inter-pupil communicative activity in pursuit of opportunities for 'having a laugh'.

In expressing these reservations, we do not wish to underestimate the merits of discourse analysis, especially in comparison with systematic observation. Indeed, we want now to emphasize a further relative advantage associated with the explicitly hierarchical organization of the analysis which derives from its linguistic roots. For it is common in linguistics for units at a given level to be combined to form others at a superior one (for example, morphemes into words). Sinclair and Coulthard adapted a rank scale from Halliday's (1961) work, and claim that it gave them the flexibility to expand their scheme whenever the need for another rank became apparent. It can be stated in simplified form:-

Rank 1	Lesson	unordered series of transactions; a social rather than a linguistic unit
Rank 2	Transaction	two classes of exchange, boundary and teaching
Rank 3	Exchange	(boundary) — framing and focusing moves (teaching) — opening, answering and follow-up moves
Rank 4	Moves	framing, focusing, opening, answering, follow up — all classes of act
Rank 5	Acts	by definition, these have no sub-classes; in the analysis of recorded lessons, 22 of these were needed to accommodate the talk.

An illustration of the scheme in action can now be provided:-

Exchanges			Moves	Acts
	T	Now,	Framing	Marker
		let me test your brains		
Boundary		Let me see if you can think of the materials that I'm going to ask you about	Focusing	Meta-statement
		If your Mummy was going to make you a frock,		
Teaching		what material would she use?	Opening	Elicitation
		Hands up		Cue
	P	(Non-verbal response)		Bid
	T	Marie		Nomination
	P	Cloth	Answering	Reply
	T	Good girl	Follow-up	Evaluate

(adapted from Sinclair and Coulthard, 1975, pp. 104–5)

Boundary exchanges may be composed of a framing move alone, though here they form a typical sequence. Within them, marker acts can be realized from a narrow set of utterances, such as 'Right', 'OK then', and 'Now', as teachers' everyday knowledge will confirm. The frequency of meta-statements in teacher discourse (that is, statements about what is being talked about) is not surprising, given the teacher's responsibility both for managing the interaction and defining knowledge. The kind of teaching exchange which we have just cited is very common indeed. It begins with a pseudo-question, and manifests the teacher's maintenance of control, both of turn-taking and topic. It also illustrates those evaluative rights of teachers (or responsibilities, in Sinclair and Coulthard's view) which are central to validating the curriculum and defining competent membership of the class through demonstrating acceptable forms of participation and expression. As we have noted in earlier chapters, it is a type of exchange which has been strongly challenged because of its persistence and pervasiveness. Thus Young (1984) notes an overwhelming tendency in such exchanges for pupils to be obliged to respond within the teacher's epistemological frame of reference and at the teacher's bidding. They are thereby excluded from posing their own validity questions, and make themselves acquiescent collaborators or partners in a process of 'indoctrination'. Young's ironic observations provoke questions about how and why so much teaching seems to be trapped in this mould.

In the extract above, the three-move exchange has embedded within it the routine sequence in which the teacher invites bids to respond, and then nominates the next speaker. It is a routine critical to that direction of turn-taking which we described, from a different research perspective, in the previous chapter. Such routines are not always so simple, of course, and often involve strategies for ignoring or correcting pupil moves which are judged to infringe interactional proprieties. They can also be characterized by inconsistency in both teachers' and pupils' adherence to the rules, as well as by changes in the rules themselves.

The exchanges to which these embedded elements belong often chain together to form lengthy transactions. The insight that each such exchange, with or without embeddings, should be regarded as a single entity is surely valuable. And, as Sinclair and Coulthard point out, the evaluative component may well be implicit, or even non-verbal; the teacher, by proceeding to the next question, may thereby imply satisfaction with the last answer, while a nod or smile or raised eyebrow may also constitute an effective judgment. The evaluation is so closely related to both question and response that treating the three moves as one sequence seems more intuitively acceptable than to treat them as overlapping 'adjacency-pairs' (Mehan, 1978). And while Mehan is justified in observing that the 'tying' of elements is strongest between question and response because that determines the nature of the evaluative move, we also suggested earlier that classroom questioning is unusual in the frequency and force with which the respondent's attention is focused on the move which follows.

The discussion of questions and questioning, which has been a recurrent theme in the two previous chapters, can gain clarity from its association with this linguistic perspective. The light which such work has shed upon the three-move exchange of initiation-reply-evaluation (or I-R-E) has not only revealed an exceptionally prevalent feature of classroom discourse but also provided a theoretical framework of enormous practical value to researchers working at different phases of schooling and with a range of subject-disciplines. Studies of reception-classes (Willes, 1983), even of nursery and reception classes (Hughes and Westgate, 1988; 1990), reveal how early in their school lives pupils have to adapt to such patterns of communication and with what implications for their development. Positive arguments for overcoming the limitations of I-R-E-dominated discourse have been offered in the context of the US elementary school (Cazden, 1988), and demonstration of those possibilities have been made powerfully available by Edwards and Mercer (1987) working mostly in English upper primary and middle schools.

Among the first to recognize I-R-E as the 'essential teaching exchange' was Mehan (for example 1979 a+b), who calculated that they constituted over half of the total interactions in the nine lessons he recorded and then analyzed in such detail. Cazden, the teacher involved, has subsequently (and on return to her professorial post at Harvard) taken the analysis beyond questions and I-R-E (1988), while accepting without modification Mehan's analysis of the 'structure and structuring' of her lessons. She also gives examples, in her own and others' teaching, of pupil-pupil discourse, according it a justifiable role on the grounds that: 'The only context in which children can reverse interactional roles with the same intellectual content, giving directions as well as following them, and asking questions as well as answering them, is with their peers' (p. 134). She also identifies certain, more open-ended kinds of teacher-pupil talk as 'scaffolding' pupils' development. There is thus common ground between Cazden's work and that of Edwards and Mercer (1987) who share the starting-point in classroom discourse and attempt to unravel its pedagogic consequences. Both represent a 'constructivist' view of knowledge; that is, of learning and knowing as jointly developed processes susceptible to qualitative judgment, rather than as a simply assessable state of fact-possession gained, for example, by rote.

From that perspective, Edwards and Mercer (1987) distinguish clearly between the kinds of teacher-pupil talk through which meanings are constructed or refined and what they refer to as 'cued elicitation'. This much-used strategy embraces such processes as preformulation, re-formulation, prompts, clues, etc., which have been described previously. They are given salience again here because teacher-directed talk of this kind can present an appearance of knowledge and understanding being elicited from pupils rather than being imposed by the teacher: as it were, a subterfuge, unmasked by analysis of teacher-pupil discourse. In that light, a familiar theme re-emerges so that, for Edwards and Mercer, classroom education often looks much more like socialization, an inculcation of pupils into a predetermined culture of educated knowledge and practice, than some unfolding development of individual cognition.

Their view accords with observations made from the same perspective in early-years classrooms, where a strong 'pedagogic agenda' (Hughes and Westgate, 1988) appears to lead teachers often to conduct 'mini-lessons' when intervening in pupils' activities and talk. Immediately putting questions from their own stand-point, those teachers leave little room for pupils to express their conceptualizations; they sometimes even spread confusion which a more conversational kind of comment might well avoid. In a more general primary context, Galton (1990) similarly finds teachers, who doubtless intending otherwise, habitually 'reconceptualize' or 'recontextualize' their pupils' contributions. What the teacher means as guidance (or scaffolding) is thus often perceived as a cognitive take-over. Galton cites one perceptive child: 'I think the teacher wants to put her view into what you are thinking which might change your mind about something. You know, instead of keeping to your own idea' (p. 23).

With more single-minded attention to questions, Dillon (1981; 1982; 1988; 1990) offers perhaps the most devastating critique of this pedagogic strategy. He has argued that the supposition that so-called higher-order questions stimulate higher levels of pupil thinking has no empirical basis in studies of the consequences of questioning. Indeed, evidence gathered from the discourse of other professions would point in the opposite direction from traditional practices in education (Dillon 1982). Social-survey interviewers, counsellors and lawyers in courtrooms all tend to use questions when they want their respondents to be brief and non-thoughtful. They use other tactics (for example, silence or declarative comment) when they wish to promote longer or more considered responses.

In his later work (for example, 1988) Dillon has addressed teachers directly, with the continuing aim of challenging persistent assumptions about the nature and value of questioning, and of helping teachers to understand the extent to which issues of teaching and learning depend on who is doing the asking. For this reason, questions from students are (quite exceptionally) taken first: Dillon maintains that 'when students ask, learning follows the answers' (1988, pp. 9–10). In normal classrooms, however, there is little room for pupils' own questions because they are too busy answering. Dillon's survey of 27 lessons showed 80 teacher-questions per hour as against 2 per hour from all students combined, even though the topics of these lessons appeared to include ones — for instance: capital punishment, divorce, child custody and sex — on which students might reasonably have been expected to have something to say or ask about. He goes on to offer, in an I-R-E framework, a persuasive explanation of why students ask so few questions. To be an asker, they must first locate a potential juncture, make a bid, gain the floor, quite possibly change the topic, and have the topic accepted as relevant. They also have to risk displaying ignorance ('You should know the answer to that by now') or being put off ('Can we come back to that later?') or even — a point Dillon might have stressed but does not — face peer comment for daring to show an interest.

His advice to teachers (1988) is to be aware of how habitual teaching methods work against pupil-questions and so deliberately to leave room for them, encourage them, welcome them, and (hardest of all) remain silent after a student has spoken. In Chapters 4 and 5, he distinguishes sharply between the contribution of teachers' questions to Recitation teaching and to Discussion. Under the former heading he includes both the 'guided discovery' and 'Socratic' approaches, as these similarly entail pursuit of a teacher-defined conclusion as well as a form of discourse in which the teacher speaks in questions and evaluations and the pupils speak in answers. The following extract illustrates, by contrast, Dillon's notion of Discussion.

T	The treatment that Louis XIV gave to the Huguenots is anything but acceptable, and yet some people say that he was justified in his treatment of the Huguenots, in respect to the point that he was trying to take care of his country. Do you feel that Louis was justified in his treatment of the Huguenots? — Rosa.
Rosa	I think, you know, they had their religion and stuff like that. I don't think he should have gone as far as totally kicking them out of the country and giving them, like, social disgrace, you know, like taking their jobs away from them. If they wouldn't interfere with his way of ruling, and their religion, why should he interfere with them? [T: Ken.]
Ken	He's partially right in what he did, but I don't feel he should've kicked them out, like she said. 'Cause who is he to say how they can — you know? Even though it's all Catholics, he gave 'em, like, religious freedom. [T: Barb.]
Barb	I feel, I feel that he had hardly any justification at all. He wound up at the end, as Lydia said, having to almost be persuaded by all the people around him that were saying, 'Well, look at the Huguenots.' You know, 'Why don't you do something about the Huguenots? We don't like the Huguenots.' [continues] It was one of the last places that he had to conquer, so he figured he'd just go out and then kill 'em. I think it was totally unfair.
T	OK, I can see where you're coming from, but I don't know

if I can totally agree with that. Is there anyone who disagrees with what these people are saying? — Marty.

Marty   I don't really disagree, but you know, we know the story, how everything worked out. [continues] They wanted to get rid of the Huguenots. And just like that, you know, us here, we don't like somebody, like, you know, Italians and Nazis — sorta the same thing, something like that, in their eyes. I don't think he was justified himself. [T: Diane.]

Diane   OK, in those days the church and state were like the same thing and everything, and so I think, well, like Louis — well, it isn't like today, when you can be a member of a country, just a member of a country. In those days, the church and the country meant the same thing, and when he saw people breaking away from the church, then he thought that they were breaking away from him. And he wanted to stop it. That was about the only thing he could do.

T   So you feel that he was justified in what he was doing, as far as he was concerned — he could justify it to himself.

Diane   Yeah, he could justify it to himself. But then, before then they really didn't have a separation. So all he could see was an allegory. And he wanted to pull back on that.

T   All right, Marty raised an interesting point just a few seconds ago. He said that [continues about Communists and Nazis in Chicago]. It's getting away from France, but again it's speaking about the same idea — acceptance of groups that are going against the norms of your society. What's your opinion on groups of this type? Should they be allowed, should they be censored, should it be washed over, should there be guidelines, stipulations — should there be control like Louis XIV tried to control them, to be done away with? — Julie.

Julie   I think that they should be allowed to speak their opinion, because [continues]. But they should be allowed to speak their opinion, you don't have to listen. [T: OK, Sean.]

Sean   I think Marty was wrong, because [continues]. Look what they did like, back I think in the 50s with the Communists, and McCarthy, and then during World War II with the Japanese. So, it's still going on today.

T   Right, and the concentration camps which we have had inside the United States during World War II, to house Japanese-Americans because you couldn't trust the Japanese. All right, so he's totally disagreeing with what you had to say, Marty.

Marty   Yeah, well — No, he brought up a good point. [continues] But I mean, I don't think Thomas Jefferson and those guys who signed the Constitution would like Nazis around here. Especially after what they did. I think that's why —

Steve   They come over here from another country for three months and they earn a ADC [welfare] check! My parents have been working for 25 some odd years, and they're not getting half the money that [ethnic epithet] are getting nowadays.

T   Yes, we know [continues].

(1988, pp. 120–21)

Here, the teacher is not taking every other turn and does not always speak in questions; the students' turns are longer than in Recitation, often referring to other students. In a subsequent publication, Dillon (1990) returns to this contextual distinction, as well as to respective features and their frequency of occurrence. He notes, for instance, that: 'After a student answers in recitation, we always hear right/wrong . . . and always from the teacher. In discussion, we hear agree/disagree, and we hear it from a student and/or the teacher' (p. 13). Comparing two brief extracts from history classes in the same school, involving students of similar ability, he finds teacher-talk contributing 69 per cent to the recitation context, as against 22 per cent to the discussion. Other features are tabulated as follows:

	Recitation	Discussion
% of question turns	78	11
% of teacher-student turns	88	6
% of student-student turns	12	94
% of students participating	41	77
Exchanges per minute	6	1
Average student utterance	4 seconds	25 seconds

While so much attention has been directed to classifying questions and their functions, surprisingly little has been paid to the parallel area of instructional discourse — that of explanations. Early studies drew more on logic than linguistics (for example, Smith and Meux, 1970). Martin (1970), however, pointed the way to a more interactional frame of reference, recognizing that to explain is not just to order arguments, but to make connections with the existing knowledge and understanding of those to whom the explanation is addressed. Using transcriptions principally of biology lessons, and analytical concepts in the same tradition as Sinclair and Coulthard, Brown and Armstrong (1978, 1984) developed a System for Analyzing Instructional Discourse (SAID) which can be applied to lessons which are 'expository' rather than 'discussion-centred'. Lessons are analyzed at five levels, in descending order of complexity

— keys, episodes, exchanges, moves and elements.

The 'keys' represent major sections of the discourse, usually turning upon a single, central question (for example, 'How does the amount of food affect the animals?'), and containing a series of episodes. Within each episode, three main kinds of exchange may be found — structuring, social, and teaching. It is the teaching exchange which was the researchers' particular concern, and which are further classified by both teaching mode and cognitive demand. Their constituent moves and elements were then examined in relation to independent measures of learning outcome so that specific features associated with 'good' or 'poor' explaining could be identified.

In the table, the starred items were found to appear more frequently in 'good' lessons:-

Elements in Moves

Structural elements	Teaching elements	Social elements
markers (now, well, OK etc)*	rephrasing*	hesitations
	explaining links*	stumbles
silence* (1)	visual aids*	
	blackboards*	
	definitions*	personal references*
	rhetorical questions	verbal mannerisms*
	multiple questions	incomplete sentences*
	inappropriate vocabulary	praise
	vagueness	chiding

(1) — though silences in the middle of 'teacher informs' were associated with 'poor' explaining' (Brown and Armstrong, 1978, p. 36)

Behind this work lie the related assumptions that some knowledge is better explained by the teacher than presented through quasi-discussion, and that the 'prime purpose of teaching' is to 'help children to learn and think'. The degree to which linguistically-oriented studies such as those considered in this present chapter can capture processes of thought beneath the discourse is a central and recurring theme. Significantly, the metalanguage which Brown and Armstrong develop to present it derives not just from linguistics, but from 'logic, psychology . . . pedagogy and everyday English as well' (1978, p. 40). In this broadening out, it is typical of other studies which have acknowledged a debt to Sinclair and Coulthard, but modified their original classification scheme in relation to the rather different questions being asked of the recorded data, or used it mainly as a starting point. To a large extent, this may be because of the highly technical (and highly time-consuming) nature of the analysis, especially if it is extended to include the fine details of intonational markers of meaning with which Sinclair and Brazil (1982) complicate matters still further. Nevertheless, the close, comprehensive analysis of discourse has opened up important aspects of the relationships between interaction, discourse and learning. Like the conversational approach examined in the previous chapter, it has provided a valuable 'alienation device', as Burton (1980) has called it — a way of making the familiar strange by forcing the observer to see everyday events in a new and analytical way. At the level of investigative theory, the distinctive contribution lies in the attempt to locate and categorize linguistic markers for interactional processes, thereby establishing a more reliable basis than what seems subjectively interesting on which to select relevant evidence.

As already hinted at, critics of discourse analysis (and some would-be users) find its very 'linguisticism' too constraining. The perspective of language-as-social action may seem little different from that of language-as-part-of-social action, yet the emphases are important. Can linguistics, or any other single discipline, unravel problems which seem to require much more general theories of human action? In comparable fields such as language development, the contribution of linguistics itself has become more valuable as the subject itself has become more broadly conceived — or, in Hymes' (1977) approving definition, more 'socially-constituted'. The work reported in Donaldson (1978), Garnica and King (1979), and Cook-Gumperz (1985) are excellent examples of this. The initial firmly linguistic orientation of Sinclair and Coulthard has itself broadened from within. Other investigations of classroom discourse have come to include a much more dynamic view of situational influences (Mehan, 1979a; Green, 1983; Cazden 1988), greater acknowledgement of the frequently multifunctional nature of utterances (Barnes and Todd, 1977) as part of the endlessly complex relationships between linguistic forms and their functions, greater attention to the interplay of cultural meanings in multicultural classrooms (Erickson and Mohatt, 1982; Heath, 1982; Ainsworth, 1984) and to contrasts and continuities in children's experience of discourse in different settings (Wells, 1987, 1985a). If the 1975 study now appears somewhat limited in its view of both discourse and classrooms, its success in highlighting some of the important features of 'normal' classrooms serves to underline how limited and limiting such classrooms can be in the options they normally make available to pupils.

3 Competence in the Classroom

Applied to a classroom, communicative competence includes not just speech used for teacher purposes, but also that used for student purposes (Lazarus, 1984, p. 225).

It will be apparent from our two previous chapters that study of classroom talk was marked, at least until the mid-1970s, by a preoccupation with teacher-performance and teacher-led interaction. Lazarus is one of many researchers who have redirected interest towards the communicative skills of children and adolescents. Under this heading comes a range of topics. These include assessment of the communicative and interactional demands typically made on pupils; identification of the situationally-appropriate skills and strategies which constitute competent membership of the classroom community; and the developmental opportunities and limitations which characterize classrooms as communicative environments. The investigation of these topics by sociolinguists was a main theme in the previous chapter, our emphasis being on broadly ethnographic studies in and around multi-cultural classrooms. We return to them now from a more linguistic per-spective, focusing again on the 'situational constraints on pupil communication which seem evident in so much recorded classroom talk.

Consider, for instance, the following two extracts from the closing stages of the same French lesson. Both are coded in a modified form of that described in the previous section to show who is initiating, responding and evaluating. The pupils are thirteen-fourteen years old. Debbie and Emma have just performed a dialogue for the whole class and are now having it constructively citicized (Westgate *et al*, 1985, pp. 274–5). The moves are coded here as follows —

    I   Teacher's initiation or invitation to respond
    R   Pupil's response
    E   Teacher's evaluation
    [R] Implicit or non-verbal response

Arrows indicate moves linked within a single conversational turn.

Extract I

Speaker	Text	Contextual notes	Moves
T	. . . When Emma was making the suggestions about peut-être qu'il est dans sa chambre, what could you have nicely said? . . . Well, whoever said it. What could they have said?	Emma silently denies authorship. Points at Nicholas, accepts offer.	I [R] I
Nicholas	D'accord.		R
T	Nn,nn . . . something that I mentioned to you earlier on. Well, there was d'accord, yeah, but there was something else. You told me . . .	Points at Michael who looks puzzled.	E ↓ I
Michael	Allons voir.		R
T	Right. Yes. Again, tell them again, Michael.		E → I
Michael	Allons voir.		R
T	Allons voir. Meaning?		E → I
Michael	Let's go and see.		R
T	Let's go and see. I think that would have enhanced yours if . . . (etc)	To Debbie and Emma.	E → . . .

Extract 2

Speaker	Text	Contextual notes	Moves
T	Right. According to me the bell's gone, but it hasn't.	Checks watch.	I
Derek	It's late.		[P]I
T	So how about, until it does, a quick game of buzz.		I
Voices	(excited chatter)	Some query about	[R]
Dawn	Buzz?	buzz included.	[P]I
T	Buzz! You mean to say this is the one class we haven't played buzz with?		[T]R ↓ I
Voices	Yeah, etc.		R
T	Well naturally, French buzz.		I
Voice	Oh . . . buzz etc.		R
T	Er, do you people along there know how to play buzz?		I
Voices	(conflicting responses)		[R]
Debbie	D— doesn't.	= Pupils from D—	[P]I
T	D— doesn't. Right . . . ah, D— saved by the bell! Right, D—, next time I'm going to tell you how to play buzz. It's really good fun.	Middle School. Bell rings.	[T]R ↓ I
Voices	(indistinct)	Includes some comment	[R] + [P]I
T	What?	from Derek. To Derek.	[T]R → I
Derek	D— saved the day.		R
T	D— saved the day, they certainly did . . . Make sure you've got your exercise books on you next time, please, so we can get this thing written down. Right.	Grins.	[T]R → E → I
Debbie	Can D— go now?		[P]I
Voice	We're all R— now.		[P]I
T	No. Yes. That's just what I was going to say. You're not D— anymore.		[T]R
Debbie	Shame.		[P]I
T	You're R— now. You're part of the greater thing.	= members of R— High School.	I
Debbie	I'd like to go back there.		[P]I
T	Would you?		[T]R/I
Debbie	The work's easier, we didn't do them dialogues.		[P]I
T	Tut.	Smiles.	[T]R/E
Dawn	You did.		[P]I
Gillian	Ah, you did. But it was harder than that last year.		[P]I
Voices	(chatter)		[[P]I]
T	She said it was harder last year.	To whole class;	[T]R → I
Dawn	It was harder . . . with Mrs M—, yeah.	pats G's head.	R → [P]I
Voices	(chatter)		[[P]I]
T	All right, never mind discussing the relative merits of all the teachers you've had, 'cos I don't really want this.		E ↓ I
Gillian	We're only chatting because we've got Maths next.		[P]I

In the first extract we see no pupil initiations. Responses are focused by the Teacher's purpose. In the second, just five minutes later, we see a markedly different pattern. Of the twenty pupil entries, fifteen are broadly initating moves, and the teacher is three times denied her normally alternate turn. (The symbols [P]I and [T]R are used to mark respectively pupil-initiations and teacher responses.)

Unsure of whether the end of the lesson has been signalled, the teacher relinquishes her pedagogic intentions, whereupon those of the pupils seem to bubble to the surface and generate a hitherto unseen interactional competence. It is this disjunction between the 'normal' and possible verbal interplay in classrooms which highlights the highly specific demands of the usual contexts in which pupils are taught and the constraints which these impose.

Within the more linguistically-oriented approaches to communicative competence which are our concern in this chapter, two related strands have been especially valuable. We shall call them the linguistic-pedagogic and the linguistic-developmental.

The first emerges clearly from evaluations of so much classroom interaction as being limited and limiting. Its 'ur-text' might be chosen as Barnes' (1976) statement that—

> Since the social functions of language go on simultaneously with the making of meanings, we have to consider how the two sets of functions interact. One would expect that the characteristics of each social context would limit the possibility of using language for the making of meanings . . . Expectations set up in a classroom, and more generally in a school, constrain . . . the pupils' participation in learning (p. 32).

Once the importance of 'talking to learn' was recognized, studies of classroom discourse pointed towards the need for pedagogic innovation and experiment, and also towards methods by which these could be monitored. If what Barnes called 'exploratory talk' was to become a more frequent and substantial part of pupils' classroom communication, then conventional classroom structures would have to change through an extension of the repertoire of learning contexts set up for them. Among these, teacher-less group-talk might be tried at appropriate stages in a sequence of experience (for example, after initial presentation of concepts but before written work was demanded). But how should such discussion be planned, integrated and conducted? How effective could it be, both intellectually and in terms of developing communicative competence? And how could teachers be persuaded that such occasions were not, simply, a waste of valuable instructional time? Barnes and Todd (1977) set out to consider such questions. Their conclusions are as relevant methodologically to the analysis of discourse as they are educationally to the promotion and management of learning through talk.

They expected to be able to show that temporarily passing control of the talk to pupils would make available (or at least possible) a 'wider range of speech roles'. These would include 'hypothesis-forming and testing, and the ability to go beyond the given information and to generate new questions and tasks' (p. 3). These expectations were largely fulfilled, though less so in an attempted second phase of recordings. In that second phase, the researchers were far more constrained by time and other factors, were not able to allow the nature of the task to determine the length of the discussions, and could not integrate the second set of tasks as carefully into the teachers' own lesson-planning nor give the pupils taking part as much explanation and 'sense of audience'. These facts are useful reminders of the sensitivity of talk to influences of many kinds. Nevertheless, among the first small groups of thirteen-year olds, there was often displayed a remarkable degree of collaboration and sense of purpose, as well as a range of social and cognitive skills.

There is a two-level analysis, distinguishing discourse moves and their associated logical processes (Level 1) from underlying abilities for managing interaction and content (Level 2). It is thus a performance-competence analysis. The following table summarizes what its authors believed they had recorded.

Social and cognitive functions of conversation

LEVEL ONE

1   Discourse Moves —
    (a)   Initiating
    (b)   Extending — Qualifying, Contradicting
    (c)   Eliciting — Continue, Expand, Bring in, Support, Information
    (d)   Responding — Accepting

2   Logical Process —
    (a)   proposes a cause   (b)   proposes a result
    (c)   expands loosely (for example, gives descriptive details)
    (d)   applies a principle to a case   (e)   categorizes
    (f)   states conditions under which a statement is valid or invalid
    (g)   advances evidence   (h)   negates   (i)   evaluates
    (j)   puts alternative view
    (k)   suggests a method   (l)   restates in different terms

LEVEL TWO

3   Social Skills

(a)	Progress through task	Given questions, shifting topic, ending a discussion, managing manipulator tasks
(b)	Competition and conflict	Competition for the floor, contradiction, joking, compelling participation
(c)	Supportive behaviour	Explicit agreement, naming, reference

back, explicit approval of others, expression of shared feeling

4 Cognitive Strategies
    (a) Constructing the question   (closed tasks, open tasks)
    (b) Raising new questions
    (c) Setting up hypotheses   (beyond the given, explicit hypotheses)
    (d) Using evidence   (anecdote, hypothetical cases, using everyday knowledge, challenging generalities)
    (e) Expressing feelings and recreating experience   (expressing ethical judgments, shared recreation of literary experience)

5 Reflexivity
    (a) Monitoring own speech and thought   (own contributions provisional)
    (b) Interrelating alternative viewpoints   (validity to others, more than one possibility, finding overarching principles)
    (c) Evaluating own and others' performance
    (d) Awareness of strategies   (audience for recording, summarizing, moving to new topic)

(Barnes and Todd, 1977, pp. 20–1)

At both levels in this analytical scheme, a further distinction is made between the interactional and the logical (or 'ideational', to use Halliday's antecedent term). The analysis therefore expresses a view of talk in which there is 'simultaneous interplay' between the 'content frames' and the 'interaction frames'; the participants 'say', in effect, 'As I talk to you I tell you what I think, or what I want you to believe I think (content frame), and I also give you evidence of my attitude towards what I think, as well as my view of each of us and our relationship (interaction frame)'. Such explicit integration of content and interaction, logic and discourse seems full of potential for analyzing educational talk — not only, of course, in teacherless settings. It should provide a way of accounting for both the cohesion of the talk (from the attention which speakers pay to what previous speakers have said, including the quoting of words, intonational details and so on), and the coherence of the talk (from the attention paid to the function of previous utterances — for example, giving an answer to a question. It is cohesion and coherence in the sense which Widdowson (1979) defines as complementary aspects of the organized sequence of discourse, and to which we referred in our general discussion in Chapter 1. Barnes and Todd present an example analyzed in this way, which we reproduce in part as an illustration. The reader may find it useful to analyze the transcript on pages 145–7 in a similar way.

	Utterance	Interaction Frame	Content Frame
Barry	All right, if a piece of rock hit a spaceship and made a hole in it, what would happen to the air?	Taking over the gatekeeping role, Barry signals a change of topic, and reads a new question (no. 3).	Although chosen by the teacher, this question has not been discussed before, so is open to interpretation.
	All't air would come rushing out, wouldn't it. Er, all the air would come rushing out.	Answers question, asking for support, but excluding others from the floor.	Assumes sufficient consensus about the content frame implied in question for a brief answer, without any detailed explication to be acceptable.
	⌈What would happen to the spaceman if he stepped out into space without a spacesuit on?	Reads next question (4), still acting as gatekeeper.	This is also open to interpretation.
Alec	Would suck everything ⌊out with it.	Challenges Barry's monopoly of the floor, both speaking at once.	Specifies as relevant to Q. 3 details not mentioned by Barry, so modifying the implicit content frame.
Barry	⌈Oh, He'd he, all his body would explode.	Trying to hold the floor.	Briefly indicates a Frame.
Graham	⌊He'd explode.	Competing for the floor.	Has now accepted move to Q4. Frame so far common with Barry.
Barry	⌈He'd expand wouldn't he? He'd explode.	Competing for the floor.	Adds alternative construction to Frame.
Graham	He'd just explode because erm, he's got pressure from inside the ⌊space ship inside him.	Competing for the floor.	Explicates the Frame he is offering by starting to analyze process.
Barry	Yeah, yeah, he's not he's not used to it really is he?	Weakening his ploy with elements of acknowledgment and appeal.	Explicates part of his Frame.
Graham	⌈Well even so, even if he breathed out or something like that there's	Graham has captured the floor	Implicitly rejects part of Barry's Frame on basis of previous utterance
Barry	⌊Yeah.	Reduced to supporting role	Preparing to accept Graham's frame.
Graham	Still't pressure that he's used to, inside him and there isn't any pressure outside at all, so he gets, he just explodes.	Holds the floor	Continues to expound in detail (without indicating whether its status is hypothetical)
Barry	Yeah . . . How, does a pace, space suit stop it? Is there air inside?	Asks for information, thus implicitly conceding expertise to Graham.	Abandons own Frame and tries to grasp Graham's Frame

(Barnes and Todd, 1977, pp. 104–6)

Barnes and Todd recognize 'failures and limitations' as well as strengths in group talk, both as an educational device and as an activity for analysis. In some of the discussions they recorded, for example, they were able to identify ways in which rivalry and 'competition for the floor' impeded some individual pupils, or in which an exaggerated concern for social harmony and for not offending friends prevented a particular view from being questioned (signs of that second process may be present in the second extract). On other occasions, it appeared that confusion was being compounded in the absence of teacher-inputs, or that learning opportunities were being missed because implicit aspects of the given task were not perceived at all. It is understandable that in a 'linguistic-pedagogic' study such as this, the researchers should wish to offer practical guidance as to how such problems could be minimized. But the guidance is carefully grounded in the evidence which they cite. Moreover, the relative modesty and tentativeness of the analysis enhances its credibility. In particular, their doubts about whether linguistic forms 'should ever be assigned unique functions' leads them to acknowledge the 'many diverse systems of meaning available to members of a speech community', and the consequent limits on researchers' certainties (p. 15).

Subsequent research has returned to the attractions of group talk, and to the inherent difficulties which it presents both to researchers trying to understand its mechanisms and to teachers wishing to harness its potential. Phillips (1985) finds children's perceptions of their peers more conducive to exploratory talk than their perceptions of 'unchallengeable' teachers. This potentially less threatening interaction may make group talk especially appropriate for low-achievers. Certainly the eleven-year old boys whose talk was recorded by Wade and Wood (1980) demonstrated an unexpected variety of purpose and degree of initiative when left to make the running. Difficult questions remain however about how to set up such talk, especially if there is reason to suspect that the most (cognitively) productive discourse strategies may be the least certain to emerge. In Phillips' study, the most 'popular' styles were those which he labelled the 'operational' and the 'argumentative' — the first marked by such discourse-organizing devices as deictics ('this', 'those' etc.), imperatives and forms of running commentary on what was taking place, and the second by direct statements of disagreement ('Yes but . . .'). At the other end of his value-scale, but less spontaneously used, came the 'hypothetical' ('What about the . . .' 'What if . . .') and the 'experiential' ('I remember when . . .' 'You know Mr Smith, well . . .'). The reliability of his markers may be doubtful, but they represent a commonsense set of indicators which teachers might well evaluate and augment.

Evidence allowing evaluation of pupil talk in general, but especially of pupil-pupil talk in small groups, has understandably been much sought after, both by teachers seeking to maximize the value of the talk they promote and by researchers seeking answers to potentially sensitive questions about teaching methods. Groups of teachers working in association with the UK's National Oracy Project have frequently shown interest in Phillips' categories described above, or in variants such as that developed by members of the Wiltshire Oracy Project (1989). The latter's analytical procedures are based on the not-unreasonable assumption that certain cognitive processes deemed to be significant (and probably rare) will be identifiable in the forms of the discourse. Since only a limited set of such 'cognitive functions' of the talk ('speculating', 'making connections' between ideas, etc.) is coded on transcripts, their frequency over time, and in relation to comparable contexts, can be considered indicative of desirable process-features. Similar attempts to identify qualitative aspects of talk itself, within a range of contexts experienced by very young pupils, has been made by Hughes and Westgate (1988; 1990). Modified use of Sinclair and Coulthard's moves and acts can, it is claimed, reveal levels of diversity in communicative functions which the children engage in (and hence aspects of communicative competence being exercised) across various activities; for instance: 'Table-games, which might have been thought likely contexts for collaborative talk, tend rather to produce somewhat elliptical, context-dependent exchanges. On the other hand, activities based on shared imagination have a particular potential for practice and development of communicative skills' (1990, p. 47). An instance of the latter is presented in the following extract recorded in the home corner of a reception class:

p^1	'Where is the ambulance where is the ambulance?'	Initiation of pretence.
p^2	'This is the ambulance yes this is the ambulance 'cos it's called the ambulance.'	Response. (Language reflects pattern of previous initiation.)
p^3	'You got some bandages?'	Initiation.
p^1	'I'll be the doctor.'	Asserting self.
p^4	'You in the ambulance sit down drive you've got a bad feet.'	Extending pretence. Directing.
p^2	'Are you dying?'	Introducing new topic.
p^1	'No.'	Response.
p^3	'I'm the doctor to the patient . . . stay there I'll get some bandages where are the bandages?'	Establishing relationship. Extending pretence.
p^1	'They're in they're up there.'	Collaborating.
p^3	'It's my lunch time.'	Initiating new topic.
p^1	'You're not allowed to stop only when it's dinner time.'	Informing. Reasoning
p^3	'I need the medicine.'	Re-initiation of role play.
p^4	'Hey no that's my box.'	Protecting rights.

p³ 'Can I can I have can I take it   Negotiating.
as well?'

p⁴ 'Yes.'   Collaborating.

p³ 'Oh . . . that's the medicine . . .   Asserting self.
you're not allowed.'

p² 'Sit down in the bit of the   Directing.
hospital don't run.'

p³ 'Open mouth wide ah . . . wide   Extending role play.
. . . all down . . . gone.'

(Hughes and Westgate, 1990, p 42)

In our second strand of competence studies, the 'linguistic-developmental', the main questions are about what children have to learn and do in order to 'become pupils' at all. While there is a natural tendency to focus on the first years of schooling, the skills and knowledge acquired then provide the base (as we argued earlier) for the wide range of specific procedural competence demanded at subsequent stages in the educational enterprise. These are then partly rules-of-the-game studies and partly studies of children's more general sociolinguistic development.

Teachers commonly observe a wide divergence in communication ability among pupils, but how do they account for these differences? The predominant tendency has been to seek explanations in the extent to which children from different social backgrounds bring with them to the classroom the vocabulary, grammar and habits of verbalizing thought which are believed to be necessary for educational success.

Advances in sociolinguistics outlined in chapter 5, and developmental studies of the kinds referred to in the section which follows, have tried to delineate more precisely the skills needed to play the language games typical of classrooms most readily. These skills should not be thought of as a static repertoire brought in from outside, but rather as skills constituted in the process of interaction, and in behaviour validated or sanctioned as it occurs. They are skills which need to be frequently enlarged and adapted to cope with all the shifts between teachers (and within the lessons of the same teacher) which children experience. Thus young children spending most of their time with the same teacher learn to 'read' her moods, interpret apparent inconsistencies, and recognize the often-sudden switches from one set of micro-rules to another ('All right, if you can't co-operate, from now on we'll have everyone put their hands up and no shouting out'). Older children build up expectations of what 'communicative etiquette' to expect in one subject relative to another, as well as extending their knowledge of the fine-grained differences between the talk permissible in (for example) practical work or 'discussion', and that normally allowed in more evidently teacher-centred activities.

The linguistic dimensions of such competence are extensive. Mehan (1979a), for example, whose view of competence broadly coincides with the one so far described, emphasizes both appropriate forms of talk and the skills needed by pupils wishing to enter the talk at appropriate moments and to good effect. So while 'interaction is not isomorphic with speaking', discourse skills are central (p. 132). Mehan's account highlights three particular areas of skill — 'getting the floor', 'holding the floor', and 'introducing news'. The first included the ability to recognize the teacher's initiating moves in all their varied forms, and to locate those junctures (for example, in a series of I-R-E sequences) where a pupil contribution was required or allowed. This in turn involves 'formal' competence skills in 'reading' pausing, intonational, grammatical, non-verbal and other cues. The other skill areas relate to the use made of those entries which are achieved. Many pupil initiatives were simply ignored. Those who successfully held the floor did so by virtue of voice modulation, tone, speed and length of utterance, choice of appropriate words or (of course) through the basic virtue of being 'right'. Introducing 'news' (that is, facts and ideas from outside the teacher's immediate frame of relevance) depended heavily, as we mentioned in an earlier reference to this study, on recognizing the 'joins' between one teacher-controlled sequence and the next within which a pupil initiative could be more readily accommodated.

Wide individual differences in such classroom competence have been identified by Willes (1981b, 1983) among children of similar chronological age. Her study of nursery and reception classes indicated clearly, first that 'newcomers to the discourse of the classroom do not start at a common level of ignorance and inexperience', and secondly that the differences between them were not readily susceptible to direct instruction from teachers. Pupils' readiness to learn what to expect of classroom discourse seemed hard to predict and the remediation of difficulties consequently hard to prescribe, despite the possibly enduring effects of teachers' negative evaluations of those who remained baffled and silent. The whole process of acquiring classroom competence seemed to Willes surprisingly indirect and even haphazard.

> I found that the teacher of these newcomers to the educational system expected and tolerated from the children answers that were unexpected or inappropriate, or indeed quite inaudible, and would select from a babel of sound a response she regarded as satisfactory; or, if none was discernible, would impose upon the chorus of sound the answer that she hoped to hear, in very much the same way that the mothers in Snow's studies (1972; 1977) would interpret a sound or look or movement from their babies as if these constituted a turn at talking that could properly elicit another turn in reply. Teachers behave as if children were already the participating pupils they will soon become (1981, p. 57).

This process resembles the induction of a new player into many rule-governed games: that is, minimal explication of the rules, but a temporarily

Exchange type	Opening		Answering		Follow-up	
direct	Come and sit down.	dir.				
direct	Come on, come and sit down.	dir.	N.V.	rea.	That's it.	ev.
elicit	What has it been doing today?	el.	Raining.	rep.	Raining.	ev.
elicit	And what do we sometimes get with rain?	el.	(babel of sound — not transcribable)			
re-initiate	No . . . a noise . . .	el.	Teacher: thunder	rep.	Yes.	ev.
direct	Are you ready?	dir.	(teacher and pupils sing 'I hear thunder')		That thunder carries on an awful long time.	
direct	Dean and Neil, I shan't tell you again to turn round and sit up please.	d. [n.]				
direct	Come on, sit up please.	d.	N.V.	rea.	Thank you.	ack.
elicit	Hello. Have you come to look for your sister?	el.	Not yet.	rep.	Not yet.	ack.
elicit	Where's one little finger?	el.				
elicit	How many?		(inaudible)	rep.	Four. Good.	ack. ev.
elicit	How many Amanda?	el. [n.]	Five.	rep.	Five.	ack.
direct	Ready?	d.				
elicit	Mark, what would you like to sing?	el. [n.]	(inaudible)	rep.	Oh, not again. We'll sing that again tomorrow.	ev. com.
elicit	All right. What would you like to sing?	s. el.	(noise, in which can be discerned) 'Jack and Jill', 'Mary Mary'		Mary Mary.	ack.
direct	All right.	d.	(children and teacher sing)		Very good I didn't know you knew that one	ev. com.

(Willes, 1983, pp. 110–12)

lenient interpretation of transgressions by those being initiated. The patterns of that game are evident from the start. Our illustration (p. 160) from a reception class, reveals them clearly. It is the patient but firmly insistent directing moves, and the 'closed' question-forms requiring simple, manageable replies (for example, 'What . . . ? or 'How many?') which characterize the establishment of such routines at this early stage.

In classrooms, the game is run by one authority; it is by gradually recognizing and responding to her many rulings that there gradually emerges 'the understanding, the ability to distinguish the appropriate from the inappropriate answer, that distinguishes the capable, active and participating, even if silent, pupil from the bewildered, and silent, child who does not know what he should do' (1981, pp. 58–9). Although Willes' linguistic orientation is evident in her use of methods of discourse analysis derived from the work of Sinclair and Coulthard, the presence of 'silent' children compelled her to use other methods of data collection, such as role-play and story-completion tasks. From these she observed, for instance, that even the silent could have recourse to what she calls the fall-back rule for a pupil suddenly aware of an adult's scrutiny in the classroom — 'Stop, attend, look to see what others are doing, and do that'.

We have suggested that teacher-pupil interaction involves continuities as well as differences in structure compared with children's talk with other adults. Pupil-pupil interaction presumably involves more continuities still between 'home' and school settings. Yet realization of what young children learn from one another has been relatively recent (for a useful collection of studies, see Garnica and King, 1979), and it has superseded the view associated with Piaget that their talk would be essentially egocentric and largely linked to direct action. The transcripts analyzed by Rosen and Rosen (1973) provided an early basis for revising that view (see also Martin *et al*, 1976). Later work has described the wide range of strategies which even very young children employ, not only to get their own way and get other children to do their bidding, but also to seek aid, make and repair friendships, and cope with strangers (Ervin-Tripp, 1982; Hatch, 1984). The picture still lacks, however, detailed accounts of pupil-pupil interaction in the less formal school settings (Borman, 1979, Cheshire, 1982b and Pollard 1985a are among the exceptions). A useful step in that direction was taken by Lazarus (1984), who recorded individual pupils through whole sessions at kindergarten. Her evidence provided a warrant for three areas of sociolinguistic skill. The first concerned children's awareness of regularities in classroom language use — appropriate address forms, greetings, question-and-answer routines, conventional directives and so on. The second related to interactional skills, such as those involved in gaining help with a problem (if only at the level of saying, 'I'm stuck') or sorting out who was to reply when the teacher directed questions at a group. Thirdly, children's competence was 'most dramatically revealed by their artful variation of components of ways of speaking to convey or mark their intent' — for example, by covering their embarassment at a mistake by a sudden shift of topic or a funny voice, using attention-gaining devices for introducing news ('Teacher, guess what I once was'), or using politeness formulas to achieve their ends. As Hatch (1984) has argued, teachers and educators may remain only dimly aware of this repertoire of skills.

4   A Language Gap Between Home and School?

Much of the work on the study of language in relation to social class and school failure has claimed that the difference between home and school language is responsible. The majority of the discussion has been carried out in the absence of any systematic comparison of the uses of language in these two settings. The notable exceptions are the work of Heath in the US and Wells in Britain (Romaine, 1984, p. 167).

Among the effects of the situation accurately summarized by Romaine has been a powerful tendency to place the main weight of explanation on the communicative inexperience of children from certain backgrounds in relation to the demands typically made on them in classrooms. We referred to this tendency, and the debate which has increasingly surrounded it, in our second chapter. We also raised there, in a preliminary way, the suspicion which so much classroom research supports — that in critical respects, classrooms may be too undemanding as contexts for pupil talk, making available too limited a range of communicative options. Having continued that discussion in chapter 5, with particular reference to Shirley Heath and other ethnographically-oriented observers of classroom talk, we return to it through the more linguistic orientation adopted by Gordon Wells and his co-workers at Bristol. (See, for instance, Wells and Nicholls, 1985; Wells, 1987.)

We begin with some disturbing conclusions from this research and comment briefly on the methods of investigation and analysis which produced them, considering finally their implications for classroom practice.

In their interactions with the external world, the young children whom Wells recorded seemed to be 'compulsive and creative seekers after meaning', and most of their homes provided at least some experience of interactions 'characterized by collaboration in the negotiation of meaning and intention' (Wells and Wells, 1984, pp. 191–2). Yet in their classrooms, these same children were *not* encountering a

> linguistically rich environment able to provide compensation for those believed to be deprived at home. On the contrary, there were no homes that did not provide richer opportunities than the schools . . . for learning through talk with an adult. Clearly there is

a mismatch between teachers' aims and the reality of classroom practice (*ibid.* p. 194).

This observation effectively turns some previous assertions about homes and schools upside down. It shifts the focus for reform firmly towards schooling in general, and towards its early years in particular.

To understand how the Bristol project arrived at these conclusions, it is important to note, first, that the data were drawn from recordings made in both types of setting, and second, that analysis was concentrated on differences within each of them. We ourselves suggested earlier that a most salient difference for children exists between those contexts which involve approximate equality of status, and those in which one (normally adult) participant claims superior or prior knowledge of the matters in hand. In this respect, some homes and some classrooms are clearly more asymmetrical than others, depending on the parents' and teachers' managerial styles or their framing of knowledge. Thus, in some contexts more than others, children enjoy a measure of freedom both to initiate dialogue and to formulate meanings in their own terms — two aspects of relative freedom of special interest to Wells.

Drawing on the naturally-occurring talk recorded in the children's homes and schools, Wells and Montgomery (1981) identify in the discourse a range of exchange-structures within the broad I-R-E type noted by Sinclair and Coulthard. They reserve the term 'display exchange' for the type of question which we discussed in detail in the previous chapter, one in which 'the child is asked . . . in order that he may show whether he knows the answer, rather than that the questioner should obtain some new information'. Scanning the home-data, they find grounds for doubting the 'accepted wisdom' that this feature is exclusively and significantly the mark of the classroom. The following is one of many such exchanges recorded in a child's home.

Mother	What's the time?
Rosie	. . . . . .
Mother	Now what number's that? (pointing to the hands on the clock)
Rosie	Number two.
Mother	No it's not. What is it? It's a one and a nought.
Rosie	Nought — one and a nought.
Mother	Yeah. Well, what's a one and a nought?
Rosie	. . . . . .
Mother	What is it?
Rosie	There one.
Mother	Yeah, what is it?
Rosie	One. One and a nought.
Mother	What's one and a nought?

Rosie   Um, that.
Mother   A ten.
(simplified from Wells and Montgomery, 1981, pp. 211–12)

Data from the project as a whole indicated interactional differences which seemed to arise from differences in the child's personality and in how rewarding he or she was as what Shirley Heath terms a 'conversational partner'. For example, adults addressed to 'more rapidly developing children' more acknowledgments of the child's contributions, and a larger number of utterances related to either the child's activity or to the joint activity of child and adult. There was also evidence of adults' 'characteristic preferences for particular styles of interaction', a reference which clearly applies to both parents and teachers, and which was particularly evident in their willingness to accept and develop the child's contributions (Wells, 1978).

In a well-known paper, Wells (1979) analyses in detail two episodes of mother-child dialogue so as to show the impact of the mother's strategies. In the first, the child (aged just over two) is playing with some clothes which are about to be washed, while her mother is washing dishes. The child's comments on her own activity, and her invitation to her mother to show interest, meet with a series of prohibitions instead. In the second, taken from the same recording of the same participants, the mother is seen to engage very clearly with what her daughter is trying to say; from their dialogue, there emerges an apparently negotiated version of the child's meaning which 'represents a compromise between what seem to have been the separate intentions of the two participants' (p. 148). In both episodes, the mother's speech is displayed as being directly relevant to the child's expression of meaning, and it is the second which illustrates that characteristic of 'mutual relevance in a child's experience of conversation that we think may be important for his success on entry to school' (p. 148). Conversely, and from this perspective, relative disadvantage lies not in linguistic resources, nor in differences of dialect and accent, but in experience of participating in dialogue defined in this way as the negotiating and exploring of 'mutual relevance'. Ideally, the child familiar with being treated as a conversational partner at home would continue to be taken seriously as a partner in dialogue at school.

The importance given to the Bristol study by Romaine and other commentators is based both on its abundance of naturalistic recording and the systematic analysis of the transcribed data. Its authority derives in part from the very volume of the data base (128 children recorded at intervals over two and a half years until they entered school full-time; together with a sub-group who were followed right through their primary schooling). The time-consuming labour of transcription and analysis usually confines such linguistic research to far fewer, more limited and more artificially contrived 'cases'. Here, the basic material of recording and transcript was not only abundant in quantity, it was also subjected to highly complex coding which involved details at every linguistic level.

The data thus differs qualitatively too from those in most other studies — for example, from the research project 'Communication Skills in Early Childhood' directed by Joan Tough, which partly overlaps in time with the Bristol work. There are some useful comparisons to be made between them. In Tough's Project, sixty-four children divided by their parents' educational and occupational backgrounds into 'advantaged' and 'disadvantaged' groups, were observed at the ages of three, five and a half and seven. Recordings were made under controlled conditions — either with a researcher 'interviewing' individual children, or in playsettings designed for small groups. The linguistic measures focused first on surface features of the children's utterances — for example, their mean length or their syntactic complexity — and then on the functions which utterances were categorized as displaying. Although the first published work dealt with children's development of meaning, the Project soon moved into more prescriptive publications aimed at enabling teachers of the young to provide a more supportive and demanding context for their pupils' language development (Tough, 1977b). The fullest account of it (Tough, 1977a) presented findings which reflect what, in an analogous context, Shuy (1984) has described as a 'reductionist' rather than a 'holistic' view of language. Such a view is typically concerned with the 'nuts and bolts' of language, but not really seen as integral with social interaction.

Other weaknesses attributed to this Project have been energetically argued over, and do not essentially concern us here (see, for example, MacLure and French, 1982). But we are ourselves doubtful about the confidence which Tough places in a limited range of recordings as a source of evidence about young children's functional range. Her main conclusions were that the socially-disadvantaged group spoke no less than their advantaged contemporaries; that while their speech was generally less complex structurally, all the main grammatical patterns of English were understood by them and most were used on occasions; that observed differences in performance seemed therefore to be caused not by a 'lack of resources of language' but by inexperience in certain ways of verbalizing thought; and that inexperience was evident in the more limited use they made of language to refer to the past, contemplate the future, to reason and to imagine. The firmness of these conclusions (unmodified by the possible constraining effects of the contrived settings and the researchers' own presence) involved extending the findings to settings in which the children were not recorded at all. Indeed, Tough has argued that naturalistic recording wastes time, and can gather data quite irrelevant to the specific research purposes being pursued. Yet without them, it is hard to see how the evidence will begin to capture the range and complexity of children's competence, or their capacity to make meaning in their own terms.

Our purpose in highlighting the methodological strengths of the Bristol study has been to stress its credentials for making the kind of statement about classrooms with which we began this section. Indeed, it seems uniquely well placed to provide the evidence, being able to refer to recordings of a target group of thirty-two children in their various classrooms, matched with recordings of each of them in their homes just before entry to school. Comparisons of the children's utterances across the settings provided results which Wells and Wells (1984, p. 193) describe as — 'clear-cut and, in the light of the ideals of the teachers, very disconcerting'. They are presented in table form as follows —

Comparison of Adult-Child Conversation at Home and School (n = 32)

	Home	School	Sig.level of difference
Absolute values			
Mean no. of child utterances to adults	122.0	45.0	p < .001
Mean no. of adult-utterances to child	152.7	128.7	n.s.
Mean no. of child turns per interaction	4.1	2.5	p < .001
Mean child syntactic complexity	3.1	2.4	p < .001
Mean adult syntactic complexity	3.5	4.3	p < .001
Mean no. of categories of semantic content in child speech*	15.5	7.9	p < .001
Proportional values (child)			
Initiation of interaction	63.6 per cent	23.0 per cent	p < .001
Exchange-initiating utterances	70.2 per cent	43.8 per cent	p < .001
Complete statements	31.2 per cent	28.0 per cent	n.s.
Questions	12.7 per cent	4.0 per cent	p < .001
Requests	14.3 per cent	10.4 per cent	p < .05
Elliptical or moodless utterances	29.4 per cent	49.4 per cent	p < .001
Utterances in text-contingent exchanges	9.4 per cent	6.3 per cent	p < .10
References to non-present time	9.1 per cent	6.4 per cent	p < .05
Proportional values (adult)			
Exchange-initiating utterances	59.9 per cent	78.7 per cent	P < .001
Complete statements	26.2 per cent	24.5 per cent	n.s.
Questions	14.3 per cent	20.2 per cent	p < .01
Requests	22.5 per cent	34.1 per cent	p < .001
Elliptical utterances	5.7 per cent	5.8 per cent	n.s.
Requests for display	2.1 per cent	14.2 per cent	p < .001
Extending child's meaning	33.5 per cent	17.1 per cent	p < .001
Developing adult's meaning	19.3 per cent	38.6 per cent	p < .001

*For this comparison only, n = 16
(Wells and Wells, 1984, p. 193)

It is worth quoting in full the commentary by which these data are summarized:-

> ... children at school were found to play a much less active role in conversation. They initiated fewer interactions, asked fewer questions, and took fewer turns per interaction. Their utterances were syntactically simpler, contained a narrower range of semantic

content, and less frequently referred outside the here and now. Indeed almost half their utterances were elliptical or moodless sentence fragments, often being minimal responses to requests for display (for example — 'T: What do we call cats, sheep and horses? P: Animals. T: That's right.'). In contrast with their parents, these children's teachers dominated conversation, initiating the majority of interactions, predominantly through requests, questions, and requests for display. They were also more than twice as likely to develop their own meanings as they were to extend those contributed by the children, this ratio being almost the exact opposite of that found in the speech of the parents (*ibid.* pp. 193–4).

These researchers go on to suggest three main explanations for the 'impoverished talk between teacher and pupils' which they recorded, explanations which are very similar to those we have discussed extensively in earlier chapters of this book. They are —

1   The number of children which classrooms contain, leading to a high percentage of talk devoted to management matters.
2   The curriculum itself, or a 'highly structured' conception of it, as ground to be covered to meet public expectations.
3   A 'less than whole-hearted belief in the value that pupils' talk has for their learning' (p. 194).

This last factor is recognized to be both the most serious, and yet the most susceptible to change if teachers can be encouraged and helped to monitor how language is used in their classrooms. Through appreciating from the evidence of recordings and transcripts that they may talk and question too much, repeat themselves unnecessarily, and allow children too little time to respond, they can undoubtedly develop an impetus for change. For example, they may reorganize resources of space and time so as to extend the range of participant structures and alter their relative frequency, thereby giving more prominence to pupils' talk and more scope to exercise those rights normally reserved for the teacher. Since the first edition of the present book was written, the rationale for such developments in pedagogy has been further elaborated and summarized by Wells (for example 1987; 1992). His work draws its authority from the Bristol research while going beyond it to form explicit links with the Oracy Project and to articulate with special clarity the constructivist view of language in processes of learning and teaching. While the scope of the 1987 book is very broad, it nevertheless possesses a unified theoretical basis. It encompasses many of the themes we have ourselves alluded to: children's language development in relation to their backgrounds, verbal aspects of their transition from home to school, the role of their talk in 'making knowledge their own', the kinds of talk which might best 'scaffold' their learning, various factors associated with differences in achievement, literacy, the significance of story, and so on.

Because of the age-focus of the Bristol research, Wells' work has had a special appeal to primary educators. Many aspects of classroom talk which have been identified as being significant for young learners, however, also have their counterparts for other age-groups. For example, the 'language gap' which Hull (1985) identified from observation of secondary-school classes shows a similar perception of the curriculum as sets of facts to be transmitted under pressure of time, and similar consequences for the shaping of pupils' answers to questions towards predetermined and non-negotiable semantic destinations. Indeed, that theme runs through most of the work we have reviewed. Transmitting knowledge involves special rights and responsibilities which are evident throughout the organization of normal classroom talk, in the variety of ways we have specified. Receiving knowledge involves a largely subordinate communicative role in which turns are allocated, answers evaluated, and 'official' meanings formulated, at the discretion of the teacher. Clearly there are many times when such direct instruction is necessary and appropriate and indeed unavoidable. We concluded the first edition of this book by noting 'disturbing evidence from classrooms across the age-range and across the curriculum' of a persistent shortage of opportunities for pupils to engage in the kinds of dialogue through which the 'shared construction and negotiation of meaning' (Wells and Nicholls, 1985, p. 18) might be achieved. Since that time such possibilities have become more tantalizingly realizable, and the message has taken an influential hold among a growing number of teachers. What has become disturbing is the re-emergent strength of the traditionalist lobby, mostly outside education, whose ignorance of research on classroom talk is only exceeded by their scorn for what they neither know nor understand. For their part, teachers now have available to them some well-developed strategies and advice: for instance, in works such as Edwards and Mercer, 1987; MacLure *et al*, 1988; Wray, 1990, and Norman, 1992. Then, too, the Oracy Project and the English Working Group, as well as providing striking examples of what professional cooperation can achieve, have given a highly positive lead.

7   Conclusion

> Education is to be given credit for recognizing small glimmers, from time to time, of the fact that learning relies heavily on language. The journey towards understanding this fact, however, has been ponderously slow and difficult, not simply because of the invisibility of the subject, but also because of the false information, incomplete knowledge, and stereotypes of language which educators inherit and pass along to future generations with discouraging faithfulness (Shuy, 1984, p. 167).

If not exactly 'invisible', language is easily taken for granted. Regrettably, moreover, misconceptions and views based on stereotypes persist in some school staffrooms — for example, that 'the only good classroom is a silent one', or 'When they (particular categories of pupils) come to us, they just don't have any language'. Certainly too, the knowledge that we have is harder to put into practice when schools are facing increasing demands for greater accountability, relevance and innovation at the same time as they have to cope with diminishing resources. But Shuy is surely correct in asserting that the centrality of language in educational processes has gained recognition, however patchily and controversially. The last ten years or so have yielded significant advances in the available professional knowledge-base, not least in respect of *spoken* languages as the vital medium for communication and learning.

One purpose of the present book has been to draw together, from widely different research traditions, some of the insights which have contributed to our understanding and to the undermining of prejudice. In reviewing this work, we have made an assumption which we believe to be increasingly necessary if teachers are to resist effectively both oversimplified appraisals of what they do and over-simplified prescriptions of what they should do. The assumption is that the boundary between the roles of teacher and researcher can become, and ought to become, less sharply defined than in the past. We agree therefore with many others who have promoted concepts of 'teachers as researchers' (for example, Elliott, 1985; Ebbutt and Elliott, 1985; Pollard, 1985b; Altrichter *et al*, 1993, Walker, 1985; Woods, 1989). While there are clearly forms of enquiry which can only be carried out effectively by specialist researchers because of their technical demands or their scale, teachers' own involvement or collaboration in research brings an enhanced capacity to reflect systematically upon the complex situations they confront, and thereby extend their 'practical judgment' and their repertoire of professional skills. While we have cited several instances of such research which have found a wider public (for example, Talk Workshop Group, 1982), we also value highly the best small-scale case-study work done by teachers as being potentially a potent reinforcement of their 'practical judgment'.

Classroom language would seem to provide an especially useful focus for such work. We have set out, particularly in chapters 3–6, some of the topics which language data can illuminate, the variety of research perspectives which can be adopted, and some of the theoretical and technical problems associated with them. Some of the technicalities involved, as in discourse analysis or conversational analysis, can appear either daunting in themselves or more complex than is really necessary for the kinds of enquiry which teachers might undertake. These technicalities may be dismissed as 'art for art's sake' by impatient practitioners seeking practical guidance, and no less firmly defended by the researchers as being required by the theoretical frame of reference within which they work. Certainly some of the approaches we have discussed have such deep roots in linguistic or sociological theory that teachers are unlikely to adopt them even when persuaded of the practical relevance of some of the 'findings' those approaches have produced. On the other hand, we have emphasized the time-wasting frustration of laboriously recording and transcribing classroom talk only to wonder in the end if there was 'anything there' to be found, displayed, and warranted by evidence.

Apparently 'over'-theoretical methods of analysis may also be a valuable device for 'making strange' something as familiar as teachers' own practices — for placing a distance between them and what they normally take for granted. And they may be used pragmatically, to an extent which the more 'pure-minded' researcher might well deplore. Westgate *et al* (1985), for example, found that a modified form of discourse analysis, taken down to the level of 'move', was sufficient to highlight those aspects of teacher-dominated foreign language teaching which were initially of interest. More detailed coding of 'acts' added less additional value than was gained by far less 'technical' (and laborious) assessment of non-verbal communication displayed in the video-record. Teachers may also take heart from many worthwhile instances of 'low-technology' observation of teaching which still contrive to challenge conventional understandings of classroom practice (for example, Evans, 1985; Hull, 1985; MacLure *et al*, 1988; Norman, 1992; Pollard, 1984).

In the course of writing about investigations of classroom talk, we have tried to integrate methods and findings, theoretical contexts and practical implications. Our starting point was a set of three related propositions —

1 that no single conceptual framework, or metalanguage, for the description of teaching is available;
2 that no research is atheoretical;
3 that in view of the pervasive influence of theoretical assumptions at every stage of the research, principled choices of method have to be made, also of data collection and of data analysis.

We have indicated that such choices may lead, deliberately, to open-ended enquiry, eclecticism, or to immersion in one of the main traditions we have identified. Much will depend on the kinds of question being asked about classroom talk. We have suggested that some questions can be answered by inspection of the surface features of talk (for example, who speaks, in what order, and for how long?). Other questions make it necessary to go 'behind' the talk for the cultural assumptions and attitudes which it manifests, or require complex analysis of its linguistic structure or its structure as discourse.

Uncertainty in 'reading off' interpersonal perceptions and strategies from the surface of talk arise from a fundamental variability in the relationship between linguistic forms and their functions in discourse. We have emphasized the high degree of obliqueness and indeterminacy which characterizes conversation, and which also marks a great deal of talk even in more formal, institutionalized settings like classrooms. We have also emphasized that no talk can be interpreted without reference to its context, and that fact brings its own severe problems once it is accepted that contexts are not fixed frames of reference within which talk takes place and has its meaning, but are themselves talked into being, renewed or challenged. All these difficulties in investigating talk have to be recognized, and they indicate the need for caution in coming to 'conclusions'. But no context can ever be completely 'penetrated', nor can the researcher expect full access to what those observed understand by and through their interaction. If perfection were required, no research would get published. A stage is reached in any project when the researcher either believes sufficient evidence has been assembled to 'warrant' conclusions being drawn, or tries another approach. In some of the approaches we have considered, especially in chapters 5 and 6, it is more appropriate to speak of 'insights' than 'findings'. Indeed, where the object of investigation is as complex as language, it is a mistake to look for too easy and rapid results from research. What the best classroom research has done is to deepen understanding of that complexity.

Annotated Bibliography

ADELMAN, C. (Ed.) (1981) *Uttering, Muttering: Collecting, Using and Reporting Talk for Social and Educational Research*, London, Grant McIntyre.

A particularly valuable methodological collection which offers a range of perspectives on talk, with educational settings providing the common theme. Nearly all the contributors are repeatedly referred to in the present book.

BARNES, D. (1976) *From Communication to Curriculum*, Harmondsworth, Penguin.

An accessible and influential statement of Barnes' case for pedagogic reform. At its centre lies the identification, based on teachers' attitudes towards classroom language, of 'transmission' and 'interpretation' styles of teaching.

BARNES, D. and TODD, F. (1977) *Communication and Learning in Small Groups*, London, Routledge and Kegan Paul.

The authors report upon experiments in integrating teacher-less discussions into secondary school learning. There is considerable methodological interest in their discussion of the interpretation of transcripts, and in the combination of interactional and cognitive 'frames' for coding the pupils' talk.

BROWN, G. and YULE, G. (1983) *Discourse Analysis*, Cambridge, Cambridge University Press.

This has a claim to being the standard work. Its authors' dynamic process-view of discourse and contexts, which is clearly set out, has proved important and influential.

BURGESS, R. (Ed.) (1985) *Field Methods in the Study of Education*, Lewes, Falmer Press.

A series of critical reflections upon studies in educational settings by researchers who have undertaken them. Particularly relevant to the present book are the contributions on ethnographic and 'mixed' approaches.

CAZDEN, C.B. (1988) *Classroom Discourse: The Language of Teaching and Learning*, Portsmouth, N.H., Heinemann.

A classic in the field, this book is the fruit of reflections prompted by its author's return to the classroom and by her cooperation with Hugh Mehan who exhaustively analysed some of her lessons. It combines copious evidence from practice with mature scholarship to produce a wide-ranging account of classroom discourse and its bearing on practice.

CORSON, D. (1988) *Oral Language Across the Curriculum*, Clevedon, Multilingual Mattters.

A thorough review of the involvement of talk in learning, from both teaching and learning perspectives; also contains useful guidance for related professional development.

Coulthard, M. (Ed.) (1987) *Discussing Discourse*, Birmingham, University of Birmingham English Language Research Unit.

This collection refines some of the ideas, as well as broadening the scope, of the important work begun in the 1970s at Birmingham. It covers aspects of discourse found in contexts other than classrooms but shows a continuing concern for educational applications, particularly in connection with languages-teaching.

Dillon, J.T. (1988) *Questioning and Teaching*, London, Croom Helm.

Perhaps the most comprehensive of Dillon's accounts of this persistent and dominant feature of classroom discourse. It combines subtle analysis of questioning with practical guidance about the benefits which alternatives may provide.

Edwards, A.D. and Furlong, V.J. (1978) *The Language of Teaching*, London, Heinemann.

Based on recordings of humanities lessons and discussions with teachers in a secondary comprehensive school, the analysis sheds light on the 'normal' features of classroom talk, on their surprising persistence even in innovative settings, and more generally on problems in researching classroom talk.

Edwards, D. and Mercer, N. (1987) *Common Knowledge: the Development of Understanding in the Classroom*, London, Methuen.

This book has proved highly influential in the context of teachers' own exploration of talk in their teaching. It has, for instance, been widely-cited and discussed within the National Oracy Project, based as it is upon a linguistic approach to classroom research and upon a constructivist view of learning which is coherently explained.

Heath, S.B. (1983) *Ways with Words: Language, Life and Work in Communities and Classrooms*, Cambridge, Cambridge University Press.

A lucid, humane and intriguing account, from an ethnographic perspective, of cultural contrasts across two (US) communities and their implications for the often problematical interaction between the teachers and young people concerned.

Hull, R. (1985) *The Language Gap: How Classroom Dialogue Fails*, London, Methuen.

Written by a teacher-researcher for other teachers, Hull's book considers many of the barriers to genuine 'dialogue' forms of teaching and learning. A richly illustrated argument for reform, particularly in secondary schooling.

Maclure, M., Phillips, T. and Wilkinson, A. (Eds.) (1988) *Oracy Matters: the Development of Talking and Listening in Education*, Milton Keynes, Open University Press.

A very influential collection of essays, arising out of a conference on oracy but transcending it. The book is given a very clear context by its introduction and by several contributors who provide background detail. It contains particularly challenging accounts of small-group talk and of the relationship of classroom communication to learning.

Mehan, H. (1979) *Learning Lessons: Social Organisation in the Classroom*, Cambridge, Mass., Harvard University Press.

This distinguished book is based on a year's field-work in a Californian elementary school. Principally, however, it offers a developed account of Mehan's 'constitutive ethnography' set in a clear discussion of broader issues in classroom research. It also contains a valuable analysis of pupils' classroom competence.

NORMAN, K. (Ed.) (1992) *Thinking Voices: the Work of the National Oracy Project*, London, Hodder and Stoughton.

A wide range of authors, all contributors to the work of the National Oracy Project, combined to create this most substantial record of that undertaking. It reflects powerfully the active involvement of teachers in classroom investigations prompted by the Project. It also contains cross-referencing between contributions which highlight the individuality of each as well as views which are shared or diverge.

SINCLAIR, J. McH. and COULTHARD, M. (1975) *Towards an Analysis of Discourse: the Language of Teachers and Pupils*, London, Oxford University Press.

The fullest account of the origins and development of the English Language Research Group's pioneering work in Discourse Analysis. It contains full details of their analytical scheme.

STUBBS, M. (1983) *Discourse Analysis: the Sociolinguistic Analysis of Natural Language*, Oxford, Blackwell.

A clear and comprehensive review of the study of discourse and thus a reliable work to refer to for all the major themes and approaches in general talk-analysis.

WELLS, G. (1987) *The Meaning Makers: Children Learning Language and Using Language to Learn*, London, Hodder and Stoughton.

In this very influential book, Wells draws together many threads from what is often called the Bristol Project. The insights it conveys about children's language development are set in a wide and pedagogically-sensitive context, uniting developmental, constructivist and discourse perspectives.

WILKINSON, A., DAVIES, A. and BERRILL, D. (1990) *Spoken English Illuminated*, Milton Keynes, Open University Press.

Valuable for its commentary on the growing acceptability of the whole notion of oracy (of which Andrew Wilkinson is the acknowledged originator), and for the official recognition given it by the separate 'Speaking and Listening' Attainment Target in National Curriculum English, the book contains numerous insights into the promotion and assessment of talk.

WOOD, D. (1988) *How Children Learn and Think*, Oxford, Blackwell.

A highly recommended and readable account of cognitive development from the perspective of constructivist psychology.

WRAY, D. (Ed.) (1990) *Talking and Listening*, London, Scholastic Publications.

A useful summary of research, with sound advice on the gathering of evidence and many pointers to the educational implications of particular forms of classroom talk.

References

ADAMS, R. and BIDDLE, B. (1970) *Realities of Teaching: Explorations with Videotape*, New York, Holt, Rinehart and Winston.

ADELMAN, C. (1981) 'On first hearing' in ADELMAN, C. (Ed.) *Uttering and Muttering*, London, Grant McIntyre.

AINSWORTH, N. (1984) 'The cultural shaping of oral discourse', *Theory into Practice* 23, 2. pp. 132–7.

ALLWRIGHT, D. (1988) *Observation in the Language Classroom*. Harlow, Longman.

ALTRICHTER, H., POSCH, P. and SOMEKH, B. (1993) *Teachers Investigate their Work: An Introduction to the Methods of Action Research*, London, Routledge.

AMIDON, E. and HUNTER, E. (1967) *Improving Teaching: the Analysis of Verbal Interaction*, New York, Holt, Rinehart and Winston.

ANDERSON, D. (1982) 'The teacher as classroom researcher: a modest method for a new opportunity', in PAYNE, G. and CUFF, E. (Eds.) *Doing Teaching*, London, Batsford.

ANDRESKI, S. (1974) *Social Science as Sorcery*, Harmondsworth, Penguin.

ATKINS, M. (1984) 'Practitioner as researcher: some techniques for analysing semi-structured data in small-scale research', *British Journal of Educational Studies* 32, 3, pp. 251–61.

ATKINSON, J.M. and HERITAGE, J. (1984) *Structures of Social Action: Studies in Conversation Analysis*, Cambridge, Cambridge University Press.

ATKINSON, P. (1981) 'Inspecting classroom talk' in ADELMAN, C. (Ed.) *Uttering and Muttering: Reporting and Using Talk for Social and Educational Research*, London, Grant McIntyre.

ATKINSON, P. (1985) *Language, Structure and Reproduction: an Introduction to the Sociology of Basil Bernstein*, London, Methuen.

AUSTIN, J. (1962) *How to Do Things with Words*, Oxford, Oxford University Press.

BALL, S. (1980) 'Initial encounters in the classroom and the process of establishment', in WOODS, P. (Ed.) *Pupil Strategies: Exploration in the Sociology of the School*, London, Croom Helm.

BALL, S. (1985) 'English for the English since 1906', in GOODSON, I. (Ed.) *Social Histories of the Secondary Curriculum*, Lewes, Falmer Press.

BARKER-LUNN, J. (1984) 'Junior school teachers, their methods and practices', *Educational Research* 26, 3, pp. 178–187.

BARNES, D. (1976) *From Communication to Curriculum*, Harmondsworth, Penguin Books.

BARNES, D. (1980) 'Situated speech strategies: aspects of the monitoring of oracy', *Educational Review* 32, 2, pp. 123–31.

BARNES, D., BRITTON, J. and ROSEN, H. (1969) *Language, the Learner and the School*, Harmondsworth, Penguin Books.

BARNES, D. and TODD, F. (1977) *Communication and Learning in Small Groups*, London, Routledge and Kegan Paul.

BARNES, D. and TODD, F. (1981) 'Talk in small learning groups: analysis of strategies', in ADELMAN, C. (Ed.) *Uttering and Muttering*, London, Grant McIntyre.

BARNES, D. (1988) 'The politics of oracy', in MACLURE, M. *et al* (Eds.) *Oracy Matters*, Milton Keynes, Open University Press.

BARNES, D. (1992) 'The role of talk in learning', in NORMAN, K. (Ed.) (1992) *Thinking Voices: The Work of the National Oracy Project*, London, Hodder and Stoughton.

BARNES, D. and SHEERAN, Y. (1992) 'Oracy and genre: Speech styles in the classroom', in NORMAN, K. (Ed.) (1992) *Thinking Voices: The Work of the National Oracy Project*, London, Hodder and Stoughton.

BARR, M., D'ARCY, P. and HEALY, M. (1982) *What's Going On: Language/Learning Episodes in British and American Classrooms*, Montclair, N.J., Boynton Cook.

BELLACK, A., KLIEBARD, H., HYMAN, R., and SMITH, F. (1966) *The Language of the Classroom*, Columbia, Teachers College Press.

BENNETT, N. (1976) *Teaching Styles and Pupil Progress*, London, Open Books.

BENNETT, N. (1978) 'Recent research on teaching: a dream, a belief, and a model', *British Journal of Educational Psychology* 48, pp. 127–47.

BENNETT, N., ANDREAE, J., HEGARTY, P., and WADE, B. (1980) *Open-Plan Schools*, Slough, National Foundation for Educational Research.

BENNETT, N., DESFORGES, C., COCKBURN, A., and WILKINSON, B. (1984) *The Quality of Pupil Learning Experiences*, London, Erlbaum.

BENNETT, S.N. and DUNNE, E. (1990) *Talking and Learning in Groups*, London, Macmillan.

BERNSTEIN, B. (1990) *The Structuring of Pedagogic Discourse, (Class, Codes and Control, Volume 4)*, London, Routledge.

BERRILL, D. (1988) 'Anecdote and the development of of oral arguments in sixteen-year olds', in MACLURE, M., PHILLIPS, T. and WILKINSON, A. (Eds.) (1988) *Oracy Matters*, Milton Keynes, Open University Press.

BERRILL, D. (1990) 'Adolescents arguing', in WILKINSON, A., DAVIES, A., and BERRILL, D. (1990) *Spoken English Illuminated*, Milton Keynes, Open University Press.

BEYNON, J. and ATKINSON, P. (1984) 'Pupils as data-gatherers: mucking and sussing', in DELAMONT, S. (Ed.) *Readings on Interaction in the Classroom*, London, Methuen.

BIGGS, A. and EDWARDS, V. (1991) 'I treat them all the same: Teacher-pupil talk in multi-ethnic classrooms', *Language and Education*, 5, 3, pp. 161–176.

BLEASE, D. (1983) 'Observer effects on teachers and pupils in classroom research', *Educational Research* 35, 3, pp. 211–17.

BLOM, J. and GUMPERZ, J. (1972) 'Social meaning in linguistic structure: code-switching in Norway', in GUMPERZ, J. and HYMES, D. (Eds.) *Directions in Sociolinguistics: the Ethnography of Communication*, New York, Holt, Rinehart and Winston.

BORMAN, K. (1979) 'Children's situational competence', in GARNICA, O. and KING, M. (Eds.) *Children, Language and Society*, Oxford, Pergamon Press.

BOURDIEU, P. and PASSERON, J-C. (1977) *Reproduction in Education, Society and Culture*, London, Sage.

BOUSTED, M. (1989) 'Who talks?', *English in Education*, 23, 3, pp. 41–51.

BOYDELL, D. (1975) 'Systematic observation in informal classrooms', in CHANAN, G. and DELAMONT, S. (Eds.) *Frontiers of Classroom Research*, Slough, National Foundation for Educational Research.

BRAZIL, D. (1981) 'Discourse analysis as linguistics', in FRENCH, P. and MacLURE, M. (Eds.) *Adult-Child Conversation*, London, Croom Helm.

BRITTON, J. (1970) *Language and Learning*, London, Allen Lane, Penguin.

BRITTEN, J. (1987) 'Vygotsky's contribution to pedagogical theory', *English in Education*, 21, 3, pp. 22–26.

BROOK, A., DRIVER, R. and JOHNSTON, K. (1988) 'Learning processes in science: A classroom perspective', in WELLINGTON, J. (Ed.) *Skills and Processes in Science Education: A Critical Analysis*, London, Methuen.

BROWN, G. and YULE, G. (1983) *Discourse Analysis*, Cambridge, Cambridge University Press.

BROWN, G. and ARMSTRONG, S. (1978) 'SAID: a system for analysing instructional discourse', in McALEESE, R. and HAMILTON, D. (Eds.) *Understanding Classroom Life*, Slough, National Foundation for Educational Research.

BROWN, G. and ARMSTRONG, S. (1984) 'Explaining and explanations', in WRAGG, E. (Ed.) *Classroom Teaching Skills*, London, Croom Helm.

BRUMFIT, C. and MITCHELL, R. (1989) *Research in the Language Classroom*, London, British Council and Modern English Publications.

BRUNER, J. (1984) 'Interaction, communication and self', *Journal of the American Academy of Child Psychiatry* 23, 1, pp. 1–7.

BURGESS, R. (1984) *In the Field*, London, Allen and Unwin.

BURGESS, T. (1984) 'The question of English', in MEEK, M. and MILLER, J. (Eds.) *Changing English*, London, Heinemann Educational Books.

BURGESS, T. (1988) *Review of Investigating Classroom Talk*, in *Language in Education*, 2, 2, pp. 133–6.

BURTON, D. (1980) *Dialogue and Discourse: a Sociolinguistic Approach to Modern Drama Dialogue and Naturally-Occurring Conversation*, London, Routledge and Kegan Paul.

BURTON, D. (1981) 'Analysing spoken discourse', in COULTHARD, M. and MONTGOMERY, M. (Eds.) *Studies in Discourse Analysis*, London, Routledge and Kegan Paul.

CARRE, C. (1981) *Language, Teaching and Learning in Science*, London, Ward Lock.

CAZDEN, C. (1971) 'The neglected situation in child language research and education', in WILLIAMS, F. (Ed.) *Language and Poverty*, Chicago, Markham.

CAZDEN, C. (1972) *Child Language and Education*, New York, Holt, Rinehart and Winston.

CAZDEN, C. (1977) 'Concentrated versus contrived encounters: suggestions for language assessment in early childhood', in DAVIES, A. (Ed.) *Language and Learning in Early Childhood*, London, Heinemann Educational Books.

CAZDEN, C. (1988) *Classroom Discourse: The Language of Teaching and Learning*, Portsmouth, New Hampshire, Heinemann.

CAZDEN, C., JOHN, V., and HYMES, D. (1972) *The Functions of Language in the Classroom*, New York, Teachers College Press.

CHERRY, L. (1979) 'A sociocognitive approach to language development and its implications for education', in GARNICA, O. and KING, M. (Eds.) *Language, Children and Society*, Oxford, Pergamon.

CHESHIRE, J. (1982a) 'Dialect features and linguistic conflict in schools', *Educational Review* 34, 1, pp. 53–67.

CHESHIRE, J. (1982b) 'Linguistic variation and social function', in ROMAINE, S. (Ed.) *Sociolinguistic Variation in Speech Communities*, London, Arnold.

CHESHIRE, J. (1984) 'The relationship between language and sex in English', in TRUDGILL, P. (Ed.) *Applied Sociolinguistics*, London, Academic Press.

CHESHIRE, J. and JENKINS, N. (1991) 'Gender issues in the GCSE Oral English Examination' (part 2), *Language and Education*, 5, 1, pp. 19–40.

CHILVER, P. and GOULD, G. (1982) *Learning and Language in the Classroom: Discursive Talking and Writing across the Curriculum*, Oxford, Pergamon.

CHOMSKY, N. (1965) *Aspects of the Theory of Syntax*, Massachusetts Institute of Technology Press.

CHRISTIE, F. (1987) 'Young children's writing: from spoken to written genre', *Language and Education*, 1, 1, pp. 3–14.

CHRISTIE, F. (1990) 'The "morning news" genre', *Language and Education*, 4, 3, pp. 161–179.

CICOUREL, A. (1973) 'Interpretive procedures and normative rules in the negotiation of status and role', in CICOUREL, A. *Cognitive Sociology*, Harmondsworth, Penguin Books.

COOK-GUMPERZ, J. (Ed.) (1985) *The Social Construction of Literacy*, Cambridge, Cambridge University Press.

COOK-GUMPERZ, J. and CORSARO, W. (1977) 'Social-ecological constraints on children's communicative strategies', *Sociology* 11, 3, pp. 411–34.

COOK-GUMPERZ, J. and GUMPERZ, J. (1982) 'Communicative competence in educational perspective', in WILKINSON, L. (Ed.) *Communication in the Classroom*, New York and London, Academic Press.

CORDEN, R. (1992) 'The role of the teacher', in NORMAN, K. (Ed.) *Thinking Voices: The Work of the National Oracy Project*, London, Hodder and Stoughton.

CORSARO, W. (1979) 'Young children's conception of status and role', *Sociology of Education* 52, pp. 46–59.

CORSARO, W. (1981) 'Entering the child's world: research strategies for field entry and data collection in a preschool setting', in GREEN, J., and WALLAT, C. (Eds.) *Ethnography and Language in Educational Settings*, Norwood N.J., Ablex.

CORSON, D. (1985) *The Lexical Bar*, Oxford, Pergamon Press.

CORSON, D. (1988) *Oral Language across the Curriculum*, Clevedon, Multilingual Matters.

CORSON, D. (1991) 'Language, power and minority schooling', *Language and Education*, 5, 4, pp. 231–254.

COULTHARD, M. (1977) *Introduction to Discourse Analyses*, London, Longman.

COULTHARD, M. and MONTGOMERY, M. (1981) *Studies in Discourse Analysis*, London, Routledge and Kegan Paul.

COULTHARD, M. (Ed.) (1987) *Discussing Discourse*, Birmingham, University of Birmingham English Language Research Unit.

COX, B. (1991) *Cox on Cox: An English Curriculum for the 1990s*, London, Hodder and Stoughton.

CRAFT, M. and ATKINS, M. (1985) 'Teacher education and linguistic diversity', *Educational Review* 37, 2, pp. 153–64.

CROLL, P. (1986) *Systematic Classroom Observation*, Lewes, Falmer Press.

CUFF, E. and HUSTLER, D. (1981) 'Stories and story time in an infant classroom', in FRENCH, P. and MacLURE, M. (Eds.) *Adult-Child Conversation*, London, Croom Helm.

CULLEY, L. (1988) 'Girls, boys and computers', *Educational Studies*, 14, pp. 3–8.

DANIELS, H. (1989) 'Visual displays as tacit relays of the structure of pedagogic practice', *British Journal of Sociology of Education*, 10, 2, pp. 123–140.

DAVIES, B. (1983) 'The role pupils play in the construction of classroom order', *British Journal Sociology of Education* 4, 1, pp. 55–69.

DELAMONT, S. (1981) 'All too familiar: a decade of classroom research', *Educational Analysis* 3, 1, pp. 69–83.

DELAMONT, S. (1983) 'The ethnography of transfer', in GALTON, M., and WILLCOCKS, J. (Eds.) *Moving from the Primary Classroom*, London, Routledge and Kegan Paul.

DELAMONT, S. (Ed.) (1984) *Readings on Interaction in the Classroom*, London, Methuen.

DELAMONT, S. and HAMILTON, D. (1984) 'Revisiting classroom research: a continuing cautionary tale', in DELAMONT, S. (Ed.) *Readings on Interaction in the Classroom*, London, Methuen.

DENSCOMBE, M. (1980) 'Paupil strategies and the open classroom', in WOODS, P. (Ed.) *Pupil Strategies*, London, Croom Helm.

DENSCOMBE, M. (1985) *Classroom Control: a Sociological Perspective*, London, Allen and Unwin.

DEPARTMENT OF EDUCATION AND SCIENCE (1975) *A Language for Life*, (Report of the Bullcok Committee of Inquiry) London, HMSO.

DEPARTMENT OF EDUCATION AND SCIENCE (1982) *Education 5 to 9*, London, HMSO.

DEPARTMENT OF EDUCATION AND SCIENCE (1988) *Report of the Committee of Inquiry into the Teaching of English Language (the Kingman Report)*, London, HMSO.

DEPARTMENT OF EDUCATION AND SCIENCE (1989) *English for Ages 5 to 16 (the Cox Report)*, London, DES and Welsh Office.

DILLON, D. and SEARLE, D. (1981) 'The role of language in one first-grade classroom', *Research in the Teaching of English*, 15, 4, pp. 311–28.

DILLON, J. (1981) 'The effects of questions in education and other enterprises', *Journal of Curriculum Studies* 14, 2, pp. 127–52.

DILLON, J. (1982) 'Cognitive correspondence between question/statement and response', *American Educational Research Journal*, 19, 4, pp. 540–51.

DILLON, J.T. (1988) *Questioning and Teaching*, London, Croom Helm.

DILLON, J.T. (1990) *The Practice of Questioning*, London and New York, Routledge.

DOMINGOS, A. (1989) 'Influence of the social context of the school on the teacher's pedagogic practice', *British Journal of Sociology of Education*, 10, 3, pp. 351–366.

DONALDSON, M. (1978) *Children's Minds*, London, Fontana.

DOYLE, W. (1983) 'Academic work', *Review of Educational Research*, 53, 2, pp. 159–200.

EBBUTT, D. and ELLIOTT, J. (1985) 'Why should teachers do research?', in EBBUTT, D., and ELLIOTT, J. (Eds.) *Issues in Teaching for Understanding*, London, School Curriculum Development Committee and Longman.

EDWARDS, A. (1976) *Language in Culture and Class: the Sociology of Language and Education*, London, Heinemann Educational Books.

EDWARDS, A. (1978) 'The language of history and the communication of historical knowledge', in DICKINSON, A. and LEE, P. (Eds.) *History Teaching and Historical Understanding*, London, Heinemann Educational Books.

EDWARDS, A. (1980) 'Patterns of power and authority in classroom talk', in WOODS, P. (Ed.) *Teacher Strategies*, London, Croom Helm.

EDWARDS, A. (1981) 'Analysing classroom talk', in FRENCH, P., and MACLURE, M. (Eds.) *Adult-Child Conversation*, London, Croom Helm.

EDWARDS, A. (1987) 'Language codes and classroom practice', *Oxford Review of Education*, 13, 3, pp. 237–247.

EDWARDS, A. and FURLONG, V.J. (1978) *The Language of Teaching*, London, Heinemann.

EDWARDS, A. and FURLONG, J. (1985) 'Reflections on the language of teaching', in BURGESS, R. (Ed.) *Field Methods in the Study of Education*, Lewes, Falmer Press.

EDWARDS, D. (1990) 'Classroom discourse and classroom knowledge', in ROGERS, R. and KUTNICK, P. (Eds.) *The Social Psychology of the Primary School*, London and New York, Routledge.

EDWARDS, D. and MERCER, N. (1987) *Common Knowledge: The Development of Understanding in the Classroom*, London, Methuen.

EDWARDS, J. (1989) *Language and Disadvantage* (Second edition), London, Arnold.

EDWARDS, J. and GILES, H. (1984) 'Applications of the social psychology of language: sociolinguistics and education', in TRUDGILL, P. (Ed.) *Applied Sociolinguistics*, London, Academic Press.

EDWARDS, V. (1979) *The West Indian Language Issue in British Schools: Challenges and Responses*, London, Routledge and Kegan Paul.

EDWARDS, V. (1981) 'Dialect and reading: a case study of West Indian children in Britain', in EDWARDS, J. (Ed.) *The Social Psychology of Reading*, Silver Spring, Maryland, Institute of Modern Languages.

EDWARDS, V. (1986) *Language in a Black Community*, Clevedon, Multilingual Matters.

EGGLESTON, J., GALTON, M. and JONES, M. (1976) *Processes and Products of Science Teaching*, London, Macmillan.

EGGLESTON, J. (1983) 'Teacher-pupil interactions in science lessons: explorations and theory', *British Educational Research Journal*, 9, 1, pp. 113–26.

ELLIOTT, J. (1985) 'Facilitating action research in schools: some dilemmas', in BURGESS, R. (Ed.) *Field Methods in the Study of Education*, Lewes, Falmer Press.

ENRIGHT, L. (1982) 'Only talking', in BARR, M., *et al* (Eds.) *What's Going On? op. cit.*

ERICKSON, F. and MOHATT, G. (1982) 'Cultural organization of participation structures in two classrooms of Indian students', in SPINDLER, G. (Ed.) *Doing the Ethnography of Schooling*, New York, Holt, Rinehart and Winston.

ERICKSON, F. and SCHULTZ, J. (1981) 'When is a context? Some issues in the analysis of social competence', in GREEN, J. and WALLAT, C. (Eds.) *Ethnography and Language in Educational Settings*, Norwood, N.J., Ablex.

ERVIN-TRIPP, S. (1982) 'Structures of control', in WILKINSON, L. (Ed.) *Communicating in the Classroom*, New York, Academic Press.

ERVIN-TRIPP, S. and MITCHELL-KERNAN, C. (Eds.) (1977) *Child Discourse*, New York, Academic Press.

EVANS, G. (1988) 'Those loud black girls', in SPENDER, D. and SARAH, E. (Eds.) *Learning to Lose: Sexism and Education* (revised edition), London, Women's Press.

EVANS, J. (1985) *Teaching in Transition: the Challenge of Mixed-Ability Groupings*, Milton Keynes, Open University Press.

FISHER, E. (1993) 'Characteristics of children's talk at the computer and its relationship to the computer software', *Language and Education*, 7, 2, pp. 97–114.

FARRER, R. and RICHMOND (Eds.) (1980) *How Talking is Learning*, London, ILEA.

FLANDERS, N. (1963) 'Teacher influence in the classroom', in BELLACK, A. (Ed.) *Theory and Research in Teaching*, Columbia, Teachers College Press.

FLANDERS, N. (1970) *Analysing Teacher Behaviour*, Reading, Mass., Addison Wesley.

FLANDERS, N. (1976) 'Research on teaching in improving teacher education', *British Journal of Teacher Education*, 2, 2, pp. 167–74.

FRENCH, J. (1990) 'Social interaction in the classroom', in ROGERS, R. and KUTNICK, P. (Eds.) *The Social Psychology of the Primary School*, London and New York, Routledge.

FRENCH, J. and FRENCH, P. (1984a) 'Sociolinguistics and gender divisions', in ACKER, S., *et al* (Eds.) *World Yearbook of Education 1983–4: Women and Education*, London, Kogan Page.

FRENCH, J. and FRENCH, P. (1984b) 'Gender imbalances in the primary classroom: an interactionist account', *Educational Research*, 26, 2, pp. 127–36.

FRENCH, P. and LOCAL, J. (1983) 'Turn-competitive incomings', *Journal of Pragmatics*, 7, pp. 17–38.

FRENCH, P. and MacLURE, M. (1979) 'Getting the right answer and getting the answer right', *Research in Education*, 22, pp. 1–23.

FRENCH, P. and MacLURE, M. (Eds.) (1981a) *Adult-Child Conversation*, London, Croom Helm.

FRENCH, P. and MacLURE, M. (1981b) 'Teachers' questions, pupils' answers', *First Language* 2, 1, pp. 31–45.

FURLONG, V.J. (1984) 'Black resistance in the liberal comprehensive', in DELAMONT, S. (Ed.) *Readings in Interaction in the Classroom*, London, Methuen.

FURLONG, V.J. and EDWARDS, A. (1977) 'Language in the classroom: theory and data', *Educational Research* 19, 2, pp. 122–8.

GAGE, N. (1978) *The Scientific Basis of the Art of Teaching*, New York, Teachers College Press.

GALTON, M. (1978a) 'Systematic classroom observation: British research', *Educational Research* 21, 2, pp. 109–15.

GALTON, M. (Ed.) (1978b) *British Mirrors: a Collection of Classroom observation Instruments*, Leicester, Leicester University School of Education.

GALTON, M. (1979) 'Strategies and tactics in junior school classrooms', *British Educational Research Journal*, 5, 2, pp. 197–210.

GALTON, M. (1990) 'Grouping and group work', in ROGERS, R. and KUTNICK, P. (Eds.) *The Social Psychology of the Primary School*, London and New York, Routledge.

GALTON, M. and SIMON, B. (1980) *Progress and Performance in the Primary Classroom*, London, Routledge and Kegan Paul.

GALTON, M. and WILLCOCKS, J. (Eds.) (1983) *Moving from the Primary Classroom*, London, Routedge and Kegan Paul.

GALTON, M. and DELAMONT, S. (1985) 'Speaking with forked tongue? Two styles of observation in the ORACLE Project', in BURGESS, R. (Ed.) *Field Methods in the Study of Education*, Lewes, Falmer Press.

GARFINKEL, H. (1974) 'The origins of the term ethnomethodology', in TURNER, R. (Ed.) *Ethnomethodology*, Harmondsworth, Penguin Books.

GARNICA, O. (1981) 'Social dominance and conversational interaction — the omega child in the classroom', in GREEN, J. and WALLAT, C. (Eds.) *Ethnography and Language in Educational Settings*, Norwood, N.J., Ablex.

GARNICA, O. and KING, M. (Eds.) (1979) *Language, Children and Society: the Effect of Social Factors on Children Learning to Communicate*, Oxford, Pergamon.

GOFFMAN, E. (1981) *Forms of Talk*, Oxford, Blackwell.

GOOD, T. and BROPHY, J. (1978) *Looking in Classrooms*, 2nd ed., New York, Harper and Row.

GRADDOL, D. and SWANN, J. (1989) *Gender Voices*, Oxford, Blackwell.

GREEN, J.L. (1983) 'Context in classrooms: a sociolinguistic perspective', *New York Educational Quarterly*, 14, pp. 6–12.

GREEN, J.L. and WALLAT, C. (1981) 'Mapping instructional conversation — a sociolinguistic ethnography', in GREEN, J., and WALLAT, C. (Eds.) *Ethnography and Language in Educational Settings*, Norwood, N.J., Ablex.

GRICE, H. (1975) 'Logic and conversation', in COLE, P. and MORGAN, J. (Eds.) *Syntax and Semantics 3: Speech Acts*, New York, Academic Press.

GUMPERZ, J. (1981) 'Conversational inference and classroom learning', in GREEN, J. and WALLAT, C., (Eds.) *Ethnography and Language in Educational Settings*, Norwood, N.J., Ablex.

HACKER, R., HAWKES, R. and HEFFERNAM, M. (1979) 'A cross-cultural study of classroom interactions', *British Journal of Educational Psychology*, 49, pp. 51–9.

HADLEY, E. (1980) 'The conversation of the classroom', *English in Education*, 14, 3, pp. 34–40.

HALE, A. and EDWARDS, A. (1981) 'Hearing children read', in EDWARDS, J. (Ed.) *The Social Psychology of Reading*, Silver Spring, Maryland, Institute of Modern Languages.

HALLIDAY, M. (1961) 'Categories of the theory of grammar', *Word*, 17, pp. 241–92.

HALLIDAY, M. (1978) *Language as Social Semiotic*, London, Edward Arnold.

HALLIDAY, M. (1989) *Spoken and Written Language*, Oxford, Oxford University Press.

HALLIDAY, M. and HASAN, R. (1976) *Cohesion in English*, London, Longman.

HALLIGAN, D. (1988) 'Is there a task in this class?', in MACLURE, M., PHILLIPS, T. and WILKINSON, A. (Eds.) *Oracy Matters*, Milton Keynes, Open University Press.

HAMMERSLEY, M. (1977) 'School learning: the cultural resources required by pupils to answer a teacher's question', in WOODS, P. and HAMMERSLEY, M. (Eds.) *School Experience*, London, Croom Helm.

HAMMERSLEY, M. (1981) 'Putting competence into action; some sociological notes on a model of classroom interaction', in FRENCH, P. and MACLURE, M. (Eds.) *Adult-Child Conversation*, London, Croom Helm.

HAMMERSLEY, M. (1984) 'The researcher exposed: a natural history', in BURGESS, R. (Ed.) *The Research Process in Educational Settings*, Lewes, Falmer Press.

HAMMERSLEY, M. and WOODS, P. (Eds.) (1984) *Life in School: the Sociology of Pupil Culture*, Milton Keynes, Open University Press.

HAMILTON, D. (1977) *In Search of Structure*, London, Hodder and Stoughton.

HAMILTON, D. and DELAMONT, S. (1974) 'Classroom research: a cautionary tale', *Research in Education*, 11, pp. 1–16.

HARDMAN, F. and BEVERTON, S. (1993) 'Co-operative group work and the development of metadiscoursal skills', *Support for Learning*, 8, 4, pp. 146–150.

HARGIE, O. (1978) 'The importance of teacher questions in the classroom', *Educational Research*, 20, 2, pp. 97–102.

HARGREAVES, A. (1979) 'Strategies, decisions and control: interaction in a middle school classroom', in EGGLESTON, J. (Ed.) *Teacher Decision-Making in the Classroom*, London, Routledge and Kegan Paul.

HARGREAVES, A. and WOODS, P. (Eds.) (1984) *Classrooms and Staffrooms: the Sociology of Teachers and Teaching*, Milton Keynes, Open University Press.

HARGREAVES, D. (1967) *Social Relations in a Secondary School*, London, Routledge and Kegan Paul.

HARGREAVES, D. (1984) 'Teachers' questions: open, closed and half-open', *Educational Research*, 26, 1, pp. 46–52.

HARGREAVES, D., HESTER, S. and MELLOR, F. (1975) *Deviance in Classrooms*, London, Routledge and Kegan Paul.

HASAN, R. (1973) 'Code, register and social dialect', in BERNSTEIN, B. (Ed.) *Class, Codes and Control: Volume 2 — Applied Studies towards a Sociology of Lauguage*, London, Routledge and Kegan Paul.

HATCH, J. (1984) 'Forms and functions of child-to-child interaction in classroom settings', *Childhood Education*, 60, 5, pp. 354–60.

HEATH, S. (1982) 'Questioning at home and at school: a comparative study', in SPINDLER, G. (Ed.) *Doing the Ethnography of Schooling*, New York, Holt, Rinehart and Winston.

HEATH, S. (1983) *Ways with Words: Language, Life and Work in Communities and Classrooms*, Cambridge, Cambridge University Press.

HER MAJESTY'S INSPECTORS (1978) *Primary Education in England*, London, HMSO.

HER MAJESTY'S INSPECTORS (1979) *Aspects of Secondary Education in England*, London, HMSO.

HESTER, K. (1985) *Carpet-time: a Study of Language and Social Interaction in the Reception Class*, Unpublished MEd dissertation, University of Newcastle-upon-Tyne.

HILLGATE GROUP (1987) *The Reform of British Education*, London, Claridge Press.

HOWE, A. (1988) *Expanding Horizons: Teaching and Learning through Whole Class Discussion*, Sheffield, National Association for the teaching of English.

HOWE, A. (1992) *Making Talk Work*, London, Hodder and Stoughton.

HOYLES, C. and SUTHERLAND, R. (1989) *Logo Mathematics in the classroom*, London, Routledge.

HUDSON, R. (1980) *Sociolinguistics*, Cambridge, Cambridge University Press.

HUGHES, M. and WESTGATE, D. (1988) 'Re-appraising talk in nursery and reception classes', *Education, 3–13* and 16, 2, pp. 9–15.

HUGHES, M. and WESTGATE, D. (1990) 'Activities and the quality of pupil talk', *Education, 3–13* and 18, 2, pp. 41–47.

HULL, R. (1985) *The Language Gap: How Classroom Dialogue Fails*, London, Methuen.

HUSTLER, D. and PAYNE, G. (1985) 'Ethnographic conversation analysis: an approach to classroom talk', in BURGESS, R. (Ed.) *Strategies of Educational Research*, Lewes, Falmer Press.

HYMES, D. (1972) 'On communicative competence', in PRIDE, J. and HOLMES, J. (Eds.) *Sociolinguistics*, Harmondsworth, Penguin Books.

HYMES, D. (1977) *Foundations in Sociolinguistics: An Ethnographic Approach*, London, Tavistock.

HYMES, D. (1979) 'Language in education: forward to fundamentals', in GARNICA, O. and KING, M. (Eds.) *Language, Children and Society*, Oxford, Pergamon.

INNER LONDON EDUCATION AUTHORITY (1983) *Language Census*, London, ILEA.

INNER LONDON EDUCATION AUTHORITY (1984) *Improving Secondary Schools*, Report of the Committee on the Curriculum and Organization of Secondary Schools, London, ILEA.

JACKSON, P. (1968) *Life in Classrooms*, New York, Holt, Rinehart and Winston.

JACKSON, W. (1988) 'Talking through writing', *Language and Education*, 2, 1, pp. 1–14.

JENKINS, N. and CHESHIRE, J. (1990) 'Gender issues in the GCSE oral English examinations' (Part 1), *Language and Education*, 4, 4, pp. 261–292.

JOHNSON, M. (1979) *Discussion Dynamics: an Analysis of Classroom Teaching*, Rowley, Mass., Newbury House.

JOHNSON, J., HUTTON, R. and YARD, L. (1992) 'Capturing talk', in NORMAN, K. (Ed.) (1992) *Thinking Voices: The Work of the National Oracy Project*, London, Hodder and Stoughton.

JONES, P. (1988) *Lipservice: The Story of Talk in Schools*, Milton Keynes, Open University Press.

KARWEIT, N. (1981) 'Time in school', in CORWIN, R. (Ed.) *Research on Educational Organizations*, Greenwich, Conn., JAI Press.

KELLY, A. (1988) 'Gender differences in teacher-pupil interactions: A meta-analytic review', *Research in Education*, 39, pp. 25–41.

KERRY, T. (1981) 'Talking: the teacher's role', in SUTTON, C. (Ed.) *Communicating in the Classroom*, London, Hodder and Stoughton.

KERRY, T. (1982) 'The demands made on pupils' thinking in mixed-ability classes', in SANDS, M. and KERRY, T. (Eds.) *Mixed Ability Teaching*, London, Croom Helm.

KING, R. (1978) *All Things Bright and Beautiful: A Sociological Study of Infants Classrooms*, London, Routledge and Kegan Paul.

KOCHMAN, T. (1981) 'Classroom modalities: black and white communicative styles in the classroom', in MERCER, N. (Ed.) *Language in School and Community*, London, Edward Arnold.

KRESS, G. (1985) 'Sociolinguistic development and the mature language user: different voices for different occasions', in WELLS, G. and NICHOLLS, J. (Eds.) *Language and Learning: an Interactional Perspective*, Lewes, Falmer Press.

LABOV, W. (1972a) 'Rules for ritual insults', in LABOV, W., *Language in the Inner City*, Oxford, Blackwell.

LABOV, W. (1972b) 'The study of language in its social context', in GIGLIOLI, P. (Ed.) *Language and Social Context*, Harmondsworth, Penguin Books.

LAZARUS, P. (1984) 'What children know and teach about language competence', *Theory into Practice*, 23, 3, pp. 225–31.

LEACOCK, E. (1969) *Teaching and Learning in City Schools*, New York, Basic Books.

LEECH, G. (1984) *Principles of Pragmatics*, London, Longman.

LEVINSON, S. (1983) *Pragmatics*, Cambridge, Cambridge University Press.

LINGUISTIC MINORITIES PROJECT (1985) *The Other Languages of England*, London, Routledge and Kegan Paul.

LONG, M. (1980) 'Inside the black box: methodological issues in classroom research on language learning', *Language Learning*, 30, 1, pp. 1–42.

McCARTHY, M. (1991) *Discourse Analysis for Language Teachers*, Cambridge, Cambridge University Press.

McCUTCHEON (1981) 'On the interpretation of classroom observations', *Educational Researcher*, 10, 5, pp. 5–10.

McHOUL, A. (1978) 'The organization of turns of formal talk in the classroom', *Language in Society*, 7, pp. 183–213.

McHOUL, A. and WATSON, D. (1984) 'Two axes for the analysis of "common-sense" and "formal" geographical knowledge in classroom talk', *British Journal of Sociology of Education*, 5, 3, pp. 281–302.

McIntyre, D. (1980) 'Systematic observation of classroom activites', *Educational Analysis*, 2, 2, pp. 3–30.

McIntyre, D. and Macleod, G. (1978) 'The characteristics and uses of systematic classroom observation', in McAleese, R., and Hamilton, D. (Eds.) *Understanding Classroom Life*, Slough, National Foundation for Educational Research.

Maclure, M. and French, P. (1980) 'Routes to right answers: on pupils' strategies for answering teachers' questions', in Woods, P. (Ed.) *Pupil Strategies*, London, Croom Helm.

Maclure, M. and French, P. (1981) 'A comparison of talk at home and school', in Wells, G. (Ed.) *Learning through Interaction*, Cambridge, Cambridge University Press.

Maclure, M., Phillips, T. and Wilkinson, A. (Eds.) (1988) *Oracy Matters: The Development of Talking and Listening in Education*, Milton Keynes, Open University Press.

McNamara, D. (1981) 'Teaching skill: the question of questioning', *Educational Research*, 23, 2, pp. 104–9.

Martin, J. (1970) *Explaining, Understanding and Teaching*, New York, McGraw Hill.

Martin, N., Williams, P., Wilding, J., Hemmings, S. and Medway, P. (1976) *Understanding Children Talking*, Harmondsworth, Penguin Books.

Martin, N. (1984) 'Researchers and learners', in Meek, M. and Miller, J. (Ed.) *Changing English: Essays for Harold Rosen*, London, Heinemann.

Massialas, B. and Zevin, J. (1967) *Creative Encounters in the Classroom*, New York, Wiley.

Maybin, J. (1991) 'Children's informal talk and the construction of meaning', *English in Education*, 25, 2, pp. 34–49.

Maybin, J., Mercer, N. and Stierer, B. (1992) ' "Scaffolding" learning in the classroom'. in Norman, K. (Ed.) (1992) *Thinking Voices: The Work of the National Oracy Project*, London, Hodder and Stoughton.

Measor, L. and Woods, P. (1984) *Changing Schools: Pupil Perspectives on Transfer to a Comprehensive*, Milton Keynes, Open University Press.

Medley, D. and Mitzel, H. (1963) 'The scientific study of teacher behaviour', in Bellack, A. (Ed.) *Theory and Research in Teaching*, New York, Teachers' College Press.

Medway, P. (1980) *Finding a Language: Autonomy and Learning in School*, London, Writers and Readers Publishing Co-operative.

Mehan, H. (1979a) *Learning Lessons*, Cambridge, Mass., Harvard University Press.

Mehan, H. (1979b) 'What time is it, Denise? Asking known-information questions in classroom practice', *Theory into Practice*, 18, 4, pp. 285–94.

Mehan, H. (1984) 'Language and Schooling', *Sociology of Education*, 57, pp. 174–83.

Mercer, N. (1992) 'Culture, context, and the construction of knowledge', in Light, P. and Butterworth, G. (Eds.) *Context and Cognition*, London, Harvester/Wheatsheaf.

Mercer, N. and Edwards, D. (1981) 'Ground-rules for mutual understanding: a social psychological approach to classroom knowledge', in Mercer, N. (Ed.) *Language in School and Community*, London, Edward Arnold.

MICHAELS, S. (1984) 'Listening and responding: hearing the logic in children's classroom narratives', *Theory into Practice*, 23, 3, pp. 218–24.

MILLER, J. (1983) *Many Voices: Bilingualism, Culture and Education*, London, Routledge and Kegan Paul.

MILROY, L. (1980) *Language and Social Networks*, Oxford, Blackwell.

MILROY, L. (1982) 'Social network and linguistic focusing', in ROMAINE, S. (Ed.) *Sociolinguistic Variation in Speech Communities*, London, Edward Arnold.

MILROY, L. (1984) 'Comprehension and context: successful communication and communication breakdown', in TRUDGILL, P. (Ed.) *Applied Sociolinguistics*, London, Academic Press.

MILROY, J. and MILROY, L. (1985) *Authority in Language*, London, Routledge and Kegan Paul.

MORAIS, A., FONTINHAS, F. and NEVES, I. (1992) 'Recognition and realisation rules in acquiring school science', *British Journal of Sociology of Education*, 13, 2, pp. 247–270.

MORSE, L. and HANDLEY, H. (1985) 'Listening to adolescents: Gender differences in science classroom interaction', in WILKINSON, L.C. and MARRETT, C. (Eds.) *Gender Influences in Classroom Interaction*, New York, Academic Press.

NEWMAN, D., GRIFFIN, P. and COLE, M. (1989) *The Construction Zone: Working for Cognitive Change in School*, Cambridge, Cambridge University Press.

NICHOLAS, J. (1988) 'British language diversity studies (1977–87): A critical examination', *Language and Education*, 2, 1, pp. 15–34.

NORMAN, K. (Ed.) (1992) *Thinking Voices: The Work of the National Oracy Project*, London, Hodder and Stoughton.

O'HEAR, A. (1991) *Education and Democracy: Against the Educational Establishment*, London, Centre for Policy Studies.

OBER, R., BENTLEY, E. and MILLER, E. (1971) *Systematic Observation of Teaching: An Interaction-Analysis Instructional Strategy Approach*, New York, Prentice Hall.

OCHS, E. and SCHIEFFELIN, B. (1983) *Acquiring Conversational Competence*, London, Routledge and Kegan Paul.

OPIE, I. and OPIE, P. (1959) *The Lore and Language of Schoolchildren*, London, Oxford University Press.

OPIE, I. and OPIE, P. (1975) *Children's Games in Street and Playground*, Oxford, Clarendon Press.

OPIE, I. and OPIE, P. (1985) *The Singing Games*, London, Oxford University Press.

OWEN, W. (1984) 'Teacher classroom-management communication: a qualitative case study', *Communication Education*, 33, pp. 137–42.

PAYNE, G. (1976) 'Making a lesson happen: a sociological analysis', in HAMMERSLEY, M. and WOODS, P. (Eds.) *The Process of Schooling*, London, Routledge and Kegan Paul.

PAYNE, G. (1982) 'Dealing with a late-comer', in PAYNE, G. and CUFF, E. (Eds.) *Doing Teaching, op. cit.*

PAYNE, G. and HUSTLER, D. (1980) 'Teaching the class: the practical management of a cohort', *British Journal of Sociology of Education*, 1, 1, pp. 49–66.

PAYNE, G. and CUFF, E. (Eds.) (1982) *Doing Teaching: the Practical Management of Classrooms*, London, Batsford.

PHILIPS, S. (1972) 'Participant structures and communicative competence', in CAZDEN, C. *et al* (Eds.) *The Functions of Language in the Classroom, op. cit.*

PHILIPS, S. (1983) *The Invisible Culture: Communication in Classroom and Community on the Warm Springs Indian Reservation*, New York, Longmans.

PHILLIPS, T. (1985) 'Beyond lip-service: discourse development after the age of nine', in WELLS, G. and NICHOLLS, J. (Eds.) *Language and Learning*, Lewes, Falmer Press.

PHILLIPS, T. (1988) 'On a related matter: Why "successful" small group talk depends on not keeping to the point', in MACLURE, M., PHILLIPS, T. and WILKINSON, A. (Eds.) (1988) *Oracy Matters*, Milton Keynes, Open University Press.

PHILLIPS, T. (1990) 'Structuring context for exploratory talk', in WRAY, D. (Ed.) *Talking and Listening*, London, Scholastic Publications.

PHILLIPS, T. (1992) 'Why? The neglected question in planning for small groups', in NORMAN, K. (Ed.) (1992) *Thinking Voices: The Work of the National Oracy Project*, London, Hodder and Stoughton.

PINNELL, G. (1984) 'Communication in small group settings', *Theory into Practice*, 23, 3, pp. 246–54.

PIRIE, S. (1991) 'Mathematical discussion: Incoherent exchanges or shared understandings?', *Language in Education*, 5, 4, pp. 273–286.

POLLARD, A. (1984a) 'Coping strategies and the multiplication of differentiation in infant classrooms', *British Educational Research Journal*, 10, 1, pp. 33–48.

POLLARD, A. (1984b) 'Goodies, jokers and gangs', in HAMMERSLEY, M. and WOODS, P. (Eds.) *Life in School*, Milton Keynes, Open University Press.

POLLARD, A. (1985a) *The Social World of the Primary School*, Eastbourne, Holt, Rinehart and Winston.

POLLARD, A. (1985b) 'Opportunities and difficulties of a teacher-ethnographer: a personal account', in BURGESS, R. (Ed.) *Field Methods in the Study of Education*, Lewes, Falmer Press.

RANDALL, G. (1987) 'Gender differences in pupil-teacher interaction in workshops and laboratories', in WEINER, G. and ARNOT, M. (Eds.) *Gender under Scrutiny: New Inquiries in Education*, London, Hutchinson.

REID, D. (1980) 'Spatial involvement and teacher-pupil interaction patterns in school biology laboratories', *Educational Studies*, 6, 1, pp. 31–41.

REID, E. (1978) 'Social and stylistic variation in the speech of the children: some evidence from Edinburgh', in TRUDGILL, P. (Ed.) *Sociolinguistic Patterns in British English*, London, Edward Arnold.

REID, J., FORRESTAL, P. and COOK, J. (1991) *Small Group Learning in the Classroom*, London, the English and Media Centre.

RENNIE, L. and PARKER, L. (1987) 'Detecting and accounting for gender differences in mixed-sex and single-sex groupings in science lessons', *Educational Review*, 39, 1, pp. 65–73.

RICHMOND, J. (1982) *The Resources of Classroom Language*, London, Arnold.

RICHMOND, J. (1984) 'Setting up for learning in a cold climate', in MEEK, M. and MILLER, J. (Eds.) *Changing English*, London, Heinemann.

ROBERTSON, I. (1980) *Language Across the Curriculum: Four Case Studies*, Schools Council Working Paper 67, London, Methuen.

ROMAINE, S. (1984) *The Language of Children and Adolescents: The Acquisition of Communicative Competence*, Oxford, Blackwell.

ROSEN, H. (1967) 'The language of text-books', in BRITTON, J. (Ed.) *Talking and Writing*, London, Methuen.

ROSEN, H. (1982) 'Language in the education of the working-class', *English in Education*, 16, 2, pp. 17–25.

ROSEN, H. and BURGESS, T. (1980) *Language and Dialects of London School Children: An Investigation*, London, Ward Lock.

ROSEN, H. and ROSEN, C. (1973) *The Language of Primary School Children*, Harmondsworth, Penguin Books.

ROSENSHINE, B. and FURST, N. (1973) 'The use of direct observation to study teaching', in TRAVERS, R. (Ed.) *Second Handbook of Research in Teaching*, Rand McNally.

ROSENSHINE, B. and BERLINER, D. (1978) 'Academic engaged time', *British Journal of Teacher Education*, 4, 1, pp. 3–16.

ROWE, M. (1986) 'Wait time: Slowing down may be a way of speeding up', *Journal of Teacher Education*, 37, pp. 43–50.

RUTHERFORD, R. (1976) 'Talk about Pop', in ROGERS, S. (Ed.) *They Don't Speak Our Language*, London, Edward Arnold.

SALMON, P. and CLAIRE, H. (1984) *Classroom Collaboration*, London, Routledge and Kegan Paul.

SAMPH, T. (1976) 'Observer effects on teacher verbal behaviour', *Journal of Educational Psychology*, 68, 6, pp. 736–41.

SANDS, M. and KERRY, T. (1982) *Mixed-Ability Teaching*, London, Croom Helm.

SAVILLE-TROIKE, M. (1982) *The Ethnography of Communication*, Oxford, Blackwell.

SCHEGLOFF, E., SACKS, H. and JEFFERSON, G. (1977) 'The preference for self-correction in the organization of repair in conversation', *Language*, 53, pp. 361–82.

SCHOOLS COUNCIL (1970) *The Humanities Project: An introduction*, London, Heinemann Educational Books.

SCHOOLS COUNCIL (1979) *Learning Through Talking 11–16*, (Working Paper 64) Evans/Methuen Education.

SELF, D. (1987) *Listen, Talk, Communicate*, London, Macmillan.

SHUY, R. (1984) 'Language as a foundation for education: the school context', *Theory into Practice*, 23, 3, pp. 167–74.

SILVA, K., ROY, C. and PAINTER, M. (1980) *Child-watching at Playgroup and Nursery School*, London, Grant McIntyre.

SIMON, A. and BOYER, G. (Eds.) (1967; 1970; 1975) *Mirrors for Behaviour: an Anthology of Classroom Observation Instruments*, Philadelphia, Research for Better Schools Inc.

SIMON, B. (1981) 'The primary school revolution: myth or reality?' in SIMON, B. and WILLCOCKS, J. (Eds.) *Research and Practice in the Primary School*, London, Routledge and Kegan Paul.

SIMPSON, A. and ERICKSON, M. (1983) 'Teachers' verbal and non-verbal communication patterns as a function of teacher race, student gender and student race', *American Educational Research Journal*, 20, 2, pp. 183–98.

SINCLAIR, J. and BRAZIL, D. (1982) *Teacher Talk*, Oxford, Oxford University Press.

SINCLAIR, J. and COULTHARD, M. (1975) *Towards an Analysis of Discourse: the Language of Teachers and Pupils*, London, Oxford University Press.

SINGH, P. (1993) 'Institutional discourse and practice: A case study of the social construction of technological competence in the primary classroom', *British Journal of Sociology of Education*, 14, 1, pp. 39–58.

SKELTON, P. (1991) 'We just talked', *English in Education*, 25, 1, pp. 40–47.

SMITH, B. and MEUX, M. (1970) *A Study of the Logic of Teaching*, Illinois, University of Illinois Press.

SMITH, L. and GEOFFREY, W. (1968) *The Complexities of an Urban Classroom*, New York, Holt, Rinehart and Winston.

SMITH, P. (1982) *The Language Styles of Children in Small-Group Interaction Compared with Whole-Class Interaction*, Unpublished MEd dissertation, University of Newcastle-upon-Tyne.

SNOW, C. (1972) 'Mothers' speech to children learning language', *Child Development*, 43, pp. 549–65.

SNOW, C. (1977) 'The development of conversation between mothers and babies', *Journal of Child Language*, 4, p. 199.

SPEIER, M. (1973) *How to Observe Face-to-Face Communication: a Sociological Introduction*, New York, Goodyear.

SPEIER, M. (1976) 'The child as conversationalist: some culture-contact features of conversational interaction between adults and children', in HAMMERSLEY, M. and WOODS, P. (Eds.) *The Process of Schooling*, London, Routledge and Kegan Paul.

SPINDLER, G. (Ed.) (1982) *Doing the Ethnography of Schooling: Educational Anthropology in Action*, New York, Holt, Rinehart and Winston.

STENHOUSE, L. (1975) *An Introduction to Curriculum Research and Development*, London, Heinemann Educational Books.

STUBBS, M. (1975) 'Teaching and Talking: a sociolinguistic approach to classroom interaction', in CHANAN, G. and DELAMONT, S. (Eds.) *Frontiers of Classroom Research*, Slough, National Foundation for Educational Research.

STUBBS, M. (1976) 'Keeping in touch: some functions of teacher-talk', in STUBBS, M. and DELAMONT, S. (Eds.) *Explorations in Classroom Observation*, London, Wiley.

STUBBS, M. (1981) 'Scratching the surface: linguistic data in educational research', in ADELMAN, C. (Ed.) *Uttering and Muttering*, London, Grant McIntyre.

STUBBS, M. (1983a) *Language, Schools and Classrooms*, (2nd Edition), London, Methuen.

STUBBS, M. (1983b) *Discourse Analysis: the Sociolinguistic Analysis of Natural Language*, Oxford, Blackwell.

STUBBS, M. (1984) 'Applied discourse analysis and educational linguistics', in TRUDGILL, P. (Ed.) *Applied Sociolinguistics*, London, Academic Press.

STUBBS, M. (1989) 'The state of English in the English State: Reflections on the Cox Report', *Language and Education*, 3, 4, pp. 235–50.

SWANN, J. (1992) *Girls, Boys and Language*, Oxford, Blackwell.

SWANN, M. and GRADDOL, D. (1988) 'Gender inequalities in classroom talk', *English in Education*, 22, 1, pp. 48–65.

SWIFT, J., GOODING, C. and SWIFT, P. (1988) 'Questions and wait time', in DILLON, J.T. (Ed.) *Questioning and Discussion: A Multi-disciplinary Study*, Norwood, New Jersey, Ablex.

SYLVA, K., ROY, C. and PAINTER, M. (1980) *Childwatching at Playgroup and Nursery School*, London, Grant McIntyre.

TALK WORKSHOP GROUP (1982) *Becoming Our Own Experts*, London, Talk Workshop Group.

TARLETON, R. (1988) *Learning and Talking: A Practical Guide to Oracy across the Curriculum*, London, Routledge.

TIZARD, B. and HUGHES, M. (1984) *Young Children Learning: Talking and Thinking at Home and at School*, London, Fontana.

TOBIN, K. (1986) 'Effects of teacher wait time on discourse characteristics in mathematic and language arts classes', *American Educational Research Journal*, 23, pp. 191–200.

TORBE, M. and MEDWAY, P. (1981) *The Climate for Learning*, London, Ward Lock.

TOUGH, J. (1977a) *The Development of Meaning*, London, Allen and Unwin.

TOUGH, J. (1977b) *Talking and Learning: A Guide to Fostering Communication Skills in Nursery and Infant Schools*, London, Ward Lock.

TRUDGILL, P. (1975) *Accent, Dialect and the School*, London, Arnold.

TRUDGILL, P. (1979) 'Standard and non-standard dialects of English in the UK: problems and policies', *International Journal of the Sociology of Language*, 21, pp. 9–24.

TURNER, G. (1982) 'The distribution of classroom interactions', *Research in Education*, 22, pp. 41–8.

UNDERWOOD, G., McCAFFREY, M. and UNDERWOOD, J. (1990) 'Gender differences in a cooperative computer-based language task', *Educational Research*, 32, 1, pp. 44–49.

VYGOTSKY, L. (1962) *Thought and Language*, Cambridge, Mass., MIT Press.

WADE, B. and WOOD, A. (1980) 'Assessing talk in science', *Educational Review*, 32, 2, pp. 205–14.

WADE, B. and DEWHURST, W. (1984) 'Led and unled groups', *Research Intelligence*, 16, May, pp. 2–5.

WALKER, A. (1984) 'Applied sociology of language: vernacular languages and education', in TRUDGILL, P. (Ed.) *Applied Sociolinguistics*, London, Academic Press.

WALKER, R. (1985) *A Handbook of Research for Teachers*, London, Methuen.

WALKER, R. and ADELMAN, C. (1975a) 'Interaction analysis in informal classrooms: a critical comment on the Flanders system', *British Journal of Educational Psychology*, 45, pp. 73–6.

WALKER, R. and ADELMAN, C. (1975b) *A Guide to Classroom Observation*, London, Methuen.

WALKER, R. and ADELMAN, C. (1976) 'Strawberries', in STUBBS, M. and DELAMONT, S. (Eds.) *Explorations in Classroom Observation*, London, Wiley.

WALKER, R. and WIEDEL, J. (1985) 'Using photographs in a discipline of words', in BURGESS, R. (Ed.) *Field Methods in the Study of Education*, Lewes, Falmer Press.

WATSON, K. and YOUNG, R. (1986) 'Discourse for learning in the classroom', *Language Arts*, 63, 2, pp. 126–33.

WELLS, G. (1975) *Coding Manual for the Description of Child Speech*, Bristol, Bristol University School of Education.

WELLS, G. (1979) 'Describing children's linguistic development at home and at school', *British Educational Research Journal*, 5, 1, pp. 75–89.

WELLS, G. (Ed.) (1981) *Learning Through Interaction: The Study of Language Development*, Cambridge, Cambridge University Press.

WELLS, G. (1985a) *Language, Learning and Education*, Slough, NFER-Nelson.

WELLS, G. (1985b) 'Language and learning: an interactional perspective' in WELLS, G. and NICHOLLS, J. (Eds.) *Language and Learning*, Lewes, Falmer Press.

WELLS, G. (1987) *The Meaning Makers: Children Learning Language and Using Language to Learn*, Cambridge, Cambridge University Press.

WELLS, G. (1989) 'Language in the classroom: Literacy and collaborative talk', *Language and Education*, 3, 4, pp. 251–74.

WELLS, G. (1992) 'The centrality of talk in education', in NORMAN , K. (Ed.) *Thinking Voices*, London, Hodder and Stoughton.

WELLS, G. and MONTGOMERY, M. (1981) 'Adult-child interaction at home and at school', in FRENCH, P. and MacLURE, M. (Eds.) *Adult-Child Conversation*, London, Croom Helm.

WELLS, G. and NICHOLLS, J. (Eds.) (1985) *Language and Learning: an Interactional Perspective*, Lewes, Falmer Press.

WELLS, G. and WELLS, J. (1984) 'Learning to talk and talking to learn', *Theory into Practice*, 23, 3, pp. 190–7.

WELLS, G., CHANG, G. and MAHER, A. (1990) 'Creating classroom communities of literate thinkers', in SHARAN, S. (Ed.) *Cooperative Learning: Theory and Research*, New York, Praeger.

WESTGATE, D. and HUGHES, M. (1989) 'Nursery nurses as talk partners', *Education*, 3, 13 and 17, 2, pp. 54–58.

WESTGATE, D. and CORDEN, R. (1993) ' "What we thought about things": expectations, context and small-group talk', *Language and Education*, 7, 2, pp. 115–126.

WESTGATE, D., BATEY, J., BROWNLEE, J. and BUTLER, M. (1985) 'Some characteristics of interaction in foreign language classrooms', *British Educational Research Journal*, 11, 3, pp. 271–81.

WIDDOWSON, H. (1979) 'Rules and procedures in discourse analysis', in MYERS, T. (Ed.) *The Development of Conversation and Discourse*, Edinburgh, Edinburgh University Press.

WILKINSON, A. (1965) *Spoken English*, Birmingham, Birmingham University.

WILKINSON, A. (1991) 'Evaluating group discussion', *Educational Review*, 43, 2.

WILKINSON, A., DAVIES, A., and BERRILL, D. (1990) *Spoken English Illuminated*, Milton Keynes, Open University Press.

WILKINSON, L. (Ed.) (1982) *Communicating in the Classroom*, New York and London, Academic Press.

WILLES, M. (1981a) 'Learning to take part in classroom interaction', in FRENCH, P. and MacLURE, M. (Eds.) *Adult-Child Conversation*, London, Croom Helm.

WILLES, M. (1981b) 'Children becoming pupils: a study of discourse in nursery and reception classes', in ADELMAN, C. (Ed.) *Uttering and Muttering*, London, Grant McIntyre.

WILLES, M. (1983) *Children into Pupils*, London, Routledge and Kegan Paul.

WILTSHIRE ORACY PROJECT (1989) *Oracy in Action: A Video-Based Training Package on Oracy in Secondary Schools*, Swindon, Wiltshire LEA.

WINCH, C. (1985) 'Verbal deficit and educational success', *Journal of Applied Philosophy*, 2, 1, pp. 109–20.

WOLCOTT, H. (1982) 'Mirrors, models and monitors: educator adaptations of the ethnographic innovation', in SPINDLER, G. (Ed.) *Doing the Ethnography of Schooling*, New York, Holt, Rinehart and Winston.

WOOD, D. (1988) *How Children Think and Learn*, Oxford, Blackwell.

WOOD, D. (1992) 'Teaching talk: How modes of teacher talk affect pupil participation', in NORMAN, K. (Ed.) *Thinking Voices*, London, Hodder and Stoughton.

WOOD, D. and WOOD, H. (1988) 'Questioning versus student initiative', in DILLON, J.T. (Ed.) *Questioning and Discussion: A Multi-disciplinary Study*, Norwood, New Jersey, Ablex.

WOODS, P (1990) *The Happiest Days? How Pupils Cope with School*. London Falmer Press.

WOODS, P. (Ed.) (1989) *Working for Teacher Development*, Dereham, Peter Francis.

WRAGG, E. (1973) 'A study of student teachers in the classroom', in CHANAN, G. (Ed.) *Towards a Science of Teaching*, Slough, NFER.

WRAGG, E. (1974) *Teaching Teachers*, Newton Abbot, David and Charles.

WRAGG, E. (Ed.) (1984) *Classroom Teaching Skills*, London, Croom Helm.

WRAGG, E. and WOOD, E. (1984) 'Teachers' first encounters with their classes', in WRAGG, E. *op. cit.*

WRAY, D. (Ed.) (1990) *Talking and Listening*, London, Scholastic Publications.

YOUNG, R. (1984) 'Teaching equals indoctrination: the dominant epistemic practices of our schools', *British Journal of Educational Studies* 32, 3, pp. 220–38.

YOUNG, R. (1992) *Critical Theory and Classroom Talk*, Clevedon, Multilingual Matters.

Author Index

Adams, R. and Biddle, B. 87
Adelman, C. 76
  see also Walker and Adelman
Ainsworth, N. 75, 102, 105, 149
Allwright, D. 26
Altrichter, H. *et al.* 58, 169
Amidon, E. and Hunter, E. 84, 85
Anderson, D. 122
Andreski, S. 18
Armstrong, S. *see* Brown and
  Armstrong
Atkins, M. 2
  see also Craft and Atkins
Atkinson, J.M. and Heritage, J. 23
Atkinson, P. 28, 37
  see also Beynon and Atkinson
Austin, J.L. 21

Ball, S. 12, 13, 103
Barker-Lunn, J. 43
Barnes, D. 13, 24, 58, 109, 152
  Britton, J. and Rosen, H. 13
  and Sheeran, Y. 18
  and Todd, F. 50, 74, 76, 106, 112,
    135, 136, 140, 149, 152–3, 154,
    155, 156
  et al. 1, 6, 7, 18, 35, 100, 134,
    135
Barr, M. *et al.* 111
Bellack, A. *et al.* 1
Bennett, N. 87, 88, 94–5
  et al. 43, 44, 50, 94, 96
Bennett, S.N. and Dunne, E. 50, 94
Berliner, D. *see* Rosenshine and
  Berliner
Bernstein, B. 37, 97
Berrill, D. 53, 111

Beverton, S. *see* Hardman and
  Beverton
Beynon, J. and Atkinson, P. 34, 103
Biddle, B. *see* Adams and Biddle
Biggs, A. and Edwards, V. 37
Blease, D. 77
Blom, J. and Gumperz, J. 3, 20
Borman, K. 22, 161
Bourdieu, P. and Passeron, J-C. 34
Bousted, M. 81
Boydell, D. 93
Boyer, G. *see* Simon and Boyer
Brazil, D. 27, 59
  see also Coulthard and Brazil;
    Sinclair and Brazil
Britton, J. 7, 13
  see also Barnes, Britton and Rosen
Brook, A. *et al.* 43
Brophy, J. *see* Good and Brophy
Brown, G.
  and Armstrong, S. 91, 147, 148
  and Yule, G. 24, 25
Brumfit, C. and Mitchell, R. 26
Bruner, J. 15
Bullock Report 31
  see also Bullock Committee
    (Subject Index)
Burgess, R. 42, 43, 44
Burgess, T. 15, 119
  see also Rosen and Burgess
Burton, D. 25, 27, 57, 59, 125, 140,
  149

Carre, C. 39, 91, 108
Cazden, C. 69, 115, 125, 133, 134,
  143, 149
  Hymes, D. and John, V. 36

Subject Index